LITTLE KNOWN CHAPTERS

in

FREE WILL BAPTIST

HISTORY

Robert E. Picirilli

randall house

114 Bush Rd | Nashville, TN 37217

randallhouse.com

Published by Randall House Publications
114 Bush Road
Nashville, TN 37217

Printed in the United States of America

ISBN 13: 978089265

Table of Contents

Preface

My purpose for this volume is twofold. First, as a historian of our movement, I like to research and tell the stories that are little known or not known
at all. There are many of those in Free Will Baptist history. Second, I have attempted to clear up some matters that are not correctly understood and so to
make sure we see ourselves more accurately. There are some misconceptions,
out there, about who we are and what has made us that.

My interest in Free Will Baptist history began when I was a student at Free
Will Baptist Bible College—now Welch College—during the years 1949-53.
For one of my classes, I wrote a paper on our history. I still have it. I was excited to encounter the Free Baptist Cyclopaedia, and I leaned heavily on that
big book. It opened up a world I didn't know existed: the world of far-away
New England just before the end of the eighteenth century. It was thrilling
to read about Benjamin Randall and the rapid spread of the movement that
sprang up from his preaching. I was immediately seized with the idea that this
was, indeed, the history of the Free Will Baptist people, and I was eager to
learn everything I could about Randall and Buzzell and Colby and Marks and
Bates College and Hillsdale College, and even about Free Will Baptists all the
way out to California.

It took me awhile to learn that things weren't quite that simple. After all,
the story of the Randall movement is captivating. Those evangelistic New
Englanders lit a fire that burned a place in the history of New England, swept

westward, brought people to Jesus, planted Baptist churches of the "free will" variety across the midwest, established educational institutions, and made a name for themselves in promoting causes like total abstinence, the anti-slavery sentiment, and the ordination of women and blacks to the ministry.

Like many others, I thought that this was the exciting history of my denomination, the Free Will Baptists! I took pride in their achievements. I said, along with others, that we lost all those churches and schools when the Randallites merged with the Northern Baptists in 1910-11. I sort of hated them for that, but I figured that some influential people must have led them down the wrong path, and that we could still delight in the stories they left behind them.

I still think that, to some degree. But I've come to understand that the reason we all rely on the history of the Northern Free Will Baptists so heavily is very simple: they published it, and it's available, whereas the history of the Southern movement didn't get put into writing like that.

It is true that there are segments of our contemporary Free Will Baptist denomination that owe their origins to the Randall movement. It is a mistake to downplay that. But it is equally a mistake to think that the history of the Randall movement is the history of our denomination as we know it now. That is not quite the case. Randall, Marks, and the others who were lights in that movement contributed to the Free Will Baptist people of today, yes; but they were not the ones who made us what we are now. We need to look elsewhere for our heroes and for the sources of our denominational culture.

Some of that "looking" has been done in recent years. Men like Bill Davidson and Michael Pelt (with a narrower focus than Davidson) have worked on the big picture and especially on the state of things in Eastern North Carolina from the days of Paul Palmer in 1727 until the people known as Free Will Baptists were more clearly defined as such in the early to mid-nineteenth century.

Even so, there are many, many places where research needs to be done if the full story is ever to be understood. There are heroes to be looked up to, some whose names we don't even know. There are interesting stories to be discovered and shared.

This volume unearths just a few of those. For the most part, each chapter is a separate "story," dealing with a hero here or an important set of events there. I have placed them in a more or less chronological order, although the first chapter, dealing with how we name ourselves, covers things from the beginning to the present. All of the stories involve people and things a long time ago, except for the last one. That one, which is set in the period 1949 to 1954, is the most recent one, and it involves "personal" history that I think others will find interesting. It, too, contributes something to seeing ourselves clearly.

My interest in Free Will Baptist history has been whetted to a finer edge over the last ten to fifteen years. Since I retired from Welch, I have devoted a significant part of my time to the Free Will Baptist Historical Collection. It "belongs"—in some sense of the word—to the denomination and is more or less jointly supervised by the Free Will Baptist Historical Commission and Welch College, where the Collection resides as part of its library. Even during my years as Registrar and then Dean at the College, I gave some attention to cultivating the collection, but time for that had been almost non-existent for the last many years of my tenure there. When I retired, I came to realize that nothing at all had been done to put the collection in order for many years, and that even what had been done needed to be done over. With Carol Reid's capable help, I learned basic librarianship and did the cataloging and organizing. I became, in essence, the curator of the collection or the historical librarian—without title. I re-did everything and caught up all the boxes of material that had not been cataloged. I put it all on computer. Today, everything in the collection is appropriately classified and readily accessible via the online catalog.

While doing this, certain matters captured my attention. Among them are the things I have written about in the chapters in this volume. In most cases, the chapters are not connected to each other. Even when put together, they don't even try to tell "The Free Will Baptist Story"—to borrow Damon Dodd's title for a book so precious when he wrote it and so out of date now in comparison to more recent works. My stories simply treat parts of our history, describing small matters that enable us to see a little more clearly some of the things that have shaped us.

I could not have written these stories were it not for the Free Will Baptist Historical Collection. It is a great and growing resource. The catalog can be accessed through either the college's website or a link on the site maintained by the Historical Commission, fwbhistory.com. The continued growth of that resource depends, of course, on the help of all of us. Many valuable items have been irretrievably lost, and many more will yet be lost unless people are willing to help us obtain and preserve the materials that will preserve our history for other researchers to come.

1

"Free Will Baptist": What's In a Name?

*What's in a name? that which we call a rose
By any other name would smell as sweet.
—Shakespeare, in Romeo and Juliet*

There appears to be an idea abroad that the Free Will Baptists of the North—the Randall movement—more or less consistently used "Freewill Baptist," while those in the South—the Palmer movement—more or less consistently used "Free Will Baptist."

Things aren't quite that simple, and therein lies the interesting story of the name(s) we wear.

Part One: The Randall Movement

I begin the story here, partly because it is a little easier to tell this first and partly because it's less important in the big picture. Many are aware that the Northern denomination began with the planting of a church in New Durham, New Hampshire, by Benjamin Randall in 1780. What some may not realize, however, is that neither this church nor the others that sprang from

1

this beginning used any form of *freewill* in their name for some twenty years.

When Randall wrote the covenant for the new congregation in New Durham, he gave the church no name at all.[1] "They organized simply as a Baptist church."[2] A letter dated January 13, 1783, was addressed "To the Baptist church of Christ at New Durham,"[3] and a letter from them in the same year was "From the Baptist church at New Durham."[4]

As other churches in their fellowship were planted, they "were, for many years, known only as Baptist churches."[5] A Quarterly Meeting was organized in 1783.[6] The first minutes begin, "The Baptist Quarterly Meeting convened,"[7] and a 1786 letter from that body was "From ... the Baptist Quarterly Meeting, held at New Durham."[8] A 1799 petition from the same body referred to "a member of this Quarterly Meeting of Baptists."[9]

Indeed, according to I. D. Stewart, the name *Freewill Baptist* does not appear in any old records or historical papers until 1799, when some ordination certificates spoke of "the Church of Christ, commonly known by the name of the new Durham church; also a member of the community in general, commonly termed General Provisioners, or Freewill Baptists."[10] Even in this, the authors of the certificates were merely acknowledging names that

---

1 For this covenant, see John Buzzell, *The Life of Elder Benjamin Randall: Principally Taken from Documents Written by Himself* (Limerick: Hobbs, Woodman & Co., 1827), 83-84.

2 I. D. Stewart, *The History of the Freewill Baptists, for Half a Century, with an Introductory Chapter: Volume I. from the year 1780 to 1830* (Dover: Freewill Baptist Printing Establishment, 1862), 55. There never was a volume II.

3 Stewart, 69.

4 Stewart, 70.

5 Stewart, 72.

6 Stewart, 76-77.

7 Stewart, 174.

8 Stewart, 88.

9 Stewart, 144.

10 Stewart, 175.

others used for them, not representing these as their official names. "Many of the fathers lived and died objecting to the name, but a majority finally acquiesced in its use."[11] It was five more years, in 1804, before the name would be used in any official capacity.

Different Names in New England

This seems a good place to discuss the names more generally. Indeed, several different names were used during the early years of those in the new denomination in New Hampshire and other New England states. As already noted, sometimes they were simply known as a *Church of Christ*, but this was apparently not a way of distinguishing them from any other groups of Christians.[12] As a title of difference, they were known as *Baptists*, and one simply had to know which Baptists were of the Calvinistic persuasion and which were Arminian ("free willers"). Stewart sometimes distinguishes the two by identifying the followers of Randall as "the free division of the Baptists"[13] or "Baptist churches with free principles."[14]

A simple way of specifying exactly who they were was as churches of the *New Durham Connection*[15] or *Connexion*. Spelled either way, the word meant essentially the same thing as a denomination. An 1801 letter from a church in Vermont to the Yearly Meeting (organized in 1792) was "To the Church of Christ, New Durham connection."[16] The same thing could be accomplished, and sometimes was, by identifying the churches in this con-

---

11 Stewart, 176.

12 See Stewart, 174, for discussion of this.

13 Stewart, 99.

14 Stewart, 145. Subsequently, it became popular to identify all Arminian Baptists, whatever their denominational name, as "liberal Baptists." But this was apparently not used by any denomination in its official name and so it remains a convenient and broad, generic term.

15 Stewart, 174.

16 Stewart, 175.

nection as *Randallites*.

Since *Baptist* was not enough, additional qualifiers came into use. *General Provisioners* was one, as noted above in the 1799 ordination certificates. A 1792 filing for incorporation, with the General Court of Massachusetts, referred to them as "the Baptist Quarterly Meeting, sometimes called General Provisioners."[17] This term reflected the "free will" doctrine that Jesus' atonement made provision for all men in general and not just for the elect in particular. From the beginning of Baptist history in England, those of Arminian persuasion were known as "General" Baptists, while their Calvinistic counterparts were known as "Particular" Baptists.

Freewill a Derogatory Name Finally Accepted

It was probably inevitable, however, that the Randallites ultimately came to be known as *Freewill Baptists*. Long before 1780, believers of Arminian persuasion were mocked as "free willers"—or maybe "freewillers." All the historians of the Northern movement agree that this was first a term of derision, put on them by their critics, accepted only gradually and with some reluctance. Frederick L. Wiley observes that the name, "though a contemptuous nickname, was eventually accepted by the majority of our people."[18] Stewart puts this in perspective: "So important was their estimate of this sentiment—*freewill*—that it was reproachfully forced upon them as a part of their denominational name."[19] He reports that Randall, according to John Buzzell, finally said,

> The devil always overshoots the mark when he attempts to reproach the people of God. The disciples were contemptuously

17 Hosea Quinby, Freewill Baptist Quarterly Magazine 1:3 (December 1839), 81.
18 F. L. Wiley, Centennial Souvenir of the New Hampshire Yearly Meeting of Free Baptists 1792-1892, second unnumbered page in front.
19 Stewart, 28.

4

called "Christians" at Antioch, but that has become a name of the highest national respect. So the name "Freewill" may, in process of time, become a title of high respect in the Christian world.[20]

Even so, Randall's last letter to the New Durham Quarterly Meeting, dated May 14, 1808, was addressed, simply, "To the Baptist Quarterly Meeting to be held at Andover, N. H."[21]

Regardless, it came to pass in 1804 that the Legislature of New Hampshire, in response to a request from the Randallites, passed the following resolution:

> Resolved, That the people in this State, commonly known by the name of Freewill Antipedo Baptist church and society, shall be considered as a distinct religious sect or denomination, with all the privileges, as such, agreeable to the Constitution.[22]

That, minus the "Antipedo,"[23] is the name that stuck.

Different Spellings of the *Freewill* Name

As I have said, however, things are not quite that simple. When we read the work of an author like Stewart, we should realize that, for the sake of consistency, he chose to represent the name the same way all the time and in the form he preferred. From his book, we would never learn that the *Freewill* took any other form. But it did. We also will understand that if one says "freewill" to a dozen different people, various ones may well write it down differently. At least two other variations are possible: *Free-will* (hyphenated,

20 Stewart, 176.
21 Stewart, 246.
22 Quinby, 81.
23 The "Anti-paedo" was an old name for all Baptists because they were opposed (*anti*) to infant (*paedo*) baptism.

with or without a capital on *Will*) or *Free Will* (two words).

Within the Northern denomination, even the official documents often used *Free-will Baptist* (occasionally *Free-Will*). The various editions of their *Treatise of Faith and Practices*, for example, show the variety. The 1839 edition has *Freewill* both in the title and in "Published by the Trustees of the Freewill Baptist Connection." But the 1850 edition has *Free-will* in both places. Indeed, the Introduction to the 1854 edition reports, in an abbreviated history, that the first church in the movement was reproached as *freewillers* and "Hence this church received the distinctive title, *Free-will Baptist*"—in the very same sentence that read, in the 1839 edition, *Freewill Baptist*! (This goes to show that the name will be represented, in any publication, in the form chosen by the writer, editor, or printer.) By 1869, the form reverts to *Freewill Baptist*, and in the 1886 edition, the publisher is "The F. B. Printing Establishment."[24]

The Morning Star was the Northern denomination's leading periodical, a weekly. It shows the same variety. The issue for July 15, 1835, was "Published ... by the Freewill Baptist Connexion." The one for May 26, 1852, was "Published by the Free-will Baptist Printing Establishment," with its office "in the F. W. Baptist Building, Washington St." (Dover, N. H.). By 1869, the masthead is back to saying "Published by the Freewill Baptist Printing Establishment."

The Myrtle, another of the publications from the same establishment, from 1847 to 1853, at least,[25] was "Published by the Free-will Baptist Printing Establishment." Similarly, the annual register and yearbook was *The Free-will Baptist Register* (published by the F. W. Baptist Printing Estab-

---

24 I have not footnoted these references since all one needs to do to confirm is to consult the edition of the *Treatise* identified. This observation will apply to several references to follow, including minutes of organizations, where the sources are obvious.

25 These are the only issues we possess.

lishment) from 1842-1858, and then *The Freewill Baptist Register*.

Even earlier than these was *The Free-will Baptist Magazine*, beginning in May of 1826, "Published by several elders of the R. I. Quarterly Meeting for the Free-will Baptist Connexion." [26] In 1836, *Hymns for Christian Melody* was published by the trustees "of the Free-will Baptist Connection" under the auspices of a publishing committee chosen by the "General Conference of the Free-will Baptist Connection"; but the 1853 *Psalmody* went back to *Freewill*. In 1841, *The Free Communionist* was "Published by the Trustees of the Freewill Baptist Connection, but officially registered for publication by Wm. Burr, agent of the "Trustees of the F. W. B. Connection." The 1847 *Memoirs of the Life of David Marks* uses *Free-will*, as does the 1854 *Life of Colby*. In the 1851 *Life of Clement Phinney*, author D. M. Graham, in the Preface, uses "F. W. Baptist Connexion."

It is therefore clear that *Freewill* and *Free-will* were both widely used in the Northern denomination, with *F. W. Baptist* apparently being an abbreviation for the latter (and sometimes for the former). The name of the publishing house itself changed accordingly, with *Free-will Baptist Printing Establishment* especially used during the middle part of the nineteenth century. Again, this may well have reflected the preference of the persons responsible.

Did They Ever Use Two Words?

Was *Free Will* ever used by them? Indeed, it was, although if all we had to go by were the things printed by the publishing house we wouldn't know that. (Even if I did not have evidence, I would be fairly confident that *Free Will* was used among them often, officially or unofficially.)

---

26 The *Herald of Gospel Liberty* for September 1, 1808, refers to the "Quarterly Meeting of the Free-will Baptists." (The paper was apparently published by one who was part of the Christian connection.)

Indeed, it may be that Randall himself used it this way. Buzzell relates an anecdote in which Randall said, about a certain preacher, "He has a mitten for either hand. When he is with the Predestinarians, then he is a great Predestinarian; and when he is with the Free Willers, then he is a great Free Willer."[27]

Furthermore, Buzzell quotes Randall as saying that, after he had drawn up the original covenant and put it before the members in New Durham, on June 30, 1780, "we all, in a solemn manner, by prayer and supplication to the Lord, covenanted together in the fear of God, and signed our names to the instrument. This is the beginning of the now large and extensive connection, called FREE WILL BAPTIST."[28] It is possible, of course, that Buzzell erred in extending the quotation to the last sentence,[29] or in printing the name the way he thought it ought to be printed. But at least Buzzell himself, who was baptized by and ministered with Randall, as early as 1827 regarded *Free Will* as two words. Although he personally preferred to refer to the churches more simply as "Churches of Christ," he said that Randall "laid the foundation of the connexion, now extending over a great part of North America, commonly known by the denomination of FREE WILL BAPTIST."[30]

I first thought it would be difficult to confirm the use of *Free Will* by the Randallites. But as soon as I realized where to look, it turned out to be easy enough. One simply has to look in documents, handwritten or printed, that were not printed by the Freewill (or Free-will) Baptist Printing Establish-

---

27 Buzzell, 98.

28 Buzzell, 84. The way the name is printed is original.

29 I find it difficult to think that Randall himself would have written the last sentence.

30 Buzzell, 82. Again, the way the name is printed is original. Buzzell had not been consistent in this. In his *A Religious Magazine* for August 1820, he used both *Freewill* and *Free-Will*. At that point, however, he still thought of this as a name given by others: "Our opposers will heap upon us the name of Free-Willers, a name which we have hitherto considered ourselves unworthy of."

ment. Of the references I found, I selected ten to mention[31]:

(1) In *The Life of Elder Abel Thornton*, written by himself and published in 1828 by J. B. Yerrinton in Providence, Rhode Island, for the Rhode Island Q. M., in the "Preliminary Remarks" (perhaps by Z. Tobey, the writer of the Preface), the heading says *Free-will Baptists*, but in the body of the remarks, when the group's identity is discussed, *Free Will Baptists* appears.

(2) The Hillsdale College paper, *The Advance*, for October 21, 1885, in an article about Ransom Dunn, refers to the organization of "a Free Will Baptist Church."

(3) An old handwritten journal is identified, in 1876, as the record of "Mill Creek Free Will Baptist Church" (in Kansas).

(4) Another record book, in 1882, reports that the church was organized in 1845 "and took the name of 'The Free Will Baptist Church of Green Oak' [Michigan]."

(5) There is an 1893 printed program for "The Indiana Free • Will • Baptist Association." (The bullets are original.)

(6) An 1890 publication is entitled "An Historical Sketch of the Vermont Yearly Meeting of Free Will Baptists."

(7) An early (undated) handwritten constitution of a Young People's Aid Society says that its objective "shall be to raise funds in the interest of the Free Will Babtist Society of East Andover, N. H." (*Babtist* is original.)

(8) The handwritten minutes of the Ohio River Yearly Meeting, for 1833, refer to "the Treatise on the Faith of the Free Will Baptist [sic]." Interestingly, in 1868 they resolved "to oppose dropping the word 'Will' in our denominational name."

(9) An 1883 volume describing the early history of the town of Bethlehem, New Hampshire, refers to "the Free Will Baptist building" that was

---

31 Since writing this, I have examined another large batch of material from the Randall movement and could supply many more examples of this usage.

originally located "on the main road nearly opposite the residence of Timo-thy Hildreth and his son Orville," but was later "taken down and trans-formed into a starch factory"![32]

(10) An 1846 obituary in Anson, Maine, indicates that the deceased, Rev. William Paine, was converted "under the labors of ... a Free Will Baptist preacher."[33]

These seem adequate to make the point that across the broad sweep of the Randall movement the name often appeared as *Free Will Baptist*. Even the 1898 minutes of the General Conference represent article 1 of the con-stitution as reading: "The General Conference of Free Baptists shall be composed of delegates from the several bodies now composing the General Conference of the Free Will Baptist Connection." This is obviously an er-ror—the correct reading was "Freewill Baptist Connection"—but it shows how easily varieties of the name appeared in print. Authors and publishers would consistently put the name in the form they thought "correct," regard-less how earlier users might have written it.

It is therefore not incorrect to refer to the Randallites, generically, as "Free Will Baptists." They were that. Harrison and Barfield called them that (in 1897), and so did the record of the old Bethel Conference in North Carolina (in 1832)[34]—just as publications in the North often referred to the freewillers in the South as "Freewill Baptists."

From *Freewill* to *Free* Baptists

The Randallites did, however, make yet another change, this a lasting

---

32 Simeon Bolles, *The Early History of the Town of Bethlehem, New Hampshire* (Woodsville: Enterprise Printing House, 1883), 94-95.

33 As will be noted in chapter six of this volume, the material cited in that chapter published by those that originated in the Randall movement uses all three forms of the name.

34 T. F. Harrison and J. M. Barfield, *History of the Free Will Baptists of North Carolina* (W. E. Moye, 1897), 57, 219.

one: they officially became *Free Baptists* in 1892. The roots of this extend at least to 1841 when their General Conference merged with a smaller group named Free Communion Baptists or Free Baptists.[35] As part of that union, the Conference voted that they considered "the name of Free Baptist, Free Communion Baptist, Freewill Baptist, and Open Communion Baptist as designating the same people."[36] The name *Free Baptist* was not entirely unknown before then. Stewart reports that, in 1826, a small group of "Free Baptist" churches in Vermont united with those in the Randall movement; he describes them as churches "of liberal Baptist sentiments."[37] Stewart also notes that many preferred this shorter name as "more expressive and appropriate ... since we believe, not only in free will, but *free* salvation and *free* communion."[38]

Not all the constituents of the General Conference approved this, of course. In southern Ohio, for example, Thomas E. Peden, beginning in 1895, led resistance and made the change of name a basis for contending that he and those who followed him were the true General Conference of Freewill Baptists. That story is too complex to tell here,[39] but an article in an 1897 issue of *The Church Watchman*, an Ohio paper, entitled "Free Will or Free Baptists," attempts to calm any waters troubled about the issue, saying:

> Many of us use the term Freewill or Free Baptists interchangeably, and often for mere sake of brevity drop the word "Will." It

---

35 The minutes of the General Conference for 1841 refer to them as "Free Baptists," but they were also known as "Free Communion Baptists"; see Stewart, 76-77; also Norman Allen Baxter, *History of the Freewill Baptists: A Study in New England Separatism* (Rochester: American Baptist Historical Society, 1957), 1 (n. 1).

36 Baxter, 1 (n. 1), citing the 1841 minutes of the General Conference, found in the 1859 bound volume of minutes from the beginning until that date, 192.

37 Stewart, 372.

38 Stewart, 176.

39 For this story, see chapter five of this volume.

is not very strange that some of our brethren should feel deeply sensitive about any change of name of our denomination, after honoring the old name so long. … Our principles are unchanged, rest assured. While there are honest differences about the use of above names, and some noble brethren have felt greatly excited over the legal change of names in our new constitution, personally we have not been greatly worried over these changes. "Let us have peace!"[40]

Perhaps those who resisted the change would have appreciated a later writer in the Southern denomination, I. W. Yandell, who contended that the Randall movement lost its identity by uniting with the Free Baptists of New York.[41]

At any rate, the short name gradually became accepted by most of the Northern denomination. When the merger with Northern Baptists came in 1910-11, the "General Conference of Free Baptists" completed this union and ensured that as a separate denomination the Randall movement would go out of existence.[42]

Part Two: The Palmer Movement

For contemporary Free Will Baptists, this part of the story is more important. Although there are significant parts of the denomination, now, that had their origins in the Randall movement, the larger part trace their origins

---

40 *The Church Watchman* (Ashtabula, Ohio), VIII:9 (June 1897), 3. The article was apparently written by the editor, T. H. Drake.

41 I. W. Yandell and Dovie Yandell, *The Origin, Doctrine, Identity and History of the Free Will Baptist Church*, (self-published, n. d.), 193.

42 Technically, the General Conference of Free Baptists continued to exist as a legal entity for a number of years after the merger, but it was a paper organization that held meetings as formalities for legal purposes.

to Paul Palmer in 1727 in Eastern North Carolina[43] or (to a lesser degree) to other indigenous movements in other places in the southeastern United States.

Baptist the Original Name, *Free Will* a Nickname

Interestingly, the North Carolina Free Will Baptists also did not at first call themselves by that name. Like the early followers of Benjamin Randall (but preceding them by half a century), the followers of Paul Palmer were originally known as *Baptists*, even though it was apparently not uncommon for Baptists holding to Arminian sentiments to be derided as *freewillers* (or *free-willers*, or *free willers*!).

My purpose, here, does not include extensive coverage of the background of this, but some brief observations seem appropriate. As a nickname, usually used negatively, *freewiller* goes back to England, well before the 1727 Palmer church in North Carolina. Stewart, writing for the Randallites, says, "The first controversy on predestination among the English reformers, was in queen Mary's reign [1553-1558], when those who believed in the freedom of the will were called '*freewillers*'."[44] For this, he cites Daniel Neal's history of the Puritans, although a check of the passage he cites reveals that while Neal himself called those mid-sixteenth century Arminians "free-willers," he did not quite say they were called that at the time.[45] Even so, that was probably the case. Adam Taylor notes that Thomas Helwys, the found-

---

43 Michael R. Pelt, *A History of Original Free Will Baptists* (Mount Olive: Mount Olive College Press, 1996), 20-55, has the most recent and thorough presentation of the first General/Free Will Baptists in North Carolina.

44 Stewart, 31. He is citing Neal's *History of the Puritans*, I:65, and he always spells the name as one word.

45 Daniel Neal, *The History of the Puritans; or, Protestant Nonconformists; from the Reformation in 1517, to the Revolution in 1688 [etc.]*, vol. I (Minneapolis: Klock and Klock, 1979 reprint of 1837 work), 73-74.

ing pastor of the original General Baptist church in London, "met with much opposition. The separatists, whom he had left, attacked him and his tenets with great warmth, calling his party heretics, anabaptists, and free-willers."[46]

William F. Davidson devotes helpful discussion to the use of this nickname, observing, "More recent discoveries have given weight to the conclusion that the name was in fairly common use throughout the 17th century in England."[47] He cites documents dated in 1659 and 1660, the latter written by an outsider "to the Free-Will-Anabaptists" and the former by "a small society of baptised believers, undergoing the name of Free-Willers, about the city of London." He argues convincingly that these represented the original Baptists in London who held to the doctrine of a general atonement (and are therefore often called "General" Baptists).[48] Indeed, Thomas Helwys, the founding pastor of the first Baptist church on English soil—a General Baptist church at that—published a pamphlet in 1611 that addressed "the congregation, which men called the New Frylers" while they were still in the Netherlands, and Davidson is confident that *Frylers* means *Freewillers*.[49]

Apparently, then, *freewillers* (however spelled) was not only a common term for anyone believing in the Arminian view of salvation but also a term applied specifically to the General Baptists in England and then in America. Even so, it was more likely to be used *of* them than *by* them, at least at first. When those English General Baptists wrote their "Standard Confession"

---

46 Adam Taylor, *The History of the English General Baptists*, vol. 1, *The English General Baptists of the Seventeenth Century* (London: Printed for the Author by T. Bore, 1818), 86. I have William F. Davidson to thank for this citation, found among his papers in the Free Will Baptist Historical Collection in Nashville, TN.

47 William F. Davidson, *The Free Will Baptists in America 1727-1984* (Nashville: Randall House Publications, 1985), 19.

48 Davidson, 19-20.

49 Davidson, 19. He thinks this might have been a Dutch pronunciation, but it might simply have been a contraction of the seventeenth-century English spelling of "free-willers."

in 1660, the document began, simply, "A brief confession or declaration of faith, Set forth by many of us, who are (falsely) called Ana-Baptists."[50] The document used no other name to identify them.

Baptists in the Lineage of English General Baptists

It is enough to say, here, that the Baptists who ultimately came to be called *Free Will Baptists* in North Carolina, and spreading out from there, traced their spiritual lineage to the English General Baptists. They used the Standard Confession of 1660, mentioned above, as their basic statement of belief. Like them, then, they simply identified themselves at first as *Baptists*. When they needed to distinguish themselves from Calvinistic Baptists, they said something like "Baptists holding to a general atonement." Apparently, then, the distinctive name most likely to be used for them soon came to be *General Baptists*. Lemuel Burkitt and Jesse Read, writing in 1803, testified to the fact that the early "General Baptist" churches in North Carolina used the 1660 Confession as "their Confession of Faith."[51]

In 1812, the North Carolina General Baptists produced a revision of the 1660 Standard Confession entitled, "An abstract of the Former Articles of Faith confessed by the original Baptist Church, holding the doctrine of general provision"—often called, in short form, the *1812 Former Articles*. Perhaps they were not yet using *Free Will Baptist* officially. However, subsequent editions of this document (1855, 1884, etc.) read the same way, although *Free Will Baptist* was certainly in general use by then. The 1895

---

50   The *Anabaptists* were groups of European believers—often called the "Radical Reformation"—who insisted on re-baptizing people, when converted, who had been baptized as infants. The church planted in London by Helwys had spent some time in the Netherlands where they were acquainted with and to some degree influenced by Anabaptists, but there was no organic connection between them.

51   Pelt, 69.

edition included a preface identifying the "Western Conference of Original Free Will Baptists" as the sponsor of the publication.

One cannot be absolutely sure exactly when the North Carolina General Baptists first applied the name *Free Will Baptist* (spelled one way or another) to themselves. Rufus K. Hearn said, in 1875, "We were called Ana-Baptists, Baptists, and General Baptists, until the year 1828, when we adopted the name of Free-Will Baptists."[52] For the 1828 date, he relied on a statement by Elias Hutchins—of the Northern Freewill Baptists, who visited in North Carolina during the period 1829-1833. Pelt observes, "There is no reason to doubt Hutchins' statement," which means that there is also no way to confirm it.[53] Even so, I think it likely that the North Carolina brethren decided to make "Free Will Baptist" their official name after learning this had been done in the North.[54] Regardless, *Free Will Baptist* had become the name that stuck.

Spellings of *Free Will* in the South

Once again, however, things are not quite that simple. In keeping with the opening paragraph of this article, my purpose includes showing that early Free Will Baptists in the Palmer movement, and throughout the part of the denomination that did not originate with the Randall movement, used *Free Will*, *Freewill*, and *Free-will* with equal freedom. *Free Will* may be the consistent form, more or less, in our day. It was not always so. In documenting this, I have limited myself to things published before 1900, even though

---

52 R. K. Hearn, "Origin of the Free Will Baptist Church of North Carolina," in the *Toisnot Transcript* (May 20-June 17, 1875), reprinted in D. B. Montgomery, *General Baptist History* (Evansville: Courier Company, Book and Job Printers, 1882, 148-178), 169.

53 Pelt, 107.

54 See chapter four of this volume. My opinion could easily be shown wrong by any publication or manuscript among North Carolina Free Will Baptists, dated before 1828, that used the words as part of the official name.

there is wide evidence of the variety after that.

Given that the Palmer movement began in North Carolina, that seems the best place to begin. The oldest conference we have any minutes for was the Bethel Conference. On the cover of the 1833 minutes the name is *Free Will Baptist*, but inside there is reference to *Free-will Baptist* churches. The excerpts from the 1829 minutes of this conference found in Harrison and Barfield are partial but also appear to confirm that it was the "Free Will Baptist Annual Conference."[55] This organization was apparently the source of the Hearn-Hutchins reference to the name cited above.

The North Carolina General Conference replaced the Bethel, and its minutes amply attest the variety: in 1845, the name is *Free Will Baptist*; in 1851, *Free-Will Baptist*; in 1857, *Freewill-Baptist*; in 1864, *Freewill Baptist*. Moreover, the variety continues from there, not getting back to *Free Will Baptist* (in the minutes we have) until 1886. The Cape Fear Conference shows similar vacillation, using *Free-Will Baptist* for many years, beginning in 1884 (the earliest minutes we have), and then back and forth between that and *Free Will Baptist* after 1897, with the latter becoming settled after 1901. Harrison and Barfield say that it was organized in 1855 as the "Cape Fear Free-Will Baptist Conference."[56]

Interestingly, the issue of the weekly paper published in Ayden, North Carolina, for May 27, 1896 is titled *The Free Will Baptist*. But in smaller print to the left of the masthead it is identified as the "Organ of the Freewill Baptist Church" and published by the "Freewill Baptist Pub. Co."

One of the early efforts at writing the history of Free Will Baptists in North Carolina was by Rufus K. Hearn, first published in the *Toisnot Transcript* (a forerunner of *The Free Will Baptist*) in 1875. Hearn used *Free Will* and *Free-Will* interchangeably. He discussed the origin of the name, raising

---

55 Harrison and Barfield, 199.

56 Harrison and Barfield, 349.

the question "why are we called Free-Will Baptists?" To answer, he reached back to the Gum Swamp community in 1766 when Calvinists called them "Free-willers."[57] Shortly thereafter, he said, "The name 'Free-Will,' was given us by way of reproach."[58]

Another early history of North Carolina Free Will Baptists is by Harrison and Barfield, apparently published in 1897 and relying heavily on Hearn (without acknowledgement) for part of the work. They, too, alternate between *Free-Will* and *Free Will*.[59]

Varieties Outside North Carolina

The first place outside North Carolina that the Palmer movement spread to was South Carolina. The handwritten record book of the South Carolina Conference, during the years 1858 to 1899 shows the same variety. In 1858, the form is *Freewill* and in 1860, it is *Free Will*; the rest of the years show first one and then the other.

The state of Georgia might have been the next one for the denomination to spread to. One of the oldest associations in that state is the Chattahoochee (which apparently did not originate within the Palmer movement); its 1892 minutes claim to be the 57th session. The name there is "United Free Will Baptist." Interestingly, a "circular letter" attached to the 1892 minutes, by J. M. Bray, includes: "Now, brethren, the term "Free Will" is simply a name given to us to distinguish us from other Baptists, and because we believe in the freedom of the will of man to act in obedience to the command of Christ for men everywhere to repent."

According to tradition, the first Free Will Baptist church in Alabama was begun when Ellis Gore rode horseback to Carolina to obtain basic docu-

---

57 Hearn, 166-167.
58 Hearn, 169. Harrison and Barfield, 78-80, copy this material from Hearn.
59 See Harrison and Barfield, 84-85 for a few of many such examples.

ments and returned to plant the Mt. Moriah church and eventually a conference by that name.[60] The minutes we have for the late nineteenth century (beginning 1874) sometimes use *Free-Will* and sometimes *Freewill*. *Free Will* does not appear until 1906.

The same variety shows up from the start among Tennessee Free Will Baptists, where there is definitely no connection to the Randall movement and any direct connection to the Palmer movement is not evident. The oldest association, the Cumberland, dates to 1842 or 1843, when it was named the Cumberland Association of Separate Baptists. But already an 1825 booklet entitled *The Experiences of Lucretia Patterson* had identified her as "Of the Society of Free Will or Separate Baptists." Exactly when the Cumberland changed its name officially is uncertain, but the minutes from 1876 on show at various times *Free Will*, *Free-will*, and *Freewill*.

The Bethlehem Association, now extinct, was next oldest in Tennessee, beginning in about 1850. The minutes we have are from 1871-1875. In 1871, *Free Will* appears on the outside and *Free-Will* inside. The next year *Free-will* is outside but *Freewill* inside. The next year *Free Will* is outside and *Free-will* inside.

In eastern Tennessee and western North Carolina, The Toe (or Tow) River Association was organized soon after 1850. Its handwritten record book shows both *Freewill* and *Free Will* from one year to another.

In Arkansas, the denomination has several associations that extend back into the nineteenth century. They show the same variation between *Free-will*, *Free Will*, and *Free-Will* (or *Free-will*) that is found elsewhere. The Antioch Association, in 1899, uses *Freewill Baptists*; the Polk Bayou in 1891 *Free Will* outside and *Freewill* inside; the Old Mt. Zion *Free Will* in 1891 and 1893 and *Freewill* in 1896 and 1898; the Little Missouri River *Free Will*

---

60   Given that there was a Mt. Moriah FWB Conference with churches in western North and South Carolina, Gore must have gone to one of those SC churches.

19

outside and *Free-will*, *Free-Will*, and *Free Will* inside, in 1891; the Western Arkansas *Freewill* in 1894.

Free Will Baptists in Oklahoma are confident that the work there traces its lineage back to the Palmer movement through Arkansas and Alabama. We have a few nineteenth century minutes of the oldest association there, first known as the Territorial Association.[61] The 1894 minutes use *Free Will*, but those from 1895 through 1900 use *Freewill*, with *Free Will* returning in 1905.

Much more evidence of the variety of usage could easily be shown, but this fairly traces the spread of Free Will Baptists from North Carolina southward and westward and seems to be adequate to demonstrate, beyond all doubt, that Free Will Baptists in the Palmer movement have throughout their history been very inconsistent in the spelling of the name. All three forms—*Free Will*, *Free-will* (or *Free-Will*), and *Freewill*—are equally valid and equally old.

Original Free Will Baptists

One more question arises: What about the name *Original* Free Will Baptists? To begin with, the use of *original* in front of the name is a very old tradition. I have cited, earlier in this article, the *1812 Former Articles* of the North Carolina General Baptists, entitled, "An abstract of the Former Articles of Faith confessed by the original Baptist Church, holding the doctrine of general provision." In this title, *original* is not capitalized; *confessed by the original* is all in the same small caps and *BAPTIST CHURCH* on a different line in larger type.[62]

---

61 At the time, what later became "Oklahoma" was still "Indian Territory."

62 While perhaps not of great significance, Pelt, 104, and J. Matthew Pinson, *A Free Will Baptist Handbook: Heritage, Beliefs, and Ministries* (Nashville: Randall House Publications, 1998), 143, have "Original" capitalized. This may reflect contemporary practice in typeset-

What seems clear is that in usage like this one "original" was an adjective rather than part of the proper name of the body. It was meant to identify the framers of the document with earlier Baptists like them: namely, the original English General Baptists from whose 1660 "Standard Confession" the 1812 Articles were drawn, and the early North Carolina General Baptists.

Even so, in time, *Original* came to be used widely enough, in front of *Free Will Baptists*, that it was often in effect a part of the name, used to distinguish between the bearers of the name and others who might be confused with them. A number of things, in North Carolina, might have contributed to that. Whenever an organization divides in tension, at least one of the successor groups will want to be known as the "original" ones by that name. And there were divisions, early, among North Carolina Free Will Baptists. During the years around 1840, they were invaded by the Campbell movement and according to Harrison and Barfield when that was over the remnants of the old Bethel and Shiloh Conferences organized in 1847 the "Original Free Will Baptist Conference" of North Carolina.[63] In about 1853, that body divided into two factions over the question of Masonry, with both groups claiming the name Free Will Baptist. No doubt this underscored the need for one of the groups—if not both of them!—to identify themselves as *original*. Later, in 1912, the Cape Fear Conference was divided over holiness doctrine, leading ultimately to the existence of the Free Will Baptist Holiness and Pentecostal Free Will Baptist denominations. More recently, the tensions that led to the separation between the North Carolina State Convention and the National Association of Free Will Baptists, in 1962, also brought about a rival North Carolina State Association that is part of the National Association.

---

ting titles, but it is probably not justified by the original. Pelt's explanation of the significance of *original* is correct.

63   Harrison and Barfield, 85, 234.

None of this should be taken to imply that "Original" was originally part of the name or consistently used in North Carolina or elsewhere. Hearn himself never uses "Original Free Will Baptists" as a name for the denomination or for any conference. Only in one discussion does he use *original* (uncapitalized) with the denominational name, and his purpose there is to emphasize the connection with the early North Carolina General Baptists, insisting, "I have shown who organized the original Free-Will Baptist Conference of North Carolina. ... [and] We are the original Free-Will Baptists of North Carolina."[64] He adds, discussing the aftermath of the division over Masonry, saying, "The old Conference, at the time of the division in 1853 adopted the following resolutions: "That by the help of God we will adhere to, and abide by, and keep inviolate the articles of faith, the rules of discipline and the constitution of the original Free-Will Baptist church."[65] The earliest date Harrison and Barfield use "Original" (with a capital letter) as part of the denominational name is 1847, in the records of the "Original Free-Will Baptist Conference" of North Carolina.[66]

When the various editions of the *1812 Former Articles*, discussed above, began using the fuller denominational name, the evidence is mixed. *Original* first appears, as part of the name in the Preface, in 1895. Thereafter it is usually on the title page, but the cover sometimes says, simply, *Free Will Baptist*.[67]

We have the minutes of the old Bethel Conference for 1833: *Original* is not part of the name there. For the General Conference of North Carolina, to which Harrison and Barfield refer, above, the 1845 minutes (the earliest

---

64   Hearn, 176.

65   Hearn, 177.

66   Harrison and Barfield, 236.

67   I thank Gary Barefoot for checking all the versions of this document to provide this information.

we have) also do not use the word;[68] but at least from 1851 on *Original* is included.[69] The Union Conference minutes say *Original*. The Cape Fear minutes do not use *Original* until 1912, and that marked the conference as it regrouped after the Holiness invasion had taken away many churches.[70] The Central, Western, and Eastern (all tracing back to the General Conference) apparently used *Original* from their beginnings.[71] But the North Carolina State Convention, organized in 1913, did not use *Original* until 1933, and even then for several years it appeared as "(Original)." In the 1926 United States Census of Religious Bodies, a statement "furnished by Rev. E. T. Phillips, editor of The Free Will Baptist" says that most Free Will Baptists "became known later as 'Original Free Will Baptists' and were listed as such in the 1890 census, "but have since preferred to drop the term 'Original,'" and be called simply 'Free Will Baptists'."[72] What seems to follow from all this is that *Original* was not used as part of the proper name of the denomination until about 1850 or so, was later dropped for a while, and was subsequently added again—with none of these changes being universal, even in the Old North State.

Original Outside North Carolina

As noted earlier, the Palmer movement in North Carolina first spread to

---

68   Pelt, 143, says, "The North Carolina Original Free Will Baptist General Conference met at Grimsley's Meeting House, Greene County, on November 6-9, 1845." I assume he was simply using the name that the conference soon came to have.

69   Again, thanks to Gary Barefoot for checking the minutes of the years not found in the Collection in Nashville.

70   See Pelt, 190-193 for details.

71   The original General Conference sub-divided into the Eastern and Western in 1886, and then the Eastern into Central and Eastern in 1895; see Harrison and Barfield, 322, 341.

72   *Census of Religious Bodies 1926: Baptist Bodies: Statistics, Denominational History, Doctrine, and Organization* (Washington: Department of Commerce, Bureau of the Census, Unites States Government Printing Office, 1929), 86.

South Carolina. Redding Moore and a few churches under his influence in that state were dismissed from the old Bethel Conference in 1831 to organize the South Carolina Conference. We have the handwritten record book of that Conference, 1858-1899; *Original* does not appear in the name until 1883; it has been used more or less consistently since then.

In Georgia, the associations that extend back well into the nineteenth century—like South Georgia, Midway, Martin, and Georgia Union—apparently did not use *Original* at first. Some of them added the word later and then dropped it still later. The South Georgia Association, for example, organized about 1880, apparently used *Original* only from 1944 to 1952.[73]

There is hardly any need to pursue this in other associations of churches. Here and there, especially where the North Carolina influence was felt, *Original* was sometimes added to the name. There was a time when various associations sent their minutes to the Ayden Press for printing, and that might sometimes have led to the addition of this word in one place or another.

Intermittently from 1935 until 1953, the minutes of the National Association of Free Will Baptists bore the name "Original Free Will Baptists," but *Original* was never in the official name in the Constitution. Since 1953, well before the separation from the North Carolina State Convention, the name has simply been *Free Will Baptists*.[74] North Carolina Free Will Baptists were prominent in the organization of the National Association and appropriately lent their influence to its organization. Free Will Baptists in various states apparently did not object to this form of the name even though most of them did not use the word in their own publications.

Since the separation of the North Carolina State Convention from the

---

73 I say "apparently" because we do not have *all* the minutes.

74 The *Treatise* of the National Association continued to use *Original* on the cover until 1981, probably copying from previous editions, but on the title page, the name did not have this modifier.

National Association in 1962, *Original* has become more prominent in the usage of Free Will Baptists in the State Convention: so much so that some now use "OFWB" as the abbreviation for the denominational name when that was probably not done before.[75] I recall discussion within the Executive Committee of the National Association, of which I was a member, shortly after the division, when the question about the use of *Original* was raised. The discussion was not part of any official action, but the consensus was that they deserved full freedom to use the name as a way of distinguishing themselves from Free Will Baptists aligned with the National Association. We thought it adequate to move forward with "Free Will Baptist" as our full denominational name.

What is clear, then, is that "Original Free Will Baptists" is an old and honored usage, even though it does not go all the way back to the beginnings of Free Will Baptists, not even in North Carolina. It is probably most appropriate for those conferences that descended from or were directly influenced by the old North Carolina General Conference. For the denomination in general, however, *Free Will Baptist* seems adequate and lengthy enough. On the East Coast, these days, the *Pentecostal* Free Will Baptists and Free Will Baptist *Holiness* have officially added those words to their names, and the distinction between them and us is therefore usually maintained.

Conclusion

Much more need not be said. It is appropriate that all of the denomination, for consistency, express our name in the way that has become dominant: *Free Will Baptists*. It is simpler if everyone knows that we write our name with two words!

One incidental by-product of this: as unofficial curator of the Free Will

---

75 For examples, see Pelt, 71.

Baptist Historical Collection in Nashville, I decided to use *Freewill Baptist (Randall movement)* as the standard subject-heading for things that were clearly part of the Northern denomination; and *Free Will Baptist* for things related to the Palmer movement and all other Free Will Baptists. In this, I am following the lead of Gary Barefoot, Curator of the Free Will Baptist Historical Collection at the University of Mount Olive, who first developed a list of subject-headings for a denominational historical library. At the same time, I use "FWB" (not "FB") as the abbreviation for any Free Will Baptist church or association anywhere, any time.

I feel constrained to add one less serious word to all who read this. *Free Will Baptist* and the plural *Free Will Baptists* should be used correctly! Without an "s" on the end, *Free Will Baptist* is either an adjective or a singular noun. As an adjective, it modifies some other noun in phrases like "Free Will Baptist people," "Free Will Baptist doctrine," "a Free Will Baptist preacher," or even "Cumberland Free Will Baptist Association." As a singular noun, it refers to one person, as in "I am a Free Will Baptist." But *Free Will Baptists* is a plural noun and should always be used when not modifying some other word and meaning more than one of us. It still embarrasses me to see, plastered on the front pages of the minutes of some of our associations, words like "The John Doe Association of *Free Will Baptist*." Then I cannot help asking myself, "Free Will Baptist *what?*"

We have a time-honored name, one we can wear without embarrassment. The two little four-letter words, *Free Will*, give any knowledgeable hearer a quick summation of our theology of salvation.

2

Robert Heaton and Separate Baptist Origins of Free Will Baptists in Middle Tennessee, 1808-1842

The traditional explanation of Free Will Baptist beginnings is that we owe our existence either to Paul Palmer in Eastern North Carolina in 1727 or to Benjamin Randall in New Hampshire in 1780—some of us to the first and some to the second. But things are not quite that simple. Actually, anyone who has explored how movements arise would be suspicious of that explanation anyway. The existence of Baptists who hold to free will and free salvation is too biblical and too probable to have just one or two beginnings.

Those of us who have explored the origins of Free Will Baptists are aware that the greater part of our denomination, as it is today, traces back to these two important movements, especially to that which began with Palmer. But we also know there were other streams that contributed to the rise of Free Will Baptists between 1727 and the present. This is the story of one of those, a story that had been lost sight of for a long time and has only recently been re-discovered.

This re-discovery began when Mrs. Pinkie Hudgens Christian asked me to look at a little record book that had been in the possession of her father, the Reverend J. E. Hudgens, one of the leading ministers in the Cumberland Association of Free Will Baptists during the first half of the twentieth century.[1] Miss Pinkie, as we called her, did not know what significance, if any, the book had, and neither did I. But it opened a door that further research confirmed and led to the story I relate here.[2]

On its surface, the book was the handwritten ministerial record of someone named Robert Heaton, who identified himself as a "Separate Baptist" and named churches and associations that I had never heard of. I first told Miss Pinkie that I did not think it had anything to do with Free Will Baptists. I was very wrong!

Who Was Robert Heaton?

First, a word about his last name, which in many sources is written Eaton, although both Robert and his father Amos wrote it Heaton. I would guess that the "H" was not pronounced, and this would explain why others often wrote it without the initial letter. In an 1843 letter from Lyman C. Draper to William Martin, the writer noted that some had assured him the name was Eaton, and he speculated as follows: "The peculiar mode of pronunciation as practiced in England, with the rough breathing, would make Eaton,

---

1   I met old Brother Hudgens once, probably in 1950, when I was a student at FWBBC and Henry Melvin took the quartet I was singing in to visit and sing for him in Ashland City, where he was confined to his bed. Hudgens was held in great respect by the ministers of the Cumberland Association.

2   I have published a part of this story before. See Robert E. Picirilli, "A Study of Separate, Free Will, Baptist Origins in Middle Tennessee" (*The Quarterly Review* 37:2 [Jan-Mar, 1977]), 44-52; ibid., "Free Will Baptists in Tennessee" (*Tennessee Baptist History* 1:1 [Fall 1999], 43-52; ibid., *History of Tennessee Free Will Baptists* (Nashville: Historical Commission, Tennessee State Association of Free Will Baptists, 2012), 9-12.

'Heaton'."[3] But that would not explain why those who wore the name wrote it with the H; perhaps Draper did not know they did. At any rate, it makes better sense to suppose that the written Heaton was pronounced Eaton—as it became before many generations had passed. I will write it (and say it, for that matter), with the H.

Here is what I know, now, about this man, learned from his record and from other sources that his record led me to. He was born March 15, 1765, the first of ten children of Amos and Elizabeth Heaton. The Heatons were involved in the pioneer settlement of Nashville and its environs. The main group of settlers came from the Watauga settlement in East Tennessee, led by James Robertson and John Donelson. Robertson led the men and livestock ahead, overland, from October to December 1779, crossing the frozen Cumberland to the French Lick (now Nashville) on Christmas day. Donelson led other family members, with the elderly and ailing, floating the Tennessee, Ohio, and Cumberland rivers to the spot, arriving in April of 1780.

Apparently, Amos Heaton and his family did not come with either Robertson or Donelson. Harriette Arnow says that there was "another party," led by Amos Eaton, who had migrated to East Tennessee by 1772 "from southwestern Virginia, where he had served the county as road surveyor."[4] This party arrived on the north side of the Cumberland, and made camp for the winter, near what would become Heaton's Station, on December 24, 1779, so that their trek occupied essentially the same time as that of Rob-

---

3 Draper Manuscripts 3 XX 14 (underlining original), on microfilm in the Nashville Public Library, Nashville Room, as issued by the Wisconsin Historical Society, Madison, Wisconsin. The letter is dated February 18, 1843. Lyman C. Draper traveled widely in the nineteenth century, interviewed many persons, and assembled many manuscripts about historical figures and events.

4 Harriette Simpson Arnow, *Seedtime on the Cumberland* (New York: Macmillan, 1960), 218-219. Against other accounts, Arnow's research seems the most thorough and persuasive.

ertson's party.[5] According to Donelson's journal, in an entry for the 31st of April (1780), on April 23 his group "reached the first settlement on the north side of the river, one mile and a half below the Big Salt Lick, and called Eaton's station after a man of that name, who with several other families came through Kentucky and settled there."[6]

Amos Heaton (c. 1740-1795[7]), Robert's father, had previously established a "Heaton's (Eaton's) Station" in East Tennessee, on the Holston River near what is now Kingsport. It had played the role of a makeshift fort in a skirmish with the Cherokee Indians in 1776, known variously as the Battle of Eaton's Station, or the Battle of Island Flats, or the Battle of Long Island.[8]

As part of the new settlement on the Cumberland, Amos Heaton established another Heaton's Station on the north side of the Cumberland,

---

5 Arnow, 232. Doug Drake, Jack Masters, and Bill Puryear, *Founding of the Cumberland Settlements: The First Atlas 1779-1804* (Gallatin: Warioto Press, 2009), 68, say that Robertson's party arrived "in late December to find three smaller parties already building," one of which was Amos Eaton's, that had arrived "on Christmas Day and had erected some temporary housing on the northern bank."

6 I assume all who came overland came through Kentucky. The Donelson journal can be found in various places; I have quoted from J. G. M. Ramsey, *The Annals of Tennessee to the End of the Eighteenth Century* (Kingsport: East Tennessee Historical Society, 1967 reprint), 202. See also A. W. Putnam, *History of Middle Tennessee or, Life and Times of Gen. James Robertson* (Knoxville: University of Tennessee Press, 1971), 75. W. G. Inman, *Planting and Progress of the Baptist Cause in Tennessee* (unpublished manuscript on microfilm in Nashville, Southern Baptist Historical Library and Archives), 14, seems to say that Amos Heaton and several families with him followed the route of Robertson and arrived to build "Eaton's Station" in the fall of 1780, but he must have had the year wrong.

7 Richard Carlton Fulcher, compiler, *1770-1790 Census of the Cumberland Settlements* (Baltimore: Genealogical Publishing Co., Inc., 1987) notes that Amos Heaton's will was "proved in Davidson Co., Mar. 4, 1795." We have a copy, printed from the microfilm record at the Tennessee State Library and Archives in Nashville.

8 Amos himself had been in the militia during the period. The inventory of the sale of part of his estate (recorded Sep. 2, 1814, in Davidson County, Tennessee) makes reference to "the amount of his discharge while a soldier in the war against the Creek Indians, $39.62½." A good account of the "Battle of Long Island Flats" can be found in Ramsey's *Annals*, and a briefer account in Putnam, 51-52.

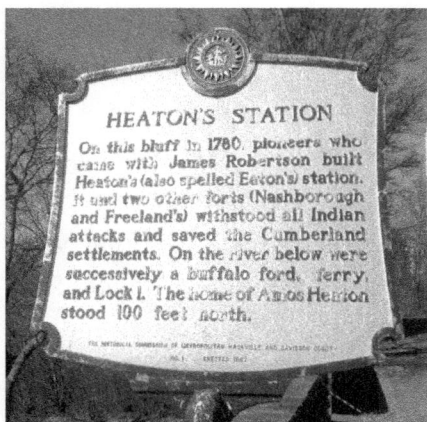

HEATON'S STATION

On this bluff in 1780, pioneers who came with James Robertson built Heaton's (also spelled Eaton's) station. It used two other forts (Nashborough and Freeland's) withstood all Indian attacks and saved the Cumberland settlements. On the river below were successively a buffalo ford, ferry, and Lock I. The home of Amos Heaton stood 100 feet north.

slightly west of the present route of U. S. Highway 41, where the Donelson flotilla arrived on April 23, 1780. A historical marker is near the spot, placed by the Historical Commission of Metropolitan Nashville and Davidson County.[9]

This means that Robert Heaton was 14 years old when he arrived, with other settlers from East Tennessee, in Nashville. Where he was born is also not clear: perhaps in Virginia from where the Heaton family had apparently moved to the Holston in the early 1770s.

What is certain is that almost thirty years after his arrival, on August 22, 1809, at the age of forty-four, "was the first time that Robert Heaton stood on the stage to endevour to preach the gospel & to spread the tydings of salvation." This is the first entry in his ministerial record, which was carefully kept—evidently in his own handwriting—from then until the final entry on July 23, 1843, shortly before his death on November 15 of that year.[10] This little book apparently provides a fairly complete account of Heaton's years as a minister of the gospel, an account that matches well, and is confirmed by, the records of the associations of churches referenced in the account.

When Heaton was converted, we do not know. Nor do we know who influenced him toward faith or to be a Baptist or to the free will doctrine that

---

9   For more detail about the site of Heaton's/Eaton's Station, see Arnow, 251 (incl. n. 12), 337. By 1792, he had moved and rebuilt his station "about five miles downriver [down the Cumberland] from his first station," on Lick Creek; see Arnow's second volume, *Flowering of the Cumberland* (New York: Macmillan, 1963), 13.

10 Throughout I will not footnote references to Heaton's record book, where the pages are not numbered. All references can easily be found by the *dates* indicated.

he espoused. Was this a heritage in his family, brought along from Virginia and East Tennessee to the new frontier? Or did he encounter a fiery evangelist among the settlers that persuaded him to follow Jesus? We will probably never know. It is clear that many Baptists, including Separate Baptists, were part of the movement to settle the frontiers, and many had come to the Holston River settlements in East Tennessee from Virginia and from North Carolina. But I cannot specifically identify the Heaton family as part of this migration.

I will return to Heaton's ministerial record, below, and build the story of him and the early Free Will Baptists in Middle Tennessee around it. Before doing that, however, it seems appropriate to relate the rest of what I have learned about the man. The Heaton family home at Heaton's Station was, according to the historical marker at the site, about 100 feet north of the marker.[11] "Evidently this was a good-sized station as we find quite a number of families living there."[12] Under the circumstances of the time, frontier families often lived close together on a "station" for mutual protection. There would have been a picket fence around most of the station to give it a fort-like quality. Ramsey relates a number of incidents when the station proved to be a refuge for the settlers who were often targeted by the Indians,[13] and it was one of the few "stations" to survive.[14] "The station...was never successfully stormed by the Indians, and remained a strongpoint for the storage of

---

11   It would have been a log house, but by Christmas of 1781, at least, it had "a floor fit for dancing, as did the other families in their station." See Arnow, *Seedtime*, 260, who provides descriptive detail about the construction and furnishing of the houses.

12   Ralph Winters, *Historical Sketches of the Winters Family*, vol. 1 (Clarksville, self-published), 13. Putnam, 190, provides insight into the comparative populations of the settlements when he provides numbers voting in regard to a 1783 treaty with the Indians: at Nashborough, 56; at Heatonsburg, 55; his numbers on p. 195 are apparently in error.

13   Perhaps the Indians had some justification for their hostility, given that they understood from some of the treaties that the land in the area was theirs.

14   Arnow, *Seedtime*, 292, including n. 40.

supplies and for refuge and reinforcement of surrounding stationers."[15] The village it became was soon known as Heatonsburg.

In 1782, the settlers in the area presented a petition for protection to the assembly of North Carolina (of which Tennessee was then part). The signature of Amos Heaton was second and Robert's was eighth. This may indicate that the petition was prepared and kept at Heaton's Station.[16]

I do not know the date of Robert's marriage, but his wife's name, like his mother's, was Elisabeth. According to a note in the back of Heaton's record, written by someone else after his death, she was about the same age as Robert, perhaps a year younger. Then she too was among the settlers of the area, but whether part of the original group, or among a large number who came in succeeding years, is not clear. Her maiden name is not indicated.

Robert and Elisabeth had at least three daughters and two sons, identified as such in his record. Since there is no list of their children, as such, there might have been others. The three daughters named were Susan, Moriller, and Sally Stewart,[17] all baptized by Heaton in May and June,1822. One son, Smith, was baptized by him in August 1822, as was Robert's wife Elisabeth. Another son, Ransom W., is mentioned in a disconnected note inside the front cover of the record book: "September the 23, 1840: Ransom W. Eaton started with his little family to move to the Missoory." While the note does not say that Ransom was Heaton's son, a contemporary descendant of Ransom, Lew Eaton, confirms that this was the case.

By the time of his death, at least, Robert Heaton was apparently a man of some means. The 1840 Census of the United States, for example, shows that at his address were a total of ten persons: Heaton and nine slaves; his

---

15 Jack Masters and Bill Puryear, *Thoroughfare for Freedom, Volume II: The Second Atlas of the Cumberland Settlements 1779-1804* (Gallatin: Warioto Press, 2011), 82.

16 Winters, 13, offers this suggestion and it seems reasonable.

17 I assume Stewart was Sally's married name.

wife had died in 1837. Among the slaves were a man and woman over 55, a man and woman 24-35, a male 10-23, and two boys and two girls under ten.[18]

He had extensive real estate holdings. The will of his father Amos had left Robert all his land lying on the east side of Lick Creek, to be equally divided with his brother Enoch. (The two of them, along with a third son Thomas, were Amos's executors.) A number of other transactions involving land deeded to Robert Heaton are recorded, which I list here (the list may not be complete).

> October 8, 1787 (Heaton was 22): 430 acres granted from North Carolina.
> July 1, 1794: 640 acres bought for 64 pounds.[19]
> July 1, 1794: 320 acres granted from North Carolina.[20]
> October 20, 1795: 396 acres bought from James Mulherin for 100 pounds.
> June 29, 1809: 256 acres granted from Tennessee.
> September 5, 1814: 40 acres bought from George Cagle for $500.
> October 12, 1815: 30 acres granted from Tennessee.
> January 1, 1820: 360 acres bought from David L. Horn for $1,000.
> February 1, 1823: 114 acres bought from Robert and William Vick for $250.[21]
> March 19, 1824: 40 acres bought from Robert Vick for $30.
> February 2, 1826: 100 acres bought from James Simmons and William Boyle for $50.
> February 26, 1834: 88.25 acres bought from Alex Lewis for $176.50.
> September 25, 1835: 500 acres granted from Tennessee.
> September 25, 1835: 400 acres granted from Tennessee.
> October 3, 1835: 120 acres granted from Tennessee.
> February 13, 1838: 112 acres granted from Tennessee.

---

18 Masters and Puryear, 144, refer to the recorded sale, in 1898, of a Negro named Mary, by Robert Heaton to Robert Weakley.

19 Ten pounds per hundred acres was the standard rate at the time; see Arnow, *Seedtime*, 311, 328.

20 This grant was "for the relief of the officers and soldiers of the Continental line" and indicates that Heaton was "one of the Commisioners Guard."

21 Robert Vick and his wife were baptized by Heaton in 1819.

The total of these acquisitions—if we assume that Heaton kept them all—is just under 4,000 acres and apparently does not count what he received as an inheritance from his father. While we must remember that land, on the frontier, was plentiful and cheap, and large holdings like this were fairly common, still it seems that Robert Heaton could be classed among the landed gentry.[22]

I do not know much else about Robert Heaton's life. According to a note in the back of his record book (entered by someone else), he died at age 78 on November 15, 1843, having been preceded in death by his wife Elisabeth at age 73 on June 17, 1837. The inventory of his estate was made on December 5, 1843, and recorded on January 5, 1844, by George E. Sanderson, his administrator. This was apparently an inventory of what is called "chattel": that is, it does not include real estate but lists one's personal property that is "movable." The list of possessions is itemized and lengthy. It includes, for example, furniture of various kinds, dishes, and different tools. The animals are listed: including three mules, one horse, and one yoke of oxen, as well as "14 head of cattle, 44 head of hogs & 20 pigs." Among the personal possessions was a "large Bible" and "3 old hymn books"; also a "saddle, bridle and blanket"—perhaps used in riding to the places where he preached.

The inventory also includes a very long list of "notes," apparently indicating that Heaton made loans to various individuals. Along with each note, the administrator has indicated whether the note was deemed "good" or "doubtful"—I assume for collection. A couple of the debtors were said to be "insolvent."

The last sentence of the inventory concerns Heaton's slaves: "The hire of the negroes subject to be called in if the court should decree a sale of them sooner than twelve months: Old Jenny hired $6.00, Lucy & little boy for $27.50 cents, Kincher for $101, Monday for $80, Jesse for $25.50." (Names

---

22   Arnow, *Seedtime*, in her chapter "The Bare Essentials" (307ff) tells the story of the land grants and purchases in Middle Tennessee, with all its drama and disappointments.

are spelled according to ability to read a handwritten note). Perhaps these amounts represent the cost of hiring them for a year? I am uncertain. Regardless, a man's slaves were part of the chattel that had value for the estate, whether for hire or for purchase. (Those were not our times!)

Robert and Elisabeth Heaton were buried in Forest Hill Cemetery in Ashland City, Tennessee. He was apparently living in that town when he died. The marker, pictured here, reads, "In memory of Rob. Heaton / Born March 15, 1765 / Died Nov 15, 1843." His wife's marker, beside his, is identical.

Between the time he first preached in 1809 and his death in 1843, however, Heaton planted the first Separate/Free Will Baptist church in the area and took part in the formation of the Cumberland Association of Separate Baptists, which has continued to this day as the Cumberland Association of Free Will Baptists. The story of all this will take up the rest of this chapter.

Robert Heaton's Ministry, May 1812 to August 1817

As already noted, the very first entry in Heaton's record is dated August 22, 1809, marking the first time he preached. The next entry is dated May 10, 1812, when he "was ordained & authorized to preach the gospel & to administer the ordinences of the house of the lord."[23] We can only wish we knew more, especially who ordained him and what church(es) were involved.[24]

---

23 One will notice that I usually copy Heaton's original spelling, which was very phonetic and inconsistent throughout his record.

24 There was a "Baptist Society," not further identified, in Davidson County at least as early as 1803 when one John Davis deeded an acre of land to the society on which to build a meeting house. No doubt, there were other Baptists, including "Separate Baptists," in the area

Heaton was at work for the Lord immediately, and on June 14, 1812, he "received" and baptized three persons. By the end of 1812, he had baptized twenty-four persons and received one by letter. These included his brother Enoch (three years younger than Robert) and several others whose names would continue to play a part in his ministry. William Seat refers to "wonderful revivals" that "swept through the churches in 1811 and 1812," and this may provide part of the context for Heaton's early success.[25]

In 1813, he baptized 14, including his brother Thomas. He also received eight persons identified as "former members" and chose Benjamin Drake and William Cradock as deacons and Thomas Heaton as clerk of the church.[26] He had baptized Cradock in 1812 and Drake early in 1813. Also among those baptized were "negro Sam" and "negro Zitter." Throughout the record, slaves are identified only by their first names and apparently were known only that way. There are, however, a number of scattered references to blacks, and sometimes the words "received" or "dismissed" are applied. I do not know what rights these were accorded.[27]

In 1814, Heaton baptized two persons and "licensed Brother Hurst to preach the gosple." In 1815, he baptized six and received five more into the church, two of the latter also being identified as "former members." In 1816, he baptized five and received two more. Of these two, one was by letter and the other by "recantation," a term apparently used to refer to

---

as soon as Nashville was settled. I know of no connections between Heaton and any others, although there were probably some.

25 William R. Seat, *A History of Tennessee Baptists to 1820-25* (Louisville: unpublished dissertation at the Southern Baptist Theological Seminary, 1931), 90-91.

26 I assume the note to mean that he is recording the *church's* choice rather than his own. Drake and Thomas Heaton were witnesses to an 1814 deed for land sold to Robert Heaton. A Benjamin Drake was among the original settlers who came in Heaton's party and was on the first Davidson County Grand Jury; see Arnow, *Seedtime*, 319, n. 52. He was one of the signers of the "Cumberland Compact"; see Putnam, 102.

27 I *assume*, without certainty, that they were regarded as members of the church.

persons who were recanting their membership in a church with different doctrine. He also recorded the deaths of two members in February, "Sister Hanah Criddle" and "Brother Elijah Hurst." Of the first, he noted that she was "leaving behind her a disconsolate companion with three little babies." In 1817, Heaton baptized seven and received two by letter.

The first note about reporting to an association occurs at this point: "August the 15, 1817 return to the association 69 members in good standing."[28] This provides a good place to stop and clarify what was taking place here.

The basic questions involve what church Heaton was serving during this period and to what association he was reporting. The answer is that he was serving Zion Church and reporting to the South Kentucky Association of Separate Baptists. These facts are confirmed in two ways. First, subsequently (in 1823) Heaton's record will show that he organized another church and the two deacons mentioned above (William Cradock and Benjamin Drake helped constitute that church. At that point, they are identified as "decons of Zion Church in Davidson County, Whites Creek, State of Tennessee." This makes clear that Heaton was serving the Zion Church as pastor in 1813 when the two deacons were chosen.

Perhaps we should also ask, on this point, whether Heaton organized Zion Church. For various reasons, it seems likely that he did, or (perhaps better) that he reorganized it. That all sixty-nine members reported in 1817 had been received into the church under his leadership seems clear from the fact that seventy-six names have appeared in his record, from 1812-1817, as either baptized or received by him. At least two have died and a few others must have dropped out, but what seems clear is that there were no active members before Heaton's ministry began to bear fruit. I suggest reorganized because some of the persons received have been identified as "former" members. This suggests a church that had ceased to function and was being

---

28 The verb *return* is being used in the sense of turning in a report.

revived by Heaton. Furthermore, the selection of two deacons and a clerk leads to the conclusion that this was a new constitution.

The minutes of the South Kentucky Association of Separate Baptists, during the period, also confirm Heaton's report. Indeed, 1817 was not the first time Heaton or his church had participated in that association. The 1812 South Kentucky minutes mention "a body of Baptists in Tennessee" who were received into the association; but they are not identified. In 1813, petitions were received from two Tennessee churches, identified as White's Creek and Sam's Creek, both in Davidson County. In the same year, a petition from Mackadoo (McAdoo) church in Tennessee asked for the ordination of a "Brother Baldra," so that church could have been the one received the previous year. (Later, in 1823, Heaton would note that Elder William Boldry of McAdoo Church helped constitute his second church.)

The 1814 minutes of the association are missing. The 1815 minutes name three churches in Tennessee as reporting: Sam's Creek, with no delegate listed; Zion, represented by "Robert Eaton"[29]; and Spring Creek, also represented by "Robert Heaton." Apparently, the McAdoo and White's Creek churches did not report. In 1816, however, five churches from Tennessee reported: Sam's Creek, Zion, Spring Creek, White's Creek (all by letter), and McAdoo Creek (represented by Wm. Boldra and G. Humphries).

Subsequently, in 1817 (when first mentioned in Heaton's record), four churches reported: Sam's Creek, Zion, White's Creek (letter only), and McAdoo Creek (represented by Geo. Humphries). The minutes also say, "The church called _____ Tennessee dissolved"—probably referring to Spring Creek. Perhaps Heaton had labored to establish a church there but had failed.

In summary, this much seems clearly established: when Robert Heaton was ordained he proceeded to (re)organize the church known as Zion, on

---

29   It is clear that this is Heaton; as noted earlier, the H was often left off.

White's Creek in Davidson County, Tennessee,[30] and was successful in doing so. (He might also have attempted to plant a church at Spring Creek that did not survive.) By 1817, his Zion church and at least three other churches in the area were affiliated with the South Kentucky Association of Separate Baptists. At least one of those churches, McAdoo Creek, would have some relationship with Heaton, but whether there was any relationship with the other two (Sam's Creek, White's Creek) churches is not indicated.

Who Were the Separate Baptists?

I diverge, temporarily, from my story of Robert Heaton to introduce the reader to the people known as Separate Baptists. Without much detail, I observe that the Separate Baptist movement traced back to a group of Connecticut colonists who settled at Sandy Creek, North Carolina, in 1755. Their two most influential leaders were Shubal Stearns and Daniel Marshall. Formerly Calvinistic Congregationalists, they had been influenced by the broad Baptist movement in the colonies and stirred by the revivalistic preaching that resulted from the ministry of men like George Whitfield. As Baptists, they strongly emphasized the importance of evangelism and conversion.

Consequently, the Separate Baptists were more moderate in their Calvinism and were tolerant of varieties of theological opinion along the Calvinistic-Arminian continuum. Apparently, they, unlike the Regular Baptists, were willing to make allowances for Arminian thinking in their fellowship.

By the 1780s, however, ideas about union among Baptists were gaining ground. In 1787, the Separate and Regular Baptists in Virginia agreed to unite and to call themselves United Baptists. The result was that this sentiment spread, and many Baptists in both the Carolinas, for example, adopted

---

30 Frederick Stump, one of the original settlers who had come with Heaton's party, "founded" the settlement on White's Creek—I assume where Zion church was. See Arnow, *Seedtime*, 251.

the same posture. For whatever reasons, however, not all the Separate Baptists were friendly to this union. Perhaps those who resisted this the most were the ones who were more emphatically Arminian in their views.

At the same time these things were happening, and before, many Baptists—especially in Virginia and North Carolina—were pressing to the westward frontier. One reason for this was the search for religious freedom. Baptists were often persecuted in the colonies as attempts to establish a state church, at one level or another, were made. Many Baptists fled from Virginia down the Appalachians into East Tennessee and beyond. Some from North Carolina joined them. Others—more of them, it seems—crossed over into Kentucky and spread out from there. Indeed, in the view of William L. Lumpkin, the Separate Baptists predominated among them and "provided religious leadership for the American frontier. ... The Separate Baptist preachers preceded most others in exploring and occupying the frontier."[31]

If the reader notices any trends, here, that parallel the account I have given of the background of Amos Heaton and the Nashville settlers, above, that is probably appropriate. I do not have any specific information about Separate Baptists among the pioneers who came to Middle Tennessee,[32] but it is not surprising that there were some, and that Robert Heaton—regardless who his influencers were—was one.

Nor should one be surprised that some Separate Baptists were definitively Arminian in their theology of salvation, even though more of them were "moderate Calvinists." Lumpkin makes clear that there were often tensions among the Separate Baptists over the differences between Calvinism and Arminianism, and this was especially true of the doctrine of the extent of the

---

31 William L. Lumpkin, *Baptist Foundations in the South: Tracing through the Separates the Influence of the Great Awakening, 1754-1787* (Nashville: Broadman, 1961), 148.

32 Lumpkin gives much information about the Separates in Kentucky, but almost nothing about Tennessee.

atonement and predestination. He relates, for example, that a query was addressed to the 1775 General Association of Separate Baptists, asking "Is salvation by Christ made possible for every individual of the human race?" As he put it, "A warm debate followed." After lengthy discussion, with powerful speakers on both sides, "it was found that the Calvinists had a small majority." The Arminians, he says, learned that their views would be considered a bar to fellowship and withdrew to form their own association. After some time, and with some compromise wording, the two groups reunited.[33] Morgan Patterson observes, "Though there is evidence that earlier Separates embraced a diluted Calvinism, most Separate Baptists of the nineteenth century in Kentucky advocated an Arminian doctrine of the atonement."[34] This would be equally true of Separate Baptists in Tennessee—and probably of Separate Baptists anywhere, that did not become United Baptists. Patterson also observes that Separate Baptists have been characterized by "opposition to all human creeds and confessions," holding that the Bible alone is an all-sufficient guide to faith and practice, and by the practice of feet-washing as an ordinance.[35] Other Baptist historians agree about the tensions among the Separate Baptists over Calvinism and Arminianism.[36]

It is clear, then, that the Baptists of the South Kentucky Association of Separate Baptists—and this includes Heaton and Zion Church and apparently the other churches in Middle Tennessee named above—were "free willers" in their theology, viewed as such by others and willing to accept the term even though it was not part of their official name. This can be confirmed from a couple of things that came along just a few years later. One of

---

33 Lumpkin, 103.

34 W. Morgan Patterson, "Small Baptist Groups in Kentucky," in Leo Taylor Crisman, *Baptists in Kentucky, 1776-1976* (Middletown: Kentucky State Convention, 1975), 150

35 Patterson, 150.

36 See, for example, Robert Baylor Semple, *History of the Baptists in Virginia*, rev. G. W. Beale (Lafayette: Church History Research and Archives, 1976), 108-110.

these is that, in 1825, a little testimony booklet was published in Nashville, at the Republican Office, entitled The Experience of Lucretia Patterson. In the front pages, Robert Heaton and other ministers whose names appear in his journal and on the pages of the South Kentucky Association minutes vouch for it. Significantly, the writer is identified as "Of the Society of Free Will or Separate Baptists."

Even earlier than that, in 1823, the minutes of the Nolin Association of Separate Baptists (organized amiably out of the South Kentucky Association in 1819) include a report by a committee that had attended a meeting where an unsuccessful attempt had been made to persuade them to unite with other Baptists in Kentucky. Their report picks up the phrase "free willers" used of them and refers to themselves, somewhat ironically, by those words. This shows both that these Separates were considered to be free willers and that they were willing, at least ironically, to identify themselves in that way.

I will return to this below, but enough is already clear to keep us from being surprised, later, when the Separate Baptists in Middle Tennessee, that were part of what I call Heaton's circle, changed their name, officially, to Free Will Baptists. I should also note that the Separate Baptists have continued to exist to this day as a small but distinct denomination. Kentucky and Indiana are probably their strongest states, but there are churches in other states.[37]

Robert Heaton's Ministry, August 1817 to 1820

Back, now, to Heaton: in 1818, he baptized three persons and wrote: "return to the South Kintucky association seventy members in good standing." (The 1818 minutes of that association are missing and so this report cannot

---

37 According to the Wikipedia article on "Separate Baptists in Christ," there are probably 100 churches in the U. S. Of special interest to readers of this chapter, the article also indicates that their missions agency has supported the ministry of Lonnie and Steve Palmer in the Ivory Coast!

be confirmed.)

If 1818 was a dry year, 1819 was not. Heaton baptized sixteen persons and received four others by letter, as well as dismissing one by letter. Of one of the five received by letter he noted, "received Sister Boldry in felowship who had bin expelled not according to the gospel." Where she had been expelled from, or why, is not indicated Of another, he noted, "received Brother Elexander Rascoe a preacher of the gospel by recommendation."

Also in 1819, Heaton made two notes about reports to the association: one of 88 members on August 20, and another of 91 members on October 20. The reason for this is that the South Kentucky Association decided to divide, amiably and because of distances. The new association was the Nolin (or No-lynn, named for the river) Association of Separate Baptists, and since it was for the more southern churches the Tennessee churches naturally became part of it.

The increase from 70 members reported in August of 1818, to 88 in August of 1819, matches the 18 listed by Heaton as baptized or received between those two notations. The increase from 88 to 91 between August and October matches Heaton's record of four received and one dismissed by letter during that period.

Yet another factor was involved, although it does not become clear in Heaton's journal until later: he had established an "arm" of Zion Church at Sycamore Creek, in Robertson County, probably in 1819. The influx of baptisms apparently was connected to that new activity, but the "arm" group, although meeting in a new location, would still be considered part of the mother church and not reported separately.

Apparently, the August report was for the South Kentucky Association and the October report for the Nolin Association. These 1819 reports cannot be confirmed by the associational minutes, simply because those minutes did not list the individual churches or their numbers that year. At any rate, it is clear that Heaton's church and others in that circle in Tennessee were active in the Nolin Association from its beginning in 1819. For that matter, the 1820 session of the Nolin convened with Heaton's Sycamore arm of Zion church, which met at Loe's Meeting House in Robertson County. The association's meeting began on the first Saturday in October.

The minutes of that 1820 associational meeting show that the Tennessee delegation played a leading role—not surprising in view of the distances from Kentucky and the methods of travel available at the time. Heaton himself was chosen Moderator. He and Alexander Rascoe (mentioned above) were appointed to write the "circular letter" that would be attached to the minutes; but subsequently that task was assigned to another brother (perhaps at their request).[38] Rascoe was also on the Business Committee, along with William Baldry (see above) and John M. Chaudoin, another Tennessee minister (see below). Chaudoin and Rascoe both preached during the session. There is no list of churches or their numbers, however, so we cannot be sure how many churches in Tennessee reported, but a "church at Macadoo Creek, Tennessee" is mentioned in a passing reference.

As for Heaton's own ministry during 1820, his record shows that he baptized four and received four others. Of these four, one was by letter, two by recommendation, and one "reclaimed & received into fellowship again." That he reported 99 members to the association on August 27, 1820, fits precisely. One of those received by recommendation is particularly significant, entered on September 3, 1920: "received Brother Cothron by recommendation & appointed him as clerk to the Sikemore arm of Zion Church."

I pause, then, to bring the account up to date with another summary. From 1817 to 1820, Heaton expanded his ministry by establishing an arm of Zion Church at Sycamore Creek. His church moved from the South Ken-

---

38 Since it is not clear that Heaton penned the circular letter, I have decided not to include it in this treatment. (A small part of the circular has been placed on a couple of websites as though it was specifically the work of Heaton.) Its chief doctrinal feature was to emphasize unlimited atonement, and we can be sure that Heaton held that position.

tucky Association to the (newly formed) Nolin Association of Separate Baptists. At least the McAdoo Creek Church was also among the Middle Tennessee churches in this circle and perhaps still the churches at Sam's Creek and White's Creek—although neither of these would ever be mentioned again in associational minutes. By 1820, at least three other ministers were in this circle: Alexander Rascoe, William Boldry, and John M. Chaudoin.

Robert Heaton's Ministry, August 1820 to 1823

In 1821, Heaton baptized four and received two by letter and one by "recantation." He reported 104 members to the Nolin Association. The 1821 minutes of the association provide no list, churches, or numbers to confirm this.[39]

The year 1822 must have been a highlight in Heaton's ministry. We can imagine his joy as he made these entries:

"May the 5-1822. Baptised my two daughters Sally Stewart & Susan Heaton."

"June the 2-1822. Baptised my daughter Moriller Heaton."

"August the 4-1822. Baptized Elisebeth Heaton my wife & Smith Heaton my son."

In all, 1822 saw him baptize fifteen, receive two by letter, and receive one former member. Among those baptized was Wilson Gower, who will become important in this account as a minister.[40] Those received by letter were John M. and Sarah Chaudon, who will also become important in subsequent events.

Heaton's 1822 report to the association was of 114 members, a number

---

39 The 1821 minutes of the South Kentucky Association note that Heaton was among those who brought greetings from the Nolin.

40 Gower was witness on a deed to Heaton in 1824. He was the grandson of Abel Gower and son of Russell Gower, both among the settlers who came with Donelson; he was also father of James W. Gower, who followed in his footsteps as a Free Will Baptist minister.

recorded both in his record and in the Nolin Association minutes. Indeed, the associational minutes show that Heaton preached and served on the Business Committee, and that the next session was scheduled to meet at "Zion at Loes M.H. in Robertson County"—which means that the Sycamore arm that met there was still considered part of Zion Church.

The 1822 Nolin minutes (for the first time since its organization) carry a list of churches and their numbers. Only two Tennessee churches are listed: Zion, in Davidson County, reporting 114 members; and McAdoo (county unclear, probably Davidson), reporting 28 members. Delegates representing Zion were R. Heaton, B. O'Daniel (perhaps Benjamin O'Donely, baptized by Heaton in 1815), H. Felts (perhaps Hardy Felts, baptized in 1821), and B. Lee (perhaps Braxton Lee, received in 1822 as a "former member"). The delegate from McAdoo Church was J. Davidson. Perhaps the Tennessee churches previously named in the South Kentucky minutes—Sam's Creek, White's Creek, and Spring Creek—had failed or affiliated elsewhere. Heaton was among those chosen to preach on Sunday.

The year 1823 was important in Heaton's ministry, primarily because it saw the Sycamore arm of Zion constituted as a church in its own right:

> *June the 14-1823*
> We the Sykemore arm of Zion church having potisioned the body of Zion church for a devision & constitution have this day met at Loes meeting house in Robertson County State of Tennessee & after singing & prayer we give ourselves to god & to each other & on the Scriptures of the old & new testament was organised constituted & pronounced a separate & independent church to our selves with our former pastor to wit elder Robert Heaton & is now known by the name of Sykemore Church at Sweet Spring meeting house Robertson County.
> Constituted by elder William Boldry of Macadoo Church & elder John M. Chaudoin Brother William Cradock & Brother Ben-

jamin Drake paster & decons of Zion Church in Davidson County
White's Creek State of Tennessee.

This decision was obviously acceptable to Zion, the mother church. It is
clear that John M. Chaudoin was now the pastor there and that Robert Heaton was pastor at Sycamore, although we cannot mark the exact date when
this became the case. It is not clear whether "Sweet Spring Meeting House"
was different from Loes Meeting House.

Before the separation of the Sycamore arm from Zion, in 1822, there had
been 114 members (above). A total of 17 persons had been recorded as
received following that report, which would bring the total at Zion (before
the separation) to 130 or so. In September 1823, Heaton (now at Syca-
more/Sweet Spring as a separate church) reports seventy-one members.
That probably left about 60 members at the original Zion.[41] The 1823 Nolin
minutes do not give any list of churches or number to help us confirm this.

At any rate, the 1823 Nolin Association met "at Loes Meeting House
in Robertson County, Tennessee, on the second Saturday in September."
Alexander Rascoe was Moderator and "John M. Shadoen" (Chaudoin, of
course) was on the Business Committee. The minutes of the association also
report that a "Union meeting" was scheduled for Zion meeting house in Davidson County, Tennessee, in June 1824. Heaton was among the ministers
named to be responsible for this union meeting.

The 1823 associational minutes are especially interesting because of the
contents of a letter attached to the minutes as a circular letter (mentioned
above in the description of Separate Baptists). Some ministers of the association who did not make the trip to Tennessee and addressed their brethren meeting in Tennessee had written the letter; they sent it by two of the

---

41 Heaton's record was not kept in such a way that we can tell which persons were baptized or
received into which of the two congregations before the separation.

ministers who were making the trip, Walter Williams and Thomas Chilton. Among other things, the letter says, "their hearts were filled with exceeding joy" when they "heard the joyful sound of salvation proclaimed by our beloved brother Heaton who visited us the last year from the realm of Tennessee. At that time much people were assembled together, and the Lord opened the hearts of the disciples called free willers."

The letter goes on to say a meeting had occurred when they had been visited by three men "who appeared to be of the sect called Calvinists, and the free willers in council gave them audience." The Calvinists had offered a "little book" with terms of union and offered "to the free will disciples" to unite with them on those terms. But the latter had offered, instead, to unite on the basis of the Old and New Testaments; to that the three men said "Nay." Afterward, according to the letter, four of their number had attended another meeting of the Calvinists where the subject of union was still being proposed. One of the Separates, named Thomas (Chilton, no doubt), who was "said to have been (by Calvinists) a ring leader of the sect called Separate Baptist" and "an enemy to creeds and decorems," urged again that there could be union only on the basis of the Scriptures alone. That had brought an end to the proceedings. The letter is lengthy, humorous, and salty. It shows that the Nolin Separate Baptists did not mind being referred to as "free-willers" and that they recognized Calvinism to be at the heart of the issues.[42] It also shows the Separates' insistence that the Scriptures alone must be the basis of any associational union.

In summary, the major development of this period is that Heaton's Zion and the Sycamore arm had now become two churches, rather than one, with John M. Chaudoin pastor at Zion and Heaton pastor at Sycamore/Sweet Spring.

---

42 Morgan Scott, *History of the Separate Baptist Church with a Narrative of Other Denominations* (Indianapolis: Hollenbeck Press, 1901), 222, refers to this meeting very briefly as including Freewill Baptists; I believe he misread the ironic references of the Separates to *themselves* as "free-willers."

Robert Heaton's Ministry, 1824-1825

In 1824, Heaton baptized seven and three died; consequently, his 1824 report to the Nolin Association does not show much gain: from seventy-one to seventy-four members. The Nolin minutes for this year do report churches by names and numbers; three were in Tennessee: (1) Sweet Spring, with 74 members, represented by Benj. O'Donald (O'Donely earlier?), H. D. Felts (Hardy?), and N. A. Williams (probably Nathan Williams, baptized by Heaton in 1821); (2) Zion, with 70 members (apparently having grown by about ten), represented by Alexander Rascoe, Reubin Chadowen (to appear later in Heaton's record), Braxton Lee (above), Kendred Jackson (not mentioned by Heaton), and John M. Chadowen (perhaps still pastor, although Rascoe might have been); (3) Liberty, with 21 members, represented by Anthony Hinkle—neither having been named elsewhere. (McAdoo Creek church and William Boldry apparently did not report that year; the church showed up again later.)

Heaton's Sweet Spring/Sycamore church only held its own in 1825. He recorded three baptisms and two deaths and reported seventy-three members to the association. Indeed, the 1825 Nolin minutes list the same three Tennessee churches as in 1824: Zion, with 70 members, represented by John M. Chadowen, apparently still the pastor; Sweet Spring, with 73 members, representing by letter, apparently; and Liberty, with 30 members, represented by F. Demombreum—probably the same as Felix Demumbro baptized by Heaton in 1812.

The 1825 associational minutes also show that Chaudoin was Moderator and that the next session was scheduled to meet at "Zion meeting house, White's Creek, Davidson County, Tennessee." These minutes have added interest because of two queries and their answers. One, from Liberty Church, asked if a church has a right to appoint a temporary moderator if their moderator (the pastor, I assume) were absent from the meeting; the answer was "They have." The other, from Zion Church, asked what to do with a member who obtains a letter of dismissal and then does not unite with another church and acts wickedly; the answer: "Deal"!

The year 1825 is also important because it saw the publication of a small testimony booklet entitled The Experience of Lucretia Patterson, A Religious Tract Written by Herself. As I have already noted in discussing Separate Baptists, above, the booklet identifies the writer as "of the Society of Free Will or Separate Baptists," thus showing the equivalence of the two names. She was obviously part of the circle of churches I have been describing, given that the names of nearly all eleven members of the "committee of Ministers and lay members of the society to which she belongs"—listed in the publication—have a role in Heaton's journal. The ministers were Wm. Bauldry, Jno. M. Chaudoin, Thomas Scaggs, Jno. Chaudoin, Reuben Chaudoin, and Robert Aeaten (Heaton, no doubt). Only Thomas Skaggs and the second John Chaudoin (perhaps son of the first?) are not in Heaton's record; Skaggs was not a Tennessean but was one of the leaders of the Separate Baptists in the South Kentucky and Nolin Associations. The lay members were Benjamin Drake, Jesse Atherly, Susannah Drake, Kitty Bauldry, and Polly T. Felts, all of whom appear in Heaton's record except for Atherly (assuming that "Kitty Bauldry" was "Mrs. Bauldry"). In her testimony, Patterson reports that she was baptized by John M. Chaudoin; she might therefore have been in the Zion Church, but that is not certain.

The Formation of Heaton's Charity Church at Marrowbone Creek, 1826-28

Perhaps it is inevitable that divisions occur. The year 1826 saw the beginning of a genuine stir among the Separate (or "free-will") brethren in Tennessee. Heaton's record gives the first indication. After a couple of blank pages, the following entry appears: "Marrowbone Church was constituted on the 10 day of January 1826 by elder Thomas Scaggs & elder Allexander Rascoe, constituted on 26 members." Then follows a list of names that must certainly be the members; but there are sixty-five names, not just twenty-six!

Apparently, Heaton allowed room for this list to grow from the original 26 to the larger number he expected to join. Indeed, he had left room to go back before this January 1826 entry and include his record of baptisms, etc., for 1826 and 1827. In October and November of 1826, he baptized two and received two, and three of the four names are in the list of sixty-five (the other perhaps omitted by oversight?). In 1827, he recorded but one baptism: namely, Lucy Heaton,[43] whose name is also among the sixty-five. So, the list of sixty-five members at Marrowbone includes the twenty-six "charter" members who were enrolled when the church was constituted on January 10, 1826, plus at least four who joined later in 1826 and 1827, plus some thirty-five others not individually recorded as "received" by Heaton.

Where did these sixty-five members for the new church come from? The plain fact is that the great majority of them had already been members of Zion or Sweet Spring/Sycamore under Heaton's leadership of those churches. The names of forty-one of the sixty-five had already appeared in his record as being baptized or received by him, and some of the other twenty-four might have been there as women with different married names. (For example, Wilson Gower's name is among the sixty-five and had been baptized by Heaton at Zion. The name of his wife, Lucindy Gower, had not appeared previously but might have been one of Heaton's converts under her maiden name.)

Further confirmation appears, indirectly, in the minutes of the Nolin Association. The 1826 minutes show reports from Zion, with fifty-three members; Sweet Spring, with twenty-seven members; Liberty, with thirty-eight members; and Macedo (McAdoo), with twenty-six members. Zion had

---

43 She is not identifiable as a member of his family.

dropped from seventy, a loss of seventeen; and Sweet Spring had dropped from seventy-three, a loss of forty-six. The total loss was sixty-three, almost the same number as Heaton's new church on Marrowbone Creek. So, Heaton had now become pastor at the new church and was no longer at Sweet Spring on Sycamore Creek. Apparently, he had ceased to be pastor at Sweet Spring near the end of 1825.

All this was probably not a friendly movement from Zion and Sweet Spring to the new church on the Marrowbone. There was serious tension between Heaton and John M. Chaudoin, and it appears for the first time in the 1826 Nolin Association minutes: "A committee was appointed to report to the association, upon examination, on the objection to admitting the Marrowbone church into this association." The following year's minutes show that Chaudoin was the one who raised this objection, but the nature of the objection is never made clear. Was Chaudoin angry over the invasion of his flock at Zion? Was there some question about doctrine or practice that was divisive? There seems no way to know.

Regardless, the association committee made its investigation and reported, later in the 1826 session, that the charges were "not sufficient to prevent the church from being received."[44] So, Heaton's Marrowbone church was received and reported the next year, although the tension continued. In 1827, the dispute reached its climax. Four Tennessee churches reported: Liberty, with forty-eight members and William Boldry delegate; Sweet Spring, with just twenty members and John Cochran delegate; Zion, with fifty-one members and delegates Alexander Rascoe, Kindred Jackson, and "Shadowen" (Chaudoin, of course); and Marrowbone with fifty-eight members and Thomas Heaton delegate. Robert Heaton's name did not appear in

---

44 Actually, the record continues by saying, "Report of the committee made to the association, upon which the association acted and determined the church should not be received." I assume the clerk, perhaps in confusing the negatives, erred in inserting the "not."

the Nolin minutes for 1826 or 1827, and he had not noted any associational report for those years in his record. But his church had been admitted and his brother represented in person in 1827.

As noted, the dispute was not quite finished. The 1827 minutes also report that a committee of twelve was appointed to report "on the difficulties between the churches in Tennessee belonging to this association." Later in the meeting, the committee provided a lengthy report, in four main parts.

(1) The problem had arisen from objections made the previous year by "Shadowen" and from new letters received from the churches who stood with him in objecting to Marrowbone's being received in the association (we do not know which churches supported Chaudoin).

(2) The conclusion of the committee was that Chaudoin had caused all the confusion and so had caused contention and acted disorderly.

(3) The reasons for this conclusion were that Chaudoin should have taken "gospel steps" with "Eaton"; that he had joined with Eaton in giving the hand of fellowship to Marrowbone (at its constitution, I assume); that he had agreed at the previous session of the Nolin that a committee should act but had then rejected its report; and that he now openly declared he would not "hear" the association.

(4) The recommendation was that Chaudoin and "the churches that justify his conduct" be disfellowshipped, although any church that desired to do so was welcome to continue in the association.

This report was adopted and so the matter was officially settled. The result was probably predictable and the next year's minutes (for 1828) show that Heaton's Marrowbone church was the only Tennessee church reporting. We do not know anything about the other three churches—Zion, Sweet Spring, or Liberty. Did they all side with Chaudoin against Heaton and accept being disfellowshiped? They do not show up in the Nolin minutes again, except that in this same year a subsequent item of business provided for a "union meeting" at "Zion meeting house" in June of 1829, to be attended by some

54

of the Nolin leaders from Kentucky. Nothing further appears about that, and the three churches are not mentioned in the Nolin minutes again.

Chaudoin himself was mentioned one final time in the Nolin minutes (1828), where a memorandum reported that he and some other individuals in Tennessee had been stirring up people for his cause and attempting "to reflect upon this association." According to this report, the South Kentucky Association had also judged Chaudoin's conduct to be improper and he had published 500 copies of a document defending himself.[45] We know nothing more about Chaudoin or the work of the three churches that apparently sided with him, except that in the January 1839, issue of The Baptist, edited by the influential R. B. C. Howell, a brief notice about Chaudoin appears, which I reproduce here in full.

Rev. John M. Chaudoin
  This brother, who now lives in this vicinity, was baptized thirty four years ago [1805] by Elder S. Woodfin and joined the church under his charge, at Muddy Creek, Powhatten, co. Va. He was then in the 19th year of his age. He subsequently moved to Adair County Ky., commenced preaching, and was ordained by Elders J. Hall and J. Jones. In 1812, in the excitements, on doctrinal subjects, which resulted in a division of the churches in that quarter, in which, brethren Chandler, Chilton &c were prominent, brother Chaudoin adhered to them, and was dropped from the General Union. He remained separate until April 1838. He then made application to the Church at Cedar Spring, Edmunson Co. Kentucky, under the Pastorship of Elder Frederick Meredith, and was received as a member. Bro. Chaudoin is now a minister of the United Baptist Church in full fellowship.

Whatever the problems in 1827-28, Heaton was vindicated. He showed

---

45 It would be helpful to find a copy of that document.

up in person for the 1828 session of the Nolin, representing Marrowbone and reporting 69 members, as noted both in his record and in the Nolin minutes. Indeed, he preached the session's introductory sermon. As for his own record, Heaton baptized three and received two others into the church during 1828; none of these were named in the original list of sixty-five Marrowbone members.

The 1828 Nolin minutes also note that a "Kerr's Creek" church in Tennessee was received and its messenger, Felix Demumbry, was seated. Surely, this was the Felix Demumbro who was baptized by Heaton in 1812 and who had represented Liberty church at Nolin in 1825 (above). Perhaps he had sided with Heaton during the tensions and that had led to the establishment of this church; but we cannot be sure of that.

Another brief summary is in order. In 1826, Heaton established a new church at Marrowbone Creek. The members he enrolled included many from Zion and Sweet Spring, and the Zion pastor, John M. Chaudoin objected to the reception of the new church into the Nolin Association. By the time the tension was over, in 1828, the three churches that had previously reported to Nolin—Zion, Sweet Spring, and Liberty—were no longer in its fellowship. The Marrowbone church was joined only by another new one, Kerr's Creek, represented by one of Heaton's friends, Felix Demonbreun (as it is properly spelled).

Robert Heaton's Ministry, 1829-1838

The year 1829 was a relatively dry one in Robert Heaton's ministry. The only entry in his record for that year was "return to the association fifty-seven members." This indicates a loss of twelve: down from 69 the previous year. Interestingly, of the sixty-five names in the original Marrowbone membership list, twelve have notes beside them saying either "removed" or "dismissed." The 1829 Nolin minutes confirm that Marrowbone reported (by letter only) fifty-seven members. These minutes also list just one other Tennessee church reporting: namely, "Republican Meeting House," with thirteen members and represented by F. Demumbro—obviously the same as the Kerr's Creek that was received in 1828.

In 1830, Heaton baptized five, received three, dismissed one, and noted the death of another. He said he was reporting 60 members; indeed, the 1830 Nolin minutes confirm that, and that both Heaton and William Fuqua, who had been identified as a deacon in the Marrowbone membership list, represented Marrowbone.[46] Heaton was chosen as Moderator for this session of the Nolin and preached. Again, the only other Tennessee church listed was Kerr's Creek, still represented by Felix Demumbro, reporting six members. This would be the last time for the Kerr's Creek church to be listed in the Nolin minutes; by 1831 and thereafter, Felix Demumbro was representing Kentucky churches. The work at Kerr's Creek/Republican Meeting House in Tennessee must have folded.

One of Heaton's 1830 entries catches our attention: "October the 4th … received Brother Antony Hinkle & Sister Hinkle by recantation." This is probably the same Anthony Hinkle—evidently a minister—who had represented Liberty Church to the Nolin in 1824 and served on the Nolin Business Committee in 1826. Liberty, of course, was one of the churches that had dropped out of Nolin following the Heaton-Chaudoin controversy. That Heaton received Hinkle and his wife in 1830 "by recantation" probably indicates that the Hinkles had repaired their relationship with him and renounced their earlier support of Chaudoin—whatever the issues were.

In 1831, Heaton baptized two and received two "by letter." One wonders if Zion and Sweet Spring were still in existence and if they would have granted letters of good standing to Marrowbone—or if Marrowbone would receive letters from those churches without "recantation." We simply do not know.

---

46 Fuqua was a witness on a deed to Heaton in 1824.

Heaton's 1831 record does not mention a report to an association. In-deed, the 1831 Nolin minutes do not list any Tennessee church—apparently the first time this had been true since Nolin's organization in 1819! Again, in 1832, the Marrowbone Church did not report to the Nolin. During that year Heaton baptized two, received one, and dismissed four. By one of those dismissed was this notation: "dismissed in disorder." Nothing like that ap-pears by any other name in Heaton's record, but we have no indication as to the nature of the misconduct involved.

The other three dismissed were "by letter," and this has some signifi-cance. The three were Wilson Gower and his wife Lucindy and John B. Demumbro. Gower had been baptized by Heaton in 1822 and had come with him to Marrowbone (as clerk of the new church) in 1826. So had his wife, and so had John Demumbro.[47] Because of what we know of subsequent events, it seems clear that this was not an unhappy parting. Probably Gower was already preaching and these three friends were going to another church to minister.

If 1829-32 were dry years in Heaton's ministry, 1833 was a revival year! He baptized no less than thirty-nine persons and received ten others (half of the ten having been baptized or received by him earlier at Zion and Sweet Spring), more than in any previous year.[48] And, after two years' absence, he once again reported to the Nolin Association. He said he was reporting 90 members, and the 1833 Nolin minutes confirm the number and note that Heaton and Wilson L. Gower represented Marrowbone.

Considering that Gower had already lettered out of Marrowbone, it may be that the Nolin clerk mistakenly listed him as representing Marrowbone simply because he was with Heaton. What seems likely to me, from all that

---

47   John B. Demonbreun is buried in the Carney Cemetery adjacent to the site of old Charity Church.

48   It would be interesting to know whether 1833 was a revival year in Middle Tennessee.

will follow, is that Gower was already serving another church (apparently Blue Spring) as pastor and that he and Heaton went to Nolin in 1833 at a time when they were evaluating whether they wished to continue to be a part of Nolin or to seek another alignment. At any rate, as far as I can tell, Heaton never reported to the Nolin again, nor did any other Tennessee church. In 1834 and 1835, the Nolin minutes note that Marrowbone and Kerr's Creek did not report. In 1836, the notation is simply, "several of the churches not represented." There are no further references to Tennessee churches, and this ends our account of the Nolin Association.

As for Heaton's personal record, in 1834 he baptized ten and received two others. In 1835, he baptized three, one of them George Head, about whom more will be said below. In 1836, Heaton baptized none, and in 1837 just three. In 1838, he baptized four, and after that entry there is a blank page, after which begins a new period of his ministry and relationships.

In summary, the decade 1829-1838 was relatively uneventful. Heaton was still serving as pastor at Marrowbone and reporting spasmodically to the Nolin Association of Separate Baptists. Wilson L. Gower, one of his converts, apparently began preaching, perhaps under Heaton's wing, at another church. If so, it was probably begun with the approval of Heaton and the Marrowbone congregation. Heaton and Gower attended the Nolin Association in 1833 for the last time.

Alignment With the Concord Association of Separate Baptists, 1839-1841

After a blank page in Heaton's record book, a new page begins with the following significant entry:

> We the Church of Christ called Separate Baptis at Charity & Zion meeting houses in Davidson County being legally constituted upon the broad bases of the Scriptures of the old & new testament

protesting against all human rules or articles of faith or decorems believing that the word of God is the only rule to govern the kingdom of Christ both in faith & practis

We have now become atached to the Concord association & represent in that body sixty nine members

September the 24 – 1839

This represents a new departure and was Heaton's first entry regarding a report to an association since 1833. Before discussing this new associational affiliation, however, other things about this entry need comment.

First is the matter of the denominational name. This was the first time "Separate Baptist" appeared in Heaton's record. But that need not concern us, since his churches had been affiliated for many years with two associations—South Kentucky and Nolin—that wore that name. This is also the first time "Church of Christ" appeared. That, too, is not especially significant: many churches, regardless of denomination, attached these words to their names entirely apart from the influence of Alexander Campbell.[49]

Second is the reference to "Charity & Zion meeting houses." Charity was the church name finally given to the Marrowbone church. Subsequent entries in Heaton's record indicate this: in 1841, he recorded 71 members from "Charity" and 53 from Good Spring (below); in 1842, he recorded 74 members from "Marrowbone" and 53 from Good Spring. The parallels and the numbers make the identification between Charity and Marrowbone certain. Indeed, a deed recorded April 9, 1840, indicates that one Asa Carney sold for ten dollars, to the trustees of Charity Church "on little Marrowbone Creek," a parcel of land measuring one and a half acres for a meeting house.[50]

---

49 We have, for example, a church letter dated in 1808 (not Free Will or Separate Baptist) that begins, "The Baptist Church of Christ at Miller's Creek ...." This was well before Alexander Campbell's influence in Middle Tennessee.

50 The five trustees were John B. Dembra [Demonbreun], Dennis Dozier, Cordy C. Peoples, Wilson L. Gower, and George S. Allen. All of them except Dozier were in Heaton's 1826-27

But what about "Zion"? Given no further references to Zion, I remain uncertain about this, but what seems likely is that the old Zion Church had closed its doors sometime after the Heaton split from Chaudoin, and that Heaton was now trying to get it going again, at the same place on White's Creek, as an "arm" of Charity. He apparently was not successful in this. This, however, remains speculative.

The third thing needing comment is the strong wording renouncing "all human rules or articles of faith or decorems" and affirming "that the word of God is the only rule to govern the kingdom of Christ both in faith and practice." This is not surprising. It was common with various Baptist groups and especially with Separate Baptists to take this stance. Lumpkin reports that one of the things that sometimes prevented the merging of Separate and Regular Baptists was the Separates' "prejudice against confessions of faith."[51]

The only new thing about this entry, then, is Heaton's affiliation with the Concord Association of Separate Baptists. In order to explain this, a digression is necessary, picking up where an earlier section in this account—Who Were the Separate Baptists?—left off. As noted there, the Regular Baptists and Separate Baptists were uniting in various places, beginning in Virginia in 1787, and calling themselves United Baptists. In the early 1800s in Middle Tennessee, then, most Baptists were apparently trying to live together in harmony, regardless of differences in the theology of salvation seen in Arminian versus Calvinistic terms.

This certainly does not mean, as affirmed by John Grime, quoting James

---

Marrowbone membership list. *Cheatham County, Tennessee: History and Families* (Paducah: Turner Publishing Co, 2001), 14, reports, "In 1796 Braxton and John Lee and Rev. Robert Heaton settled at the mouth of Marrowbone Creek, Heaton preaching at Lealand meeting house." Since Heaton did not begin preaching until 1808, this note must represent some conflation of dates. On page 34, the same publication names many "early settlers" and several of the names appear in Heaton's record; on page 33 is a 1918 map that locates the site of Charity Church on the Little Marrowbone.

51 Lumpkin, 144.

Whitsitt, that "all the Baptists of this section [Middle Tennessee] at the beginning of the nineteenth century were Calvinists"![52] In a separate article, entitled "Separate Baptists" Grime repeats this claim.[53] Interestingly, both in the book and in the article Grime shows no awareness of Tennessee churches in the South Kentucky or Nolin Associations of Separate Baptists before the split in Concord or any awareness of Heaton's circle who refused to merge with the Concord United Baptists and formed the Cumberland Association of Separate/Free Will Baptists.[54] The existence of Heaton and churches affiliated with Separate Baptist associations in Kentucky and Tennessee since 1817 certainly disproves Whitsitt's claim. John Asplund, writing in 1794 after the majority of Separate Baptists had become United Baptists, classified all Baptists into two major groups, with "Armenian [sic], Freewill, Separate, or General Baptists" in one group, contrasted with "Regular, Calvinists, or particular Baptists."[55] Given that Asplund was writing at the very time referred to, his identification of Separate Baptists shortly before 1800 as Arminian in sentiment should be taken seriously.

One of the early associations of Baptists in Tennessee was the Concord Association. However, by 1826-27 tensions about Calvinism and Arminianism led to the division of that association into two groups, both of which kept the name "Concord Association." Those on the more Arminian side—the larger group, as admitted by contemporary Baptist historians—were identi-

---

52 J. H. Grime, *History of Middle Tennessee Baptists* (Nashville: Baptist and Reflector, 1902), 539.

53 The article was not published, so far as I know. As I recall, I obtained the copy from his son. It is dated 1934, well after the book cited in the previous note.

54 This may in part be accounted for by the fact that the "Middle Tennessee" Grime focused on was nearer the plateau than to Nashville, but he did examine and refer to the minutes of the Concord Association.

55 John Asplund, *The Universal Register of the Baptist Denomination in North America, for the Years 1790, 1791, 1793, and part of 1794* (New York: Arno Press, 1980 reprint), 5-6.

fied as Separate Baptists.[56] This provided, for Heaton and others in his circle, a truly Separate Baptist association much closer home than the Nolin in Kentucky. This is what lies behind the 1839 entry in Heaton's record, quoted above. Heaton and Gower, at least, and churches in their circle, chose to leave Nolin and affiliate with the Concord Association of Separate Baptists.

As we have seen, Charity/Marrowbone last reported to Nolin in 1833, and in 1839, it was fully affiliated with the Concord. But there had been contacts with the Concord before 1839. In 1837, a church named Blue Spring was received into the Concord Association, represented by none other than W. L. Gower! Furthermore, the 1837 Concord minutes show that the pulpit, on Sunday, was occupied by Robert Heaton, W. L. Gower, and William Keele.[57] No doubt Gower, at least, and perhaps Heaton as well, had already visited the Concord and become known there.

The 1838 minutes of the Concord Association show that the Heaton and Gower circle of churches were fully participating. Not only did Blue Spring report, represented by W. L. Gower and E. Simmons, so did Good Spring (more about this church to follow), represented by J. B. Felts and T. W. Felts, and Charity, represented by R. Heaton and J. Vick.[58] Indeed, Gower served the association as Moderator. (The 1839 minutes of the Concord are missing.) Why Heaton waited until 1839 to note in his record, "We have now become attached" to the Concord, is not clear, since they had joined in

---

56 The 1831 minutes of the other Concord (which subsequently came to call itself "United Baptists") include a query as to whether it "is right to value the baptism administered by Separates." The answer ends, "There is no example in the Scripture authorising her [the church] to receive it." The Separates' version of the Concord was subsequently identified as Concord #2 and exchanged correspondence with the Duck River and Mount Zion Associations of Separate Baptists.

57 Keele was one of the influential leaders in Concord.

58 The minutes of the Baptist State Convention for 1840 make reference to the Concord Separates and include in a list of their ministers Wilson L. Gower, Thomas W. Felts, and Robert Heaton.

1838. Perhaps he had regarded the new affiliation as a trial.

The reference to Thomas W. Felts as representing Good Spring church is interesting. In a later biographical summary, Felts's son Drury said of his father, "Soon after his conversion, he and my mother united with the old Good Spring Baptist Church, Robertson county, Tenn., and were baptized in 1833 by Rev. Robert Heaton."[59] Heaton's record indicates, in fact, that Thomas Felts was "received by experience and baptism" on July 28, 1833. The son indicates that Felts had preached his first sermon "at George Head's private house" in Robertson County and had been ordained on June 27, 1838, by a presbytery called by the Good Spring Church and consisting of Robert Heaton, Wilson L. Gower, and George Hazlewood, at which time he "was called to the care of the church"—Good Spring, apparently. The account goes on to say that Felts's associates in the ministry, then, were Heaton, W. S. Baldry (mentioned several times above), and Wm. Luck; in 1840, he moved to Kentucky and became active in the ministry among Baptist churches there.[60]

As for Heaton's personal record, no entries are dated in 1839 except the lengthy one quoted above about affiliation with Concord. In 1840, he recorded five baptisms, and one in 1841. He did not record a report to the association in 1840, but in 1841, he recorded a report from Charity of 71 members and from Good Spring of 53 members. This is the first time the Good Spring church appears in Heaton's record, although it had appeared in the Concord minutes for the first time in 1838, as noted above, and was in Robertson County. When it was planted, and by whom, I do not know.[61] What is clear from Heaton's record, however, is that at least in 1841 and 1842 he was reporting both Charity and Good Spring to the association and

---

59   Joseph H. Borum, *Biographical Sketches of Tennessee Baptist Ministers* (Memphis: Rogers & Co., 1880), 247.

60   Borum, 247-48.

61   Whether this was the same as the present Good Springs FWB Church, which has had gaps in its existence, is apparently not possible to determine.

so was apparently serving both as pastor.

When Heaton became pastor at Good Spring is not certain. Since there is no reference to Good Spring in his lengthy 1839 entry quoted above (even though Good Spring had already been received in the Concord in 1838), it seems unlikely that Heaton was serving the church at that time. Perhaps he became its pastor in 1840 when Felts moved to Kentucky. It seems likely that someone in the Heaton-Gower circle planted the Good Spring Church. At any rate, there were three churches in this circle reporting to the Concord Association in 1838-1841: Blue Spring, Charity, and Good Spring. In 1840, a fourth church joined this Heaton-Gower circle in the Concord: Heads Church, represented by Charles Lankford and George Head. As noted above, Head had been baptized by Heaton in 1835, and Felts had preached his first sermon in Head's house.

Also joining the Concord in 1840 was Mt. Zion Church, represented by R. R. and William Barton. Whether this church owed its existence to someone in the Heaton-Gower circle is not clear. But if not, it subsequently became part of that circle. R. R. Barton would continue to be part of the Concord; William Barton would align himself with Heaton and Gower.

In 1841, yet another church in the Heaton-Gower circle joined the Concord: Liberty Church at "Hays Fork Meeting House" in Stewart County, represented by W. L. Gower. We simply do not know whether this was the same Liberty that had been associated with Heaton and Gower earlier, in 1824-27.[62] That church had been with them in the Nolin Association and had been represented at times by Anthony Hinkle, Felix Demumbro, and William Boldry; it had apparently sided with John M. Chaudoin against Heaton and dropped out of the Nolin. If it was the same, perhaps it had languished and Gower had led in its revival; but that is speculation. At any rate,

---

62 References to the earlier "Liberty" in the Nolin minutes did not indicate the county where it was located.

in 1841 Gower, Heaton ("R. Eaton"), and Barton served on the committee for arrangements; and Barton and Gower were the finance committee.

Another short summary is in order. During the period of 1839-1841, important developments took place. For one, Wilson L. Gower became a close associate of Heaton's and obviously shared in the leadership of the growing circle of Separate Baptists. For another, the ministers and churches in that circle changed their associational affiliation, moving from the Nolin Association of Separate Baptists, primarily in Kentucky, to the Concord Association of Separate Baptists, composed entirely of Tennessee churches. Heaton himself began to serve the Good Spring church as well as Charity at Marrowbone. Other churches were established and associated with their influence: at least Blue Spring, Heads, and Liberty in Stewart County.

A New and Permanent Organization, 1842-1843

The year 1842 was momentous for the growing band of churches associated with Robert Heaton and Wilson L. Gower. The significance, however, was not in Heaton's personal ministry but in their associational affiliation. Indeed, for Heaton's personal ministry, his record shows that he baptized four in 1842 and one in 1843. These are the only entries for these years other than the notation about reporting Good Spring (fifty-three members) and Charity (seventy-four members) to the Concord in 1842. For that matter, the 1843 baptism is the last entry in Heaton's record. He was seventy-eight years old at the time.

In the association, however, there were important developments. When the Concord convened in September of 1842, probably the primary topic of discussion was the possibility of reunion with the other Concord made up of the more Calvinistic-minded Regular or United Baptists. That possibility had been raised as early as 1840,[63] when the other Concord sent a letter to the Concord Separates promoting friendship. (They sent the same letter to the Duck River and Mt. Zion Associations of Separate Baptists.) Following that, the 1841 minutes of both Concords reflected a friendly spirit toward each other. Then in 1842, the other Concord inquired of the Concord Separates about the possibility of actual union. Consequently, during the 1842 session of the Concord Separates, a resolution approving the reunion was adopted and men were appointed to meet later that fall to consummate the merger. The reunion would take place on November 18, 1842: both Concords would become one, and there would no longer be a Concord Association of Separate Baptists.

What, then, of the Heaton-Gower circle of churches in the Concord? The 1842 minutes answer this question with the following entry, even before the final vote approving reunion with the other Concord: "Resolved, that those churches which petitioned for letters of dismission for the purpose of forming a Separate Association, be dismissed, viz. Heads church, Liberty, Blue Spring, Good Spring, and Charity." All five of these had joined the Concord, beginning in 1837, under the influence of Heaton and Gower. Later in the minutes, after the final vote approving the reunion, another note reports, "Mt. Zion Church is dismissed." Subsequent events make clear that Mt. Zion and its pastor, William Barton—even if they were not originally part of the Heaton-Gower circle—decided to join with these five churches in leaving Concord to form a Separate Baptist Association.

What is reasonably clear is that these churches, especially the five led by Heaton and Gower, were not willing to lose their identity as Separate Baptists. The reasons for this have not been recorded, but one may assume that the differences between a Calvinistic and an Arminian view of salvation were

---

63 Actually, the reunion had been suggested by R. B. C. Howell in the July 1835 issue of *The Baptist*; he had even proposed a set of articles of faith for the united body!

involved. Some have suggested that a difference of opinion about communion was the main consideration, with Heaton and Gower holding to open communion. Perhaps this was the case, but nothing in the minutes of the Concord Separates would indicate this, and so it remains speculative. Perhaps there was a combination of factors: open communion, Arminian soteriology, or even a sense of identity. After all, Heaton and Gower had spent their entire ministry as part of the Separate Baptist people. Those among the other Concord Separates who reunited with the Concord Regular/United Baptists had not.

Perhaps Heaton himself was not present at Concord in 1842 when all this transpired. His name does not appear in those minutes. At age 77, he might have been home in failing strength. It seems obvious, however, that he supported the refusal of the circle of churches to take part in the merger into United Baptists. That Gower, his protégé, would have acted contrary to his wishes is unlikely. Even more unlikely is it that the two churches he served as pastor—Good Spring and Charity—would have withdrawn from Concord without his approbation.

But Heaton was present when the newly-formed Cumberland Association of Separate Baptists met in October 1843 at Heads Church. It may well be that there had been an organizational meeting late in 1842, following the withdrawal from Concord, but that cannot be said for sure. The Free Baptist Cyclopaedia (1888) says that Heaton and Gower founded the Cumberland in 1842. Regardless, the 1843 minutes exist and show that seven churches were part of the new association: Heads, Liberty, Blue Spring, Good Spring, Charity, Mt. Zion (represented by William Barton as in 1840 at Concord, above), and Sycamore. Perhaps this last was a recent formation: might it have been a revival of the old Sweet Spring church on Sycamore Creek? We do not know.

At this meeting, Barton was Moderator and preached. Gower also preached, as did James M. Cherry. One month after this meeting, on November 15, 1843 (as reported in the first part of this article) Robert Heaton died. But he had lived to see the fruition of his thirty-four year ministry, realized in the formation of an association of churches that has existed to this present day. It seems particularly appropriate that the minutes of this meeting end thus: "So closed by prayer by Elder W. L. Gower in much peace and great harmony." I include, at the end of this article, copies (reduced) of all three pages of the minutes of the session.

One wonders whether other Baptist associations took note of the formation of the Cumberland. I did note that the Duck River Association of Separate Baptists minutes for 1845 reported receiving a "letter from B. F. Binkley, of Davidson County, ... a Separate Baptist, instructed by his ass'n (of the same faith and order) to open correspondence w. us." The Duck River named some of its ministers to visit Binkley's association, but there is no further reference to the contact in subsequent minutes. As can be seen from the 1843 Cumberland minutes below, Binkley represented Gower's Blue Spring Church when the Cumberland was formed.

The Baptist historians appear not to have learned about this band of Separate/Free Will Baptists or the formation of the Cumberland Association. The one exception I am aware of is found in an unpublished history by W. G. Inman, who described the decline of the Cumberland Baptist Association (not Free Will or Separate) in the 1840s and added: "About this time the Free Will Baptists effected, within the territorial limits of this Association, an organization, bearing the same name. ... The Free Will Baptist Association was composed of a few feeble churches but they never attained to any denominational influence."[64]

---

64 Inman, 75. His document is not dated but provides information to about 1880, by which time the Cumberland had changed from Separate to Free Will in name. Another unpublished history by O. L. Hailey, *History of the Baptists of Tennessee* (on microfilm in the Southern Baptist Historical Library and Archives), 153, makes essentially the same statement in almost the same words. One of these documents was obviously dependent on the other.

Exactly when the Cumberland Association officially changed its name from Separate Baptist to Free Will Baptist is not certain. Except for the 1843 minutes, we have no other minutes of the Cumberland until 1876, and by that time, the change had been made. We do possess a copy of the Cumberland's Constitution and Bylaws dated 1856, however, using the name Cumberland Association of Free Will Baptists. G. V. Frey, in a brief historical article attached to the 1911 Cumberland minutes, said that "Freewill" was added in about 1851 and that for a while the wording "Freewill Separate Baptist" was used. This seems reasonable, but there is no documentation for it now. The records of Bethlehem Church, near Ashland City, show that Wilson L. Gower founded it in 1847 as "The Separate Baptist church of Christ at Bethlehem," and "Free Will Baptist Church at Bethlehem" first appears in its records for 1854. Regardless, the 1876 Cumberland Association minutes show that five of the seven original churches (along with fourteen others) were still reporting to it—all but Blue Spring and Sycamore. Some of the churches involved still report to the Cumberland.

I have already indicated that, as early as 1825, "Separate Baptist" and "Free Will Baptist" were often used interchangeably, even though the two were distinct denominations. Even in 1842, at the time the Cumberland was organized, that was true. The deed to Liberty Church in Stewart County, executed by Elisha Williams, Sr., on April 19, 1842, conveyed two acres of land and the meeting house at Hayes Fork to "the Separate or Free Will Baptist Church ... called Liberty."[65]

There are things we do not know and wish we did. There may have been other individuals who should be given credit for the planting of the Free Will Baptist movement in Middle Tennessee, but if so, we do not know who they

---

65 I thank Mrs. Nelda Saunders of Dover, Tennessee, for providing a transcription of this deed, found on page 393 of Deed Book 14 in Stewart County. Liberty Church reported to the Cumberland until shortly after 1890 and was succeeded by the present Brandons Chapel and Pleasant Hill Free Will Baptist churches.

are. Surely there were persons who influenced Robert Heaton, and their role in his ministry might have been significant if we but knew.

From what we know, however, it is clear that Robert Heaton should be recognized as the father of the Free Will Baptist movement in this area. It is likewise clear that he and Wilson L. Gower, whom Heaton baptized, should be regarded as founders of the Cumberland Association of Free Will Baptists.

Therefore, it is clear that the Free Will Baptists in this part of Middle Tennessee came from Separate Baptists. I would suspect that there may be other segments of Free Will Baptists, in one place or another, who owe their origins to that people. Perhaps something will happen, like the little record book Miss Pinkie gave me, to bring that to light.[66]

---

66 The late David Joslin told me, once, that he had found evidence that Separate Baptists provided the background for some of the Free Will Baptists in Arkansas, but I have not given any attention to that.

MINUTES

OF THE

CUMBERLAND ASSOCIATION OF SEPARATE BAPTISTS,

HELD AT HEAD'S MEETING HOUSE,

Robertson County, Tenn.

On Saturday before the first Lord's day in October, 1849, and the two succeeding days.

INTRODUCTORY.

Elder William Barton delivered a Sermon from Acts, 10th ch., 34th and 35th ver., the Association was then opened by prayer by Elder Wilson L. Gower.

CHURCHES	DELEGATES NAMES.	By Experience & Baptism.	By Letter.	Restored.	Dismissed.	Excluded.	Dead.	Total.	Contribution.
Liberty,	James M. Cherry, W. W. Cherry and J. R. Williams,	44	7	10	3		1	111	1 82
Blue Spring.	J. Darrow, W. L. Gower, and B. F. Binkley,	15	1	1	3	1		56	1 00
Good Spring,	A. Williams, J. Dowlen, J. Walker,	4	4		6		1	44	1 00
Charity,	John Martin, Robert Heaton,	13	2					49	1 00
Mount Zion,	Wm. Barton, W. D. Hamlin, L. Hollin,	4		2			1	50	1 50
Heads,	M. Woodrough, W. Head, G. Head,	1						50	1 50
Sycamore,	W. Railey, Thos. Smith, J. Wingo,							16	50

1st. Called for petitionary letters received from Sycamore by the hands of William Railey, John Wingo and Thos. Smith, and they are invited to seats.

2d. Chose William Barton, Moderator, and Wilson L. Gower, Clerk. Committee of Arrangements appointed to consist of Brothers John Martin, James M. Cherry, John Dowlen, James Darrow and George Head.

Chose Elder W. L. Gower, Wm. Barton and James M. Cherry, to occupy the stand on Sabbath, who preached to a large and attentive congregation. Adjourned until Monday 9 o'clock.

Met on Monday morning pursuant to adjournment. Appointed James M. Cherry and John Dowlen, a committee of finance, who reported they received $7 32 cts. from the churches. We recommend the churches to prepare a Blank Book against the next Association.

Resolved, That our next Association be held at Liberty Meeting House, Stewart county, commencing on Friday before the first Lord's day in October next—and Brother Wilson L. Gower to preach the introductory sermon, and Brother Wm. Barton his alternate.

The Association recommend a circular letter to be prepared by our next Association, and appoint Bro. W. L. Gower and Wm. Barton to prepare it.

The Association recommend to the churches the propriety of sustaining a traveling preacher, and wish each church to ascertain the voice of said church, and send the amount they wish to contribute set out in their next letters.

Our days of communion will be as follows:—Blue Spring will hold a protracted meeting, commencing on Saturday before the first Lord's day in September. Good Spring, commencing on Friday before the fourth Lord's day in Sept. Charity, on Saturday before the second Lord's day in September. Heads', on Saturday before the third Lord's day in October. Sycamore, Old Liberty, on Saturday before the fourth Lord's day in July—the ministers of the Association are requested to attend said meetings.

Resolved, That Bro. B. F. Binkley is appointed to superintend the printing and distributing the Minutes, and that he will have at least 300 copies struck, and that he reserve fifty for general distribution. So closed by prayer by Elder W. L. Gower in much peace and great harmony.

WILLIAM BARTON, *Moderator.*

WILSON L. GOWER, *Clerk.*

3

When North Met South: Elias Hutchins, Jesse Heath, and Hutchins's Visits from New England to North Carolina, 1829-33

Many contemporary Free Will Baptists seem to think there was little if any contact between the Northern and Southern Free Will Baptists. It is true that there was not much organic union between them, although there was some. However, there were productive contacts. This chapter tells the story of the visits of Elias Hutchins from New England to the North Carolina Free Will Baptists, a story not widely known.

Our historians have treated this briefly,[1] but the letters that Heath and Hutchins wrote, describing the visits and the Free Will Baptist situation in

---

1 See William F. Davidson, *The Free Will Baptists in History* (Nashville: Randall House, 2001), 149-150; Michael R. Pelt, *A History of Original Free Will Baptists* (Mount Olive: Mount Olive College Press, 1996), 119-123. Edmundo Gonzalez, with some collaboration from L.

North Carolina at the time, have mostly gone unnoticed. Most of these letters were published in the Randall movement's weekly newspaper, the *Morning Star*. From them we learn much about the condition of Free Will Baptists in Eastern North Carolina in the early part of the nineteenth century.

Jesse Heath's Letters to the *Morning Star*

The story apparently began in 1827 in North Carolina. I. D. Stewart's history reports as follows:

> Early in the year 1827, Rev. Jesse Heath, of North Carolina, learned, by some means, that there was a Freewill Baptist Paper published in Maine, and John Buzzell, of Parsonsfield, was an editor, to whom he addressed a letter of inquiry. Buzzell answered it April 23^d, and the correspondence thus commenced, and published in the Morning Star, was continued occasionally for years. Rev. Elias Hutchins visited them in 1829, met with a cordial reception, preached in most of their churches, and visited the small branch in South Carolina.[2]

This seems straightforward enough, but the full story is much more interesting.

First, a brief biographical sketch of Jesse Heath, about whom not much is known, including the date of his birth in the latter part of the 1700s. He was from the Grimsley Free Will Baptist Church in Greene County, North Carolina, ordained to the ministry in 1807. He was active in the original Annual Free Will Baptist Conference in North Carolina and in the Bethel

---

S. Joyner, published a series of articles, entitled "'Sketches' of Religion in America," in the *Free Will Baptist* (Ayden, NC) in 1977 that told part of the story of Hutchins's visits, but not using the letters in the *Morning Star*; issue dates were June 29, July 6, 27, September 7, 28 (plus one with date of publication not yet identified).

2   I. D. Stewart, *The History of the Freewill Baptists for Half a Century, 1780-1830*, vol. 1 (Dover: Freewill Baptist Printing Establishment, 1862), 463. (There never was a vol. 2.)

and Shiloh conferences into which that conference was amiably divided in 1830-31. He was a man of some ability, as indicated in the letters he wrote. Among other things, he and Hutchins compiled a hymnal for Free Will Baptists in the South, published in 1832 under the title, *Psalms, Hymns and Spiritual Songs, Selected for the United Church of Christ, Commonly Called Free Will Baptists, in North Carolina, and for Saints in All Denominations.*[3] His name disappears from the record in 1839, although we have no records of the Shiloh conference and he was probably active there. Already in May of 1833, he was "the oldest preacher belonging to the Bethel or Shiloh conference," as a letter from Robert McNab, given later in this chapter, testifies. At any rate, newspapers in New Bern, North Carolina, began publishing notices in April of 1839 that he had mail that had not been picked up, and so it seems likely he had died by that time.[4] Davidson speaks of Heath in this way: "Without question, Heath was the foremost leader of the early Free Will Baptist denomination. His contributions as preacher, administrator, historian, and theologian were vital to the success and prosperity of the new movement. No other early leader was to contribute so much or to gain such a degree of respect."[5]

As for Heath's letters, we do not have a copy of his first letter or of Buzzell's answer. But Heath's next letter was published in the *Morning Star*, dated at Cox's Bridge, North Carolina, May 28, 1827.[6]

---

3 Davidson, 188.

4 I thank Gary Barefoot, curator of the FWB Historical Collection at the University of Mount Olive, for much of this sketch.

5 Davidson, 153. By "new" movement, he means after the transition from the original General Baptists to those officially using the name *Free Will Baptists*.

6 *Morning Star*, June 28, 1827. I reprint as found in the *Morning Star*, except that I have added some paragraph divisions to relieve the reader. Throughout this chapter, I will take only minimal liberties with the text, making occasional corrections in spelling or punctuation.

Dear Brother—Your communication dated the 23d of April was duly received by the last mail. I rejoice to learn that your connexion is so large, and that it is pleasing to you to open a correspondence with us. As to Principle, there is not the least difference, and I hope there will be none in Practice.

We baptise none but such as confess their sins, believe in Jesus, and consider baptism by immersion as a duty deeply impressed. We think that no person can feel baptism deeply impressed on their minds as a duty, and still be in an unprepared state to comply with it. We have not been in the habit of practising Open Communion, because, no application has been made for liberty to eat and drink with us; but if any in good standing were to ask that liberty, they would not be denied. At our meetings we often invite others to the stage, and when invited we labor amongst them.

We practice the imposition of hands on all newly baptized members, according to the examples of St. Peter, John, and Paul. We also practice washing of feet, believing it to be a gospel ordinance, but there is no compulsion if any are not disposed to wash with us, we do not compel them. We sometimes commune and wash feet in the day and sometimes at night.

We have a book of discipline which contains a few articles of faith and rules of discipline—the constitution of our annual conference—the ordination of a minister—the constitution of a church—and the form of matrimony. The principal use that we make of this book, is in the government of the annual conference—the ordination of our ministers—the constitution of our churches, and in the solemnization of matrimony.

Our annual conference is composed of two delegates from every church, and all the preachers both ordained and licensed, and the general treasurer. The conference meets annually, and returns are made from all the churches so that once a year we know the state of the whole connexion. Our minutes are taken and printed and distributed among our members.

And now brother I have given you all the necessary information respecting our discipline, belief, &c. and I hope there is nothing that will be offensive, if there should be let us try to remove it. Twenty years ago, when I first came to the ministry, there was but three ministers and five small churches, but bless the Lord, latterly we have been highly favored, and the work at this moment is gloriously reviving among us. But I must tell you something of our situation in the ministry; we are all men of families, of little property and not a single scholar* amongst us, so that the work is of God and not of us.

You requested me to give you the names of a few of our most useful ministers, and the probable number of our baptised members. The names of the most useful ministers, are as follows: Frederick Fonville, Isaac Pipkin, Henry Smith, Levi Braxton, Nathaniel Lockheart, Reading[7] Moore, Jesse Alfin, Jeremiah Heath, Jeremiah Rowe, James Moore, and Robert Bond; and the probable number of our church members, is eight hundred. This calculation is made from the returns of 1825. On account of its being very sickly in this section of our country last fall, all the churches were not represented at the last conference.

I must conclude. May the Great Head of the church bless you, and all in connection with you; may we be happily united in time, and saved in eternity, through Jesus Christ, is the prayer of your unworthy servant.

Respectfully yours in gospel bonds,
JESSE HEATH.

The editor attached this note: "*We presume that their privileges to obtain a common school education have not been so great in that country, as ours have been in this." Also, in the same issue, the following editorial note

---

7 Usually spelled *Redding*. Redding Moore was apparently my great-great-grandfather!

appears, probably by associate editor S. Burbank rather than by senior editor J. Buzzell:

> It will be perceived by this day's paper, that a correspondence is opened betwixt Eld. Jesse Heath of Cox's Bridge, North Carolina, and the senior editor. The letter which is published is the second. By this, we learn that there are many churches, ministers, and brethren in N. C. in sentiment similar to us. It appears, however, that with respect to discipline there is a little difference. This does not cause us to marvel. The exact age of that connexion is not given us by Eld. Heath. He observes that when he first came to the ministry, (twenty years ago) there were only three ministers and five small churches. From this circumstance we draw the conclusion, that their connexion is several years younger than ours.[8] Had our connexion been in a situation to have sent some ministers to North Carolina thirty years ago, the connexion of which Eld. H. is a prominent member, and our own, would, doubtless, have been one in *every* respect. In answer to Eld. Buzzell's first letter, which gives a general account of our doctrinal views, Eld. Heath says, "there is no difference in sentiment." Speaking of discipline, he hopes there is nothing offensive. "If there should be," says he, "let us try to remove it." Eld. Heath discovers a humble, conciliating spirit. May we possess a good degree of the same; then will our correspondence be beneficial to the churches, and for the edification and union of the whole body.
>
> This circumstance argues conclusively, the propriety of sending laborers into all parts of the Lord's vineyard, so much as in us lies.
>
> We presume it was through the medium of the Star that Eld. Heath learned the name and residence of Eld. Buzzell.

The *Morning Star* did not publish Buzzell's replies to Heath's letters,

---

8 This conclusion was, of course, incorrect. The North Carolina Free Will Baptists traced their origins to Paul Palmer in 1727.

nor can we be absolutely certain of the number of letters written.[9] The next letter from Heath, written before December 13, 1827, was not published in its entirety but was reported in some detail, as follows.[10]

OUR BRETHREN IN NORTH-CAROLINA

Eld. Buzzell has recently received a letter from Eld. Jesse Heath of Snow Hill, Green County, North Carolina; which brings some interesting information. A preceding letter from Eld. H.,[11] giving a general account of the people in connexion with him, was published in the Star. We are informed in this, that a short time previous to its being written, their Annual Conference was in session. This meeting was attended by *nineteen* ministers, and about as many churches were represented by letter. Most of which gave accounts of refreshing revivals, and additions. It was agreed by the Conference that the first letter addressed by Eld. Buzzell, (which contained a summary statement of the sentiments of the Free-will Baptist people,) to Eld. Heath, should be published in their minutes for the present year.[12]

"We abundantly rejoice," says Eld. Heath, "that we have so many brethren in your part of the country, of sentiments similar to ours. We have frequently been told, that there were no people on earth, like ourselves. Your letter has been laid before our Conference, and every part of it approved." Eld. Heath was appointed by the Conference to correspond and cultivate a more general acquaintance with us.

---

9   This applies to letters from Heath or Hutchins, below. The ones I report are, simply, the ones I found in the pages of the *Morning Star* as I worked through the periodical on difficult-to-read microfilm.

10   *Morning Star*, December 13, 1827.

11   Heath's letter of May 29, transcribed above.

12   This apparently refers to the 1827 annual conference in N. C., which would have met in November. The minutes for this session do not presently exist to confirm that Buzzell's letter to Heath appeared there.

It was by means of the Star that this correspondence was first opened, which paper Eld. Heath has regularly received for some months past, and with which he is well satisfied. He has lately sent us 15 more subscribers from among his brethren and friends in N. C., and says that he will do all that he can to procure subscribers in that country.[13] He thinks it will be beneficial in the cause. We cheerfully accord with him in this opinion.

The next letter that appeared from Heath was dated in Snow Hill, North Carolina, April 25, 1828, some four or five months later.[14]

Br. Buzzell,—Yours of January 2nd, was duly received. I should have written sooner, had I not been absent from home on a tour in the lower part of this state, when I had a pleasing interview with Eld. Smith[15] and many respectable brethren, with whom I spent some time, and attended several meetings with much satisfaction. In the following places religion has recently gloriously revived among us, viz: Poly Bridge,[16] Duplin co. under the care of Eld. Alfin[17]; Gum Swamp, Pitt co. under the care of Eld. Lockham[18]; Newbern, Craven co. under the care of Eld. Pipkin,[19] and in Poiny Nick,[20] Newbern co. under the care of Eld. Hollace.[21] The additions in all these places have been considerable. Blessed be the Lord.

---

13 During this period, both Heath and Thomas J. Latham were listed in the *Morning Star* as "agents" for the paper in North Carolina.

14 *Morning Star*, May 28, 1828.

15 Henry Smith.

16 The church name does not match any in Harrison and Barfield, listed in 1829. The only church they listed for Duplin County was North East.

17 Jesse Alfin.

18 Probably Nathaniel Lockhart.

19 Isaac Pipkin.

20 Apparently Piney Neck in Craven County.

21 Brinson Hollace.

I am also happy to state that a gradual work appears to be progressing generally among us. On the second Saturday in this month at the Grimesly meeting house in Green co. I baptized four; and while administering the ordinance of baptism, many were in a flood of tears; I hope the Lord will pour out of his spirit upon that place.

I have just received a letter from Br. Elias Hutchins now in the state of Indiana, and from what he states I am encouraged to hope that he will pay us a visit, probably next winter. I have also recently received a letter from a preacher in West Florida, Jackson co. who wishes to be taken into connexion with us. A special conference has been called for that purpose. After considering his case, we agreed to receive him as a member and preacher in connexion with us until our next Annual Conference, which meeting we have invited him to attend, in order that he may receive ordination and form some acquaintance with the people of his choice. His name is Elijah H. Callaway.

I remain your brother in the best of bonds.

JESSE HEATH.

A subsequent letter from Heath was not published, but the editor of the *Morning Star* made mention of it.[22]

Eld. Jesse Heath, of North Carolina, in a recent letter to Eld. John Buzzell, observes that religion appears to flourish and blossom as the rose in that country: Zion travails and brings forth children; the Redeemer's kingdom is fast advancing, and Free Salvation is spreading like fire through stubble that is fully dry. Religion is reviving in the Floridas, in Georgia and in Tennessee.

I judge that the last sentence was not part of Heath's letter but simply an (unrelated?) observation of the editor.

---

22 *Morning Star*, October 30, 1829.

Hutchins' First Visit

Heath's April 1828 letter (above) shows that Elias Hutchins had learned about these North Carolina Free Will Baptists—through the correspondence in the *Morning Star*, one assumes—and had made contact with him. D. M. Graham says that the two men had been corresponding for two years when Hutchins visited North Carolina in October 1829.[23]

Rev. Elias Hutchins.

Before telling that story, it seems appropriate to include a short biographical sketch of Hutchins. He was born in New Portland, Maine, on June 5, 1801, converted in 1818, and was licensed to preach by the Farmington (Maine) Freewill Baptist Quarterly Meeting in 1823. He was ordained as an evangelist in 1824, and for many years his ministry was primarily itinerant. Among the Randall Free Will Baptists his name came to be mentioned in the same breath with Randall, Colby, and Marks.

In November of 1826, he began a two-year tour among the Freewill Baptist churches in Ohio and Indiana. After returning to New England, he set out for North Carolina in October 1829, and remained there until June 1830, from where he went back, over land, to Ohio and Indiana and then back to New England in 1831. There he married Lucy Ambrose of New Hampshire and the two of them visited North Carolina again in the fall of 1832.

According to this account, the North Carolina brethren offered him considerable inducements in an attempt to persuade him to remain in the state, but he returned to New England and settled down in the pastorate. In 1841, his wife died, leaving him with a month-old daughter. In 1846, he married the widow of the well-known minister, David Marks. His offices included

---

23 D. M. Graham, "A Biographical Sketch of Rev. Elias Hutchins," *The Freewill Baptist Quarterly*, vol. VIII (January, 1860), 96.

stints as corresponding secretary of the Freewill Baptist Mission Society, editor of the *Myrtle* and *Gospel Rill*, president of the Home Mission Society, the Education Society, and the Sunday School Union of the denomination, and trustee and corporator of the Freewill Baptist Printing Establishment.[24]

One writer tells that his final year was dominated by serious illness. On Sunday evening, September 11, 1859, "after taking an affectionate leave of his family and friends, about five minutes before his death, exhorting them to meet him in heaven, he whispered, as the last wave passed over him: '*Trust—trust—trust.*' These were his last words." Mourners who passed by his coffin saw on his bosom a piece of satin with the words, "Remember the words I spake unto you while I was yet with you."[25]

Evangelist Hutchins was but twenty-eight years old, however, when he visited the Free Will Baptist work in North Carolina. In its issue for October 30, 1829, the *Morning Star* included this notice:

> Eld. Elias Hutchins sailed from Boston on the 8th inst.[26] for North Carolina—where, by Divine permission, he intends to spend the winter in preaching the Gospel.

The *Morning Star* mentioned this again in its next issue, published November 6, 1829:

> As recently noticed by us, Eld. Elias Hutchins, that faithful and devoted servant of the Lord, (may he always live humble and feel

---

24 The information in this sketch and photograph are from the *Free Baptist Cyclopedia*, eds. G. A. Burgess and J. T. Ward (Free Baptist Cyclopaedia Co., 1889), 283-284. For a more complete biography, see Graham, "Biographical Sketch," 84-108, and D. M. Graham, "Rev. Elias Hutchins as Pastor and Philanthropist," *The Freewill Baptist Quarterly*, vol. VIII (April, 1860), 208-229.

25 Selah Hibbard Barrett, *Memoirs of Eminent Preachers of the Freewill Baptist Denomination* (Rutland: Selah Hibbard Barrett, 1874), 191, 193. My thanks to David Crowe for a digital copy of this work.

26 = *instant*, for the present month.

his dependence upon Him who holds the seven stars in his right hand,) has gone to North Carolina with an intention, if the Lord will, to be gone two years, and to return through Ohio &c. May God Almighty preserve his life, and make him successful in the blessed cause.

Hutchins's letters back to the *Morning Star* were published there and provide information about his visit in his own words.[27] The following was dated at Newbern, North Carolina, October 26, 1829.[28]

I left Sandwich[29] for this state, Frid. the 2nd inst. and went the same day by stage to Dover,[30] where I tarried till Monday. There has lately been a precious revival in that place. I had a few meetings with the brethren there, some of which I humbly hope will be long had in remembrance. Several spake freely and feelingly of God's goodness to them, and affectionately invited their friends to seek the pearl of great price, and some penitent sinners desired the prayers of God's wrestling saints.

Mond. 5th, I went to Portsmouth,[31] in company with a young brother from Dover, where we had a meeting in the evening. We spent the night with the afflicted family of the lately deceased Asa Dearborn. Our interview with them was solemn and interesting, and I sincerely hope productive of some good. Tuesday, I went in the stage to Boston, and the next day engaged a passage to this place. On Friday we sailed, but owing to a head wind returned to the harbor. Monday morning, 12th, we again put to sea with a

---

27 Some of Hutchins's letters also appeared in another Northern publication, the *Freewill Baptist Magazine*, reprinted from the *Morning Star*.

28 *Morning Star*, November 11, 1829.

29 In New Hampshire.

30 In New Hampshire.

31 In New Hampshire.

fair wind and pleasant weather, which continued till we arrived at Ocrecock bar.[32]

Sabbath 18th. Soon after we came to anchor, a number of sailors came on board, which with the pilots and our own crew amounted to about twenty. As I was about to leave the vessel, I asked of the captain liberty to pray, which was readily granted, (a privilege I had all the time I was on the voyage, when I was able to attend to it,) and about every soul on board bowed the knee while the throne of grace was addressed. It would be something novel to our northern people to see rough swearing sailors and others kneel with christians in their devotion; it is, however, quite common here. After prayer, I took leave of the crew and all on board, some of whom seized my hand with both theirs, and by an expressive grasp, as well as by word, manifested a desire for my welfare. I was set ashore at Portsmouth,[33] and introduced to a family of Methodists, who kindly received me under their hospitable roof, where I received the kindest attention, which to me was very acceptable after the fatigue and severe sea-sickness attending my passage, and for which may God richly reward them. Soon after I went of shore, an appointment was given out for a meeting, which with a short notice was well attended. I was enabled to speak with more than usual freedom and feeling; my heart was filled with mingled emotions of love and pity for my dear hearers, and oh! how thankful I felt for the privilege of preaching the gospel to my dying fellow mortals on the shores of North Carolina.

As there is no way of communication by land between Portsmouth and Newbern, I was under the necessity of staying at the former place till the 23d, when I left my kind friends at Portsmouth and the same evening, through the mercy of God, arrived safe at Newbern, where I was joyfully received by the brethren. I

---

32 Ocracoke Island.

33 A village on the north end of the Core Banks (in North Carolina) that was an important port for ships at the time. It has since been abandoned.

think I never met with a more candid reception in all my travels than I did in this place. When I arrived, to my grief, I found that my respected correspondent, Eld. Jesse Heath, left the place on the afternoon of my arrival, without a knowledge of my being in the state. I anticipate, however, the unspeakable pleasure of seeing him to-morrow, and expect he will take me and my trunks to his plantation in the country, the day following.

There is a glorious revival among the Methodists, and some other denominations, in this place. The F. W. Baptists have had some additions, and there is now an encouraging prospect of the revival's assuming a much more interesting[34] character among them.

ELIAS HUTCHINS.

Hutchins' account picked up with his next letter, dated November 25, 1829, from Newbern North Carolina.[35]

My dear Brother,

Having a desire to address you through the medium of a letter, and through that means inform my friends of my welfare since my arrival in this state, I now take my pen for that purpose.

Wednesday morning, Oct. 28th, I left this place, in the state, for Eld. Heath's; and about half past 12 o'clock the driver gave me the joyful intelligence that Eld. H. was standing at the road, waiting my arrival, he having previously directed me by letter to meet him that day. As soon as I left the stage he affectionately took me in his arms, and in the strongest terms, expressed the satisfaction our interview[36] gave him; and you may well think that my feelings were of no common character, on this occasion, as I now had a personal interview with a worthy christian brother, with whom I

---

34 Throughout the letters, *interesting* is used to mean important or of consequence.

35 *Morning Star*, December 23, 1829.

36 As used in these letters, *interview* simply means a meeting together.

had corresponded for some length of time, and to whom I had felt particularly partial.

The day I left Newbern was cool and cloudy, and the appearance of almost every object that I beheld was something different from the likeness of the objects with which I was familiar; my health was quite reduced, and, by some, thought precarious. Nature's vernal robes were beginning to wax old, and the thoughts of being a lonely stranger, far from my native land, all conspired to fill my mind with gloom. But reflecting on the goodness of God to me, and my object in coming to this place, together with the satisfaction I had in finding myself at last in the company of those for whose welfare I had often prayed, while hundreds of miles absent, all served to prevent the dejection I must otherwise have felt.

Thurs. Nov. 5th, the Annual Conference commenced at Bay River meeting-house, in this county.[37] At that place I had the pleasure of forming an agreeable acquaintance with several preachers, also a number of loving christian brethren and sisters. Among the preachers were two brethren belonging to the *Christian Connexion*,[38] in the westerly part of this state.

Great union prevailed through the different sessions of the Conference. The business was amicably done; the preaching was evangelical and powerful, and its effects were felt by a number through the course of the meeting, some of whom, it is hoped, will obtain a pardon of sin, *become servants of God, have their fruit*

---

37 Bay River was in Craven County, according to Harrison and Barfield's list of churches for 1829. Perhaps the site is now in Pamlico County. Hutchins's journal (see the following chapter) places it "a few miles below Newbern."

38 According to the minutes, as printed in the *Morning Star*, these were "Elders Gunter and Hays, messengers from the Christian Baptist Conference in Chatham County, N. C." Chatham County is just west of Raleigh-Durham. Pelt, 120-121, thinks they were not part of the intentionally Campbellite movement known as Christian Baptists that later infiltrated the Free Will Baptists. At any rate, this might have been the very first contact with some who had imbibed some of the teaching of Alexander Campbell, initiating a relationship that eventually resulted in the loss of many Free Will Baptists to the Disciples of Christ.

unto holiness and their end everlasting life. But as the minutes of the Conference will be forwarded to you, I shall not give you a particular account of its proceedings here.[39] It has, for some time past, been very sickly at the place where the Conference met, and I am informed that 3 or 4 men belonging in the place, who attended, are now in their graves. O how little we know, when preaching, who of our hearers stand nearest the brink of death, and how careful every preacher should be to deliver his discourses, as much as possible, under a sense of the uncertainty of life, and the vast importance of faithfully warning the wicked to turn from the evil ways before it be forever too late!

The week after Conference, I rode[40] with the above mentioned Christian preachers and Eld. Heath, about 60 miles back into the country, where we attended several meetings. On week days we generally met from two to three hundred people, and on the Sabbath nearly one thousand. They generally heard with great attention; many were deeply affected, and some made to rejoice under the word; some were received as candidates for baptism, and others will probably submit to that ordinance soon.

We were together on this route about one week; were favored with much freedom in preaching the word; were kindly received by the brethren, and enjoyed with them much divine consolation.

After taking an affectionate leave of the brethren that accompanied me, I went home, on the 17th inst. with a Br. Flood,[41] with the intention of taking a little rest, and doing some writing. By candle-lighting[42] his house was full of people, to whom I gladly delivered a discourse, instead of resting myself. Some came four miles to

---

39 See below for reference to the minutes.

40 Most of Hutchins's travels were on horseback.

41 As the next letter (and Hutchins's journal) shows, this should be Hood (of Lenoir County) instead of Flood; Pelt, 121, identifies him as Thomas Hood.

42 Twilight.

see me that evening. The next night the house was full again, and altho' there was no appointment, we had another meeting.

In some of the churches that I have visited here, there has been a gradual revival for about two years past; large additions have been made to their numbers, and their prospects are still encouraging.

O, my dear brother, notwithstanding my unworthiness, I do hope that my visit here will not be in vain, as the harvest is truly great, faithful laborers few, and help much needed in these regions. I attended meetings almost every day, and was I able to preach three times where I do but once, I should not be able to answer the request for meetings.

The cause of Christ is still near to my heart, and I view no sacrifice that I can make, too dear for its promotion. I ask not for riches, honors, pleasures, or a long life; but O let me see the benevolent religion of Jesus extending its influence far and wide, counteracting the baneful effects of sin, and sweetly inclining the hearts of ungrateful, rebellious sinners to return to their God. Then let me leave the world in peace, my eyes having seen the salvation of the Lord.

I expect soon to set out on a visit to South Carolina, if the Lord will, and, should I be spared to return, shall probably soon write again.

Yours, in gospel bonds,
ELIAS HUTCHINS.

Jesse Heath also sent a brief report of the 1829 annual conference to the *Morning Star*; it was dated in Snow Hill, North Carolina, on December 1, 1829.[43]

Our last Annual Conference closed its session on Sunday, the 8th of November last; the interview was pleasing in the extreme. Through the course of the meeting ten sermons were delivered.

---

43 *Morning Star*, January 13, 1830.

The congregation for that section was large, and some were deeply affected. The letters from the churches were mostly filled with good news of prosperity in religion. The increase last year is 250; whole number, 1234. Two churches were admitted as members of the Conference, and seven licentiates added to the list of preachers. As soon as the minutes are printed I shall forward to you a copy.

As noted in Hutchins's letter, he also planned to send to the *Morning Star* the minutes of the Conference he attended. Regardless who sent them, the minutes were sent and printed in that paper in the issue for February 24, 1830.[44] They are headed as "the Free-Will Baptist annual Conference of North Carolina," meeting November 5-7, 1829. The minutes show that at noon on the first day Hutchins preached the introductory sermon, using Acts 11:22-23. He preached again on Saturday from Jeremiah 8:22, regarding which the clerk noted, "the word of salvation was dispensed with zeal and faithfulness." He preached yet again on Sunday, with 2 Corinthians 5:13, 19-20 as his text. The minutes also report: "On motion, Seven Dollars, out of the general fund, were presented to Elder Hutchins."

Of interest is the fact that the Conference reported 26 churches, 1,232 members, and 27 ministers. This compares to what Jesse Heath had reported (in his 1827 letter, above, referring to twenty years before, when he first entered the ministry) for 1807: five churches and three ministers; and to Heath's statement that in 1825 there were some 800 members.

Hutchins was also asked to prepare a circular letter to be attached to the minutes. The letter is sermonic in nature and does not deal with the events of the time. Consequently, I will only summarize it here. It asks "the all-important question—'How shall we live in this world so as to live in heaven?'"

---

44 Excerpts from these minutes, along with all of Hutchins's "circular letter," also appear in Harrison and Barfield, 197-202. Twenty-six churches are named as composing the Conference.

The conclusion summarizes the answer: "We must be christians in deed and in truth; always living in reference to the eternal world; having at all times, the glory of God in view; and we must also *follow peace with all men, and holiness, without which no man shall see the Lord.*"

It seems obvious that Hutchins made a positive impression on the brethren of the North Carolina Conference.

Apparently, the next letter from Hutchins was written in January 1830.[45]

> *Dear Brother*—Having lately returned from a journey to the south, I now set down to make good the promise I made in my last to write on my return.
>
> Sabbath, Dec. 6th. After preaching to a large and attentive congregation at Wheat Swamp meeting house, I sat out, in company with a Br. Hood, for South Carolina. That night I met a well-behaved congregation, in a place mostly destitute of preaching, to which I was enabled to speak with much freedom.[46] The next day I fulfilled an appointment at Duplin Co.[47] This was an interesting time, and many were affected under the word. I am informed that a revival has commenced there, and several have lately been baptized.
>
> Sat. 12th, we reached a place called Mt. Elon, in Darlington district, S. C.[48] Here I met with a regular Baptist preacher, who had a two days meeting appointed in the place. He invited me to take a part in the meeting: we had much freedom in dispensing the word, and, I trust, it will produce fruit in the hearts of some that heard on that occasion.

---

45 *Morning Star*, February 17, 1830.

46 Pelt, 122, thinks this must have been "in the vicinity of Whitehall, which is now Seven Springs on the Neuse River."

47 According to Hutchins's journal, this was Indian Springs in Wayne County. Why the letter and journal did not agree is not clear.

48 This is Mt. Elon Baptist Church near Lydia, S.C., in Darlington County. Thanks to Joe McKnight for pointing me to this identification.

Wednesday, 16th, we arrived at Eld. Redding Moore's, in Marion district, where we were kindly received. He moved from his brethren in this State, and took up his abode among strangers, that knew nothing of the Free-Will Baptists, and began to preach *free salvation* in South Carolina, about 13 years ago.[49] It has been his lot to encounter considerable opposition, and pass through many discouragements; but the Lord has been his support. The church of which he is pastor now consists of about fifty members[50]; and, to encourage his heart, after toiling alone for years in his Master's vineyard, two preachers have lately been raised up to assist him in this glorious work in his declining years.[51]

As Eld. M. lives about 30 miles from the church just mentioned, I was denied the pleasure of visiting it: I, however, attended several meetings with him in his own neighborhood, which were generally interesting, and in some, signs of a revival were visible.

Monday morning, 21st. We set out for N. C. and arrived at Br. Hood's, Frid. evening. 25th. The next day the Q. M. commenced at Bethel,[52] which I attended. This was indeed a refreshing time from the presence of the Lord. Two were added to the church, and one excluded. Bethel was formerly filled with dissipation of every description; consequently, with the most, religion was only mentioned as a subject of ridicule. But of late there has been a glorious revival in the place. The obscene songs of lascivious rakes and drunkards, have given place to the sweet songs of Zion: prayer has taken the place of swearing, and the Sabbath, formerly a day of revelry, drinking, gambling, fighting, horse-racing, &c. is now

---

49 This places the beginning of the work in South Carolina in about 1816; the churches in the state were dismissed from the annual North Carolina Conference to organize their own conference in 1831; see Harrison and Barfield, 212.

50 Perhaps this was old Bethel Church, the only one listed in Marion County in 1858, the earliest minutes of the South Carolina Conference now existing. If so, it is the church of my mother and grandparents.

51 One of these two was most likely Moab Hewitt; the other is uncertain.

52 In Lenoir County.

religiously observed; and the salutary influence of the religion of Jesus is too obvious to be denied by its most inveterate enemies.

Saturday, Jan. 2d. The Q. M. commenced at Luzen Swamp.[53] This was a time that will be long remembered by many that attended; and to add to the joy felt on the occasion, two respectable youth were baptized.

Tuesday night, I had a meeting at Kinston, (the seat of Justice for Lenoir Co.) I was informed that it was the largest congregation that had met in the place for meeting for some time; but the number, on this occasion, was not great; by which I was led to conclude that the people were more anxious for the riches, honors, and pleasures of this world, than they are for an inheritance in heaven.

Many were much engaged in visiting a Circus, which at this time, was at Kinston; and were much delighted with the childish sports there exhibited. Among the other boyish absurdities practised there, a lady, dressed partly in masculine habit, performed several feats of horsemanship, and, to show her dexterity in masculine performances, engaged in fencing with as much adroitness as the most experienced swordman! "O shame where is thy blush!" What would the immortal Adison say to such brazen fronted, shameless females as the one mentioned above, was he now alive?[54] But modesty, decency, and every thing that makes life desirable, and society agreeable, must be prostituted to the base purpose of supporting indolent, avaricious drones, who, too lazy to engage in a useful calling for their support, obtain their living by practices that are as degrading to the noble faculties of the soul as they are injurious to the morals of society. And at this day, such is the rage for novelty, that many spend the money due their creditors or else necessary to supply the wants of their families, in upholding the characters and

---

53 Louson Swamp, also in Lenoir County not far from Bethel.
54 Apparently a reference to Joseph Addison (1672-1719), an English poet and essayist.

practices just described, who always draw the lewd, drunkards, gamblers, &c. after them, and misery in their train.

Such as have no time to go to meeting, and are so poor that they have no money for charitable purposes, are often the most constant attendants at those nurseries of vice; and what is still more surprising, in many instances, professors of the religion of the Immaculate Jesus encourage such dissolute conduct by honoring it with their presence. In primitive days, christians were noted for their contempt of the world and its vanities, and their strict observance of the commands of their self-denying Master. But in modern times, "the intelligence of the age" is so much "in advance" of the Bible that many professors regard it more as an obsolete work, to be venerated only for its name and former worth, than as the rule of their conduct. They, of course, live as much "after the flesh" as though Christ had introduced a popular, self gratifying religion, every way calculated to please the taste, and pamper the appetites of proud, worldly-minded, avaricious, and honor seeking mortals. But let these characters look upon the cross as *"foolishness,"* and plead for *"popular amusements,"* such as *"May poles,"* *"morris dances,"*[55] &c. and mourn the *"decay of all this bloom of happiness by the withering hand of the Puritans,"* then unblushingly assert that *"where popular amusements are superessed, there man degenerates into the savage,"* as though the gospel, literature, and the arts and sciences are all incapable of raising men above the savage, without the assistance of *popular amusements*; the faithful christian enjoys that, in taking his *daily cross*, and following his adorable Master, which raises him as much above the *"savage,"* as "the foolishness of God" is above the wisdom of pleasure-loving "men." 1 Cor. i. 25.

---

55 A kind of folk dance, imported from England, in fancy costumes.

But to return. Wednesday 6th, I met a large and attentive congregation at Sandhill chapel.[56] Just as the meeting commenced, a man, under the influence of liquor and rage, approached the house, raving and swearing, in an awful manner, and pouring floods of abuse on all around him. Some were frightened, and others irritated at his conduct; and for a while, the meeting was broken up. But, in a short time, some led him off, and the rest took their seats; after which we had a solemn and peacable waiting before the Lord. With due deference to the feelings of his friends, I took occasion to caution my hearers against the intemperate use of ardent spirits, and associating with those addicted to such practices.

Thursday, I preached a funeral sermon in Lenoir Co. This interview was attended with much solemnity; sinners wept and mourned; the hearts of God's people were comforted, and two were received as candidates for baptism.

Sat. 9th, Q. M. commenced at Grimesly M. H. in this county.[57] The first day was a day of much trial and grief; but on the next day many were made to sit in a heavenly place in Christ, and his banner over them was love.

I would here inform you that this climate agrees well with my health, which, at present, is better than it was when I left the northern States. Respectfully yours, in Gospel bonds.

ELIAS HUTCHINS.

Hutchins wrote again, from Newbern, North Carolina, on April 29, 1830, but only a brief excerpt from the letter was published.[58]

The Lord is gloriously reviving his work in different parts of this state. While nature is putting on her vernal robes, Zion is put-

---

56 Harrison and Barfield did not list a church in the conference by this name.
57 Greene County.
58 *Morning Star*, May 19, 1830.

ting on her "beautiful garments," looking "forth as the morning," and enlarging her borders on every hand.

From the next letter, dated May 7, 1830, in Core Creek, North Carolina, the excerpt that appeared was a little longer and provided some specific information.[59]

> I have the pleasure of informing you that the Lord is doing won-ders for Zion in this state. Since the first of January, the numbers baptized or received as candidates for that ordinance in the sev-eral churches, are as follows: —Gum Swamp, Pitt Co. 6. Bethel, Lenoir Co. 10. Wheat Swamp, do.[60] 20. Little Swift Creek, Cra-ven Co. 9. Hookerton,[61] Green Co. 10. Little Creek, Greene Co. 20. In Beaufort Co 13 have been received, and in the lower part of Craven Co. 17. In some of the places above mentioned, several others are expected to come forward soon; and I trust that the good work will continue to spread.

Hutchins's next published letter was written from Strong Creek, North Carolina, on June 20, 1830.[62]

> *Dear Brother,*—By a letter to you of May 7th, an extract of which appeared in the Star, I did not intend to give you an exact ac-count of the number added to all the churches in this place, since the first of January, but an account of the number added to the churches mentioned in my communication, since the commence-ment of the present year.
>
> Some of the churches in other parts of the state, especially in Wayne and Duplin counties, as I am informed, are favored with in-

---

59 *Morning Star*, June 9, 1830.

60 = ditto.

61 Harrison and Barfield did not list this church.

62 *Morning Star*, July 28, 1830.

teresting revivals, as well as the churches noticed in my other letter.

Since the first of May, as I expected at that time, the good work has continued to spread in several places, and the drooping spirits of many dejected christians have been much revived, and many precious souls, formerly far from God, have been brought nigh by the blood of Christ. Soon after I wrote to you before, 7 persons were baptized at Hookerton, and three or four at Bethel. About the same time, Eld. Pipkin baptized 15, in one day, at Bay River; 5 were baptized at the last session of the Q. M. in Newbern, and one at the Q. M. at Beaver Creek.[63] On the 22nd and 23rd of May, I attended a two days' meeting at Pungo river M. H. in Beaufort Co. This was a time that will be long remembered by many in that place. Lord's day morning, Eld. H. Smith baptized 20 persons, and, among this number, was his oldest daughter. The candidates were of different ages, from nearly 80 years down to the youth of 13. Seventeen of this number joined hands on the shore and marched into the river, led by Eld. Smith: after reaching a suitable depth of water they all stood still, and the administrator commenced baptizing at the right hand, and went on to the left. They then turned about and marched back to the shore; and in a few minutes 3 others were baptized. The scene was solemn and impressive, well calculated to animate the christian, and fill the minds of sinners with sensations of a favorable character; and the large congregation that witnessed the performance by a commendable decorum evinced great respect for the ordinance. The Wednesday following, I had a meeting at Pantego: five or six persons were here received for baptism, and have probably been baptized before now. Lord's day, 30th, 3 persons were baptized by Br. Smith, at a two days' meeting, at North Creek.[64] The next Thursday, 3 or 4 were received for

---

63 In Jones County.

64 In Beaufort County.

baptism at Sandhill, and the following Lord's day, Eld. Braxton[65] baptized 8 happy converts at Wheat Swamp.[66]

After taking an affectionate leave of the brethren and friends in the lower part of this state, I set out, on Monday, 7th inst, for the western country. Frid. 11th, I arrived at Eld. Fonville's,[67] in this county, quite unwell. He received me with open arms, and bid me a cordial welcome to his hospitable dwelling, where I have been treated with much kindness, and received all the attention that the reduced state of my health required. It is a dull time with professors in this place; iniquity is abounding, and the love of too many has already waxed cold. Yet, I trust, that there are some who mourn over the desolations in Zion, and are yet praying for her prosperity.

Soon after my arrival at Eld. Fonville's, I had the pleasure of baptizing his wife: this, to them, as well as to the faithful christians who were present, was a rejoicing time.

The hearts of the people, where I have travelled in this state, are generally open to receive laborers in the Lord's vineyard; their ears are open to hear the word; and their hands are open to minister to their necessities.

My health is now much better than it was when I came here; and to-morrow morning, "if the Lord will," I intend to recommence my journey to the west.

Respectfully, Yours, in gospel bonds,
ELIAS HUTCHINS.

Hutchins had completed his visit and was on his way out of the state to Ohio and Indiana, as indicated above in the biogragraphical sketch—still on

---

65 Levi Braxton.

66 In Lenoir County.

67 Frederick Fonville, whose church was in Orange County, the farthest west of any in the conference. Harrison and Barfield name it Stony Creek; Davidson, 149, names it Strong Creek, which matches the heading of Hutchins's letter.

horseback. We are not surprised, then, that another letter from Jesse Heath appeared, sent from Core Creek, North Carolina, and dated November 13, 1830.[68]

> Our Annual Conference for 1830 ended its session last Sabbath. The interview was pleasing in the extreme. The weather was very favorable, particularly the two last days. Preachers from South Carolina, Raleigh, Pungo, and Newbern attended. The meetings of worship were truly interesting. Increase this year, 660. Whole number, 1892. The work of reformation in almost every part of the Connexion is gloriously going on. The old and the young, the rich and the poor, the black and the white are the happy subjects of the revival; and we rejoice most of all, that, while other denominations are divided, and party spirit and prejudice prevails, with us brotherly love continues. For further particulars, I shall forward a copy of the Minutes, as soon as they are printed.
>
> Respectfully yours, in Gospel bonds. Farewell.
>
> JESSE HEATH.

The historical account by Harrison and Barfield includes a fairly full description of the 1830 annual Conference in North Carolina, including the decision to divide the conference, for convenience, into the Bethel and Shiloh Conferences.[69] More important for the purposes of this chapter, the account includes yet another lengthy "circular letter" from Elias Hutchins, sent from Ohio or Indiana. Unlike his 1829 circular letter, mentioned above, this one does speak to the events of the time.

> DEAR BRETHREN:
> As it is impossible for me to attend in person at your Conference, I will attempt to communicate some of my thoughts and feelings to

---

68 *Morning Star*, December 22, 1830.

69 Harrison and Barfield, 202-211.

my friends in North Carolina, through the medium of a letter.

The many marks of kindness that I received during my visit among you, and the agreeable interviews that we have enjoyed both at the house of God, and in the domestic circle, have made impressions on my mind, that neither time nor distance can easily remove; and likewise created a solicitude for your welfare, which I trust will not cease till my anxiety for the prosperity of Zion, and the salvation of sinners, shall be lost in death.

The return of your Annual Meeting, when you are permitted to assemble from different and distant parts, for the pleasing purpose of worshiping God together, to hear of the prosperity of Zion, and to consult the best means of promoting the interests of the Redeemer's Kingdom, is well calculated to fill the devotional and contemplative mind with grateful emotions, and with sensations of the most delightful character.

Should you contrast your present situation with the standing of your brethren 65 years ago, you will discover abundant cause to be thankful for the favors that God has of late conferred upon you. About that time, the most of the Churches and Ministers composing the body to which you now belong, forsook their original principles and united themselves to a body of Christians, whose sentiments, their former brethren could not think accorded with the gospel of Christ.[70] The small number that refused to follow the seceding party, soon encountered serious difficulties, and their prospects were of a gloomy character. They were illiterate, opposed, considered as heretics, and had all manner of evil spoken of them; and at the expiration of 60 years, this little despised body consisted of only about 800 members.[71] But O, my brethren, what has God done for you in the course of 5 years that are past! The mouths of

---

70 Hutchins is referring to the proselyting work of the Calvinistic Baptists that turned most of the original churches to Particular Baptist churches that established the Kehukee Association (Primitive Baptist).

71 See Heath's letter of May 28, 1827, above.

gainsayers, in many places, have been stopped: much of the prejudice that formerly existed against you, has given place to feelings and sentiments more Christian like and refined; some that were your enemies, have become your friends; and many that were the subjects of the kingdom of darkness, and looking on religion with indifference, have been translated into the kingdom of God's Son, and can now cheerfully unite with you in the worship of the living God. O could some of the old labourers, who were themselves out in the Lord's vineyard, and had many fears, that the few churches that they left behind, would come to nothing after their death[72]; I say could they now take their seats among you, and witness the rich displays of Immanuel's power, that have been made in those regions, tears of joy would roll over their cheeks, and gratitude to God would fill their souls.

A lengthy paragraph follows in which Hutchins warned against dangers involved in spiritual prosperity. Among other things he said,

> As you increase in number, may you increase in love, humility, meekness, forbearance and in the knowledge of the Lord and Saviour Jesus Christ. O! may your peaceable and quiet lives, your godly deportment and your Christian-like conduct, convince all around you, that you know religion to be something more than a mere profession, and faith to be something more than a bare assent to the doctrine of a particular creed.

Then Hutchins moved to an urgent warning against the evils involved in the use of alcoholic beverages. Interestingly, he reports that the church at Pungo River had laid aside the practice of drinking, so that "the bottle is now no longer seen among the articles with which their friends are entertained." He added,

---

72 Surely, Hutchins was thinking of men like Joseph and William Parker.

I should rejoice to hear that this laudable effort to suppress intemperance, was well seconded by the other churches composing your Conference, and I do hope that an example so well worthy of imitation, will be faithfully copied by all the friends of morality and religion.

And then he concluded with reminiscences.

My mind retraces with peculiar pleasure, mingled with mournful sensations, many of the scenes through which it passed, while I enjoyed the pleasure of your society; and I ardently desire a recurrence of our former happy interviews. But if we are never permitted to meet in this "mournful vale," O! may we meet beyond tribulation, eternally to be delighted in the presence of Him, at whose right hand are pleasures forever more.

ELIAS HUTCHINS

Although Hutchins was away, he was still actively interested in the work in North Carolina. A subsequent letter from him, sent from Indiana and dated October 30, 1830, included the following paragraph.[73]

By letters lately received from N. Carolina, I am informed that the work of the Lord is still going on in those regions, and many souls have been taken from the kingdom of darkness, and translated into the kingdom of God's dear Son, since I left that state.

Probably the letters had come to him from Jesse Heath.

The Second Visit

Indeed, Hutchins was to realize his ardent desire for a "recurrence" of his 1829-30 visit. He returned to North Carolina, with his new wife, in 1832. As

---

73 *Morning Star*, December 15, 1830.

before, he chronicled his visit in letters to the *Morning Star*, which faithfully published them.

The first notice of this appeared in the *Morning Star* for October 19, 1832.

> We understand that Elder Elias Hutchins and his companion have commenced their journey to North Carolina, in which state and vicinity they expect to spend the ensuing winter. May the Angel of mercy attend them thither—and may our devoted brother appear among that people, as heretofore in a good degree he has done, in the fulness of the blessing of the gospel of Christ.

At about this time, a new correspondent from North Carolina became involved, perhaps taking the place of Jesse Heath. His name was Robert McNab, and he wrote to the *Morning Star* on September 27, 1832.[74]

> Dear Brethren,
>
> I have so many appointments out and so many other things to attend to, that I have but little time to write; but I must take time to tell you of what the Lord has done for this people around Piny Grove M. H.[75] (Sampson, N. C.) whereof we are glad. There is no Freewill Baptist meeting house within 25 miles of said place, neither did any of our ministers ever preach at said place before myself. A few months since, I commenced, and found that the congregation kept increasing; many appeared very much concerned, and some have recently obtained a good hope, through grace, that Jesus is their portion. Therefore I felt encouraged to open a door of reception last Saturday and Sabbath mornings. At said time, I received in all 13—nine of whom I baptized after preaching, in the presence (as was thought) of upwards of 1000 people, who appeared very solemn. The other 4 did not come prepared. We have received 1

---

74 *Morning Star*, October 28, 1832,

75 = Meeting House.

more since. I have travelled a good deal within two years past, and
have seen times of refreshing in various places; but I never yet saw
a greater prospect of a large ingathering of souls, than I now see
in this part of Sampson Co. Lord Jesus grant it. Since I withdrew
from the Calvinistic church, I have travelled through many places
where the Freewill Baptists have never been but little known; and
I think our Connexion would increase rapidly if we could only get
an itinerancy established, and have it properly conducted. If the
different Conferences were to establish an itinerancy, our numbers
throughout the country would increase at an astonishing rate. I
have faith to believe it, for we have the truth on our side, and *truth*
is irresistible. I will write you again after the constitution of said
church, which will take place shortly.

In Anson Co. our prospect of success is more gloomy at present
than at any former period—however, the darkest time of night is always just before day; and though this is the case now, I have faith to
believe it will not be the case three years hence. I stay but very little
of my time in Anson, consequently some of those who first joined,
went back again to the old church. But if this cause be of God, they
cannot overthrow it. See Acts 5:33, 39.

Yours,

ROBERT McNAB

McNab carried out his promise to write again, and his letter merited a
brief note.[76]

Br. NcNab informs us, that the revival at Piney Grove, Sampson co. N. C. of which he spoke in his last communication, still
continues to progress. He baptized 13 at that place on the 6th ult.[77]
and the prospect then looked more flourishing than ever. On the 1st

---

76 *Morning Star*, November 9, 1832.
77 = *ultimo*, for the previous month.

ult. he baptized 8 persons at north-east meeting house, Dauphin co. The church at that place has increased considerably within a few months.

I assume that McNab's correspondence did not influence Hutchins's decision to return to North Carolina, since the first one was not published until after Hutchins had departed. At any rate, Hutchins's first letter back was dated in Lenoir County, North Carolina, on November 16, 1832.[78]

> Dear Brethren,
> As some of my friends, and especially my relatives in Maine, to whom it is inconvenient for me to write, may be desirous to know something of my welfare, I wish to inform them, through the medium of the Star, that I arrived at Newbern in this state about the first of October. My health is much as it was at the north.
> As soon as time and circumstances will permit, I intend to give you some account of my travels since the commencement of the present season.
> In haste, yours in gospel bonds,
> ELIAS HUTCHINS.

As promised, Hutchins wrote on December 3, 1832, from Newbern, North Carolina.[79]

> Dear Brethren,
> I take my seat for the purpose of giving you some account of my travels and gospel labors for a few months past.

Before describing the visit to North Carolina, Hutchins first describes a period in September when he was in Maine and New Hampshire. Then he

---

78 *Morning Star*, November 30, 1932.

79 *Morning Star*, January 17, 1833.

comes to the North Carolina trip.

Monday morning, Oct. 15, as probably you recollect, I set out from Meredith, N. H., with my companion, for N. Carolina. Nothing out of the common occurrences of travelling took place on our journey till after we sailed from New York, Tuesday the 23d of October. That night the wind blew a gale, split one of the sails and made the sea very rough; the next morning the wind increased, and with it the size and violence of the waves. Towards noon I took my wife on deck to see the wonders of the deep: but the howling of the tempest, the roaring and force of the huge angry waves, the rolling of the vessel, the menacing appearance of the clouds, together with the thoughts of being hundreds of miles from home and not knowing what awaited her, sensibly affected her mind. For a few moments she viewed with astonishment the wild and confused scenes around her, then burst into tears and went below. That night the packet's boat was carried away; the next night the wind increased, we laid to in the dreaded gulf stream, with but little rest; and but little was said by the passengers or crew. Friday and Saturday it became a little more moderate; Sunday, after narrowly escaping the frying pan shoals,[80] we got into smooth water, and the next day, through the mercy of God, we arrived at Smithville, about 30 miles below Wilmington, in this state. During this storm, I felt more sensibly than I ever did before, the support and consolation of religion. It is true at times I felt much depression of spirit and distress of mind while I thought on friends that I had left, not knowing but I should sink in the briny deep, and be gorged by its scaly monsters, without ever being able to give them any account of my fate! But I was conscious that neither a prospect of riches, ease, or the honors of the world, had induced me to leave my native land and journey to the south. This indeed afforded me much consolation: but I de-

---

80 A lengthy area of shoals off the coast of Cape Fear in North Carolina, still a hazard to ships and the site of many shipwrecks.

rived still more from promises like these—"*I will never leave thee,
nor forsake thee*"—"*It is I be not afraid.*" &c. O with what light
and comfort were they applied to my mind, instantly removing my
distress and causing tears of joy to gush from my eyes. Sometimes
when my fears would return, something like what Christ said to
Peter, O thou of little faith, wherefore didst thou doubt? would
soon remove them. I trust that I shall never forget that instance of
God's favor to me.

But to return. Tuesday evening, Oct. 30, I took the stage at
Wilmington and set out for Newbern. The next morning just before day, the stage upset with six passengers beside an infant in it.
No person was hurt, excepting my wife, who had her hand considerably injured; but fortunately no bones were dislocated or broken.
That night we arrived at Newbern and were joyfully received by
our friends there, as also we have been in other places where we
have visited.

In coming to this place I had to go 100 miles out of my way, suffered much on my passage, and spent 83 dollars. But the kindness
of my friends and the satisfaction I have in preaching, in my feeble
manner, a free salvation, more than compensates me for the little
sacrifices I have made in coming here. My health, especially the
complaint in my head, is better than it was when I left the Northern states; my wife also enjoys good health. The state of religion
in some places in this country, is prosperous, but in other places
prospects are not very encouraging. The Bethel Annual Conference was very interesting: and at a three days meeting just held in
this place, three were baptized.

In haste, yours in gospel bonds,
ELIAS HUTCHINS.

The last sentence of the letter refers to the annual meeting of the Bethel Free Will Baptist Conference, held at Louson Swamp Church in Lenoir
County on November 9-11, 1832. The minutes were sent to the *Morning*

Star and a digest of them was published on February 14, 1833. The number of churches was 22, with 27 ministers, and 1,585 total members.

Interestingly, Hutchins and Heath were commissioned "to publish a history of our Connexion in this and the adjoining States"; but the proposed history was never published. The Conference voted to give Hutchins ten dollars from the general fund, and he prayed the closing prayer on Saturday. On Sunday, both Robert McNab and Hutchins preached, the latter using Deuteronomy 32:1-2 as his text. There was an enthusiastic response, with some fifty mourners coming forward for prayer. It was decided that he would preach again on Monday, after which six converts joined the church.[81]

Hutchins wrote again on December 28, 1832, but only a brief extract from it was printed.[82]

> Last night in this place, in a quarrel that originated from drinking, a Mr Hutchins was cut on the head several times by a Mr Bull. The former keeps an oyster house and dram shop, out of which he attempted to put the latter, for disturbance; and in the act he was cut with a pocket knife. It is thought that his wounds are not mortal. This circumstance must be extremely painful to the feelings of the wives and other family connexions of these, to say the least, imprudent men. O! when will ardent spirits be banished from the land, and both its buyer and seller be doomed to the ignominy that they justly deserve!

Another letter from Robert McNab, written from Coxes Store, North Carolina, on February 9, 1833, appeared.[83]

81　Some of this paragraph is from "Elias Hutchins in North Carolina" (*The Freewill Baptist Quarterly*, vol. X [July 1862]), 307, where a lengthy excerpt from the minutes is cited. See the following chapter in this book.

82　*Morning Star*, January 24, 1833.

83　*Morning Star*, March 7, 1833.

There still appears to be a prospect of a large ingathering in this section of country, and I may safely remark a brighter prospect than ever. I have constituted 3 churches in Sampson county since I joined the Freewill Baptists, viz: The Piny Grove, Ten Mile, and Roan M. H. I see a prospect of constituting more churches, but I shall have to slack travelling or my health I find will become impaired. I have baptized in all 130 who have been added to these three churches. Tomorrow, if spared, I shall baptize several persons at the Ten Mile m. h. We have formed a Temperance Society at the Piny Grove, which bids fair to flourish. We got the first day 27 members. I have no doubt but we shall have 100, or more, in less than six months. I intend to form a society of this kind in all the churches of which I have the pastoral care. Brethren Hutchins and Lewis Hartsfield attended the constitution of the Ten Mile church, which took place the 12ᵗʰ of last month. This visit which Br. Hutchins has paid us will be of lasting benefit to our Connexion. He appears to manifest a zeal for the glory of God and for the salvation of sinners, and those are the kind of preachers we want. I wish that his friends and companion would consent to let him spend the remainder of his days among us—for the harvest is truly great and the laborers are few. I shall before long tell you how we come on in the temperance cause.

ROBERT McNAB

The next letter from Hutchins was dated in Greene County, North Carolina on January 22, 1833.[84]

Dear Brethren,
I have just returned from Sampson and Duplin counties in this state, where I have lately spent a few days in our Master's cause,

and now take my seat to give you a hasty sketch of the religious state of things in those places.

Previous to last summer there was no F. W. B. church in Sampson Co. But of late the labors of Br. McNab have been greatly blessed, and he has been instrumental of doing much good there, especially in the vicinities of Piney Grove and Ten Mile meeting houses. It may emphatically be said that many in those regions have *turned to the Lord*. Some houses in which the votaries of sinful pleasure formerly met for revelry and mirth, are converted to houses of religious worship; some among the people have left the race paths, the tiplers' shop, &c for the house of God; some have exchanged their cards for the bible, their oaths and vain songs for the sweet songs of Zion, and their former associates for the people of God; and among these characters there are some who have left the *broad and* UNCERTAIN *way* in which they formerly hoped to go to heaven whether they served God or themselves and satan, for the *narrow and* CERTAIN *way* of the cross. Some of all classes have shared in this good work, and many have united with the brethren there whose names would honor any religious society. The first Friday in this month a four days' meeting commenced at Piney Grove, which closed very favorably to the cause of religion. Saturday a temperance society was formed consisting of 26 members; Lord's day morning, Br. McNab immersed 18 believers in Christ, and on Monday 8 persons were received for the same ordinance.

The succeeding Friday, a three days' meeting commenced at Ten Mile, which likewise resulted in good. On Saturday a church was constituted there consisting of 14 members who had belonged to the Piney Grove church; the next morning 12 believers were immersed and added to this church, and this is an encouraging prospect of a continuance of the good work at that place. Last Monday Br. McNab had an appointment at Roan M. H. for baptism, and he will probably soon constitute a church there. The churches at North East and Probability in Duplin county, were, a few months since, favored with large additions. But of late the church at Probability has passed through some trials. The church at North East is still enjoying a good degree of prosperity. A church has lately been constituted at Salem, Duplin county, by Eld. Lewis Harts-field, which is in a prosperous way.

In some places in this country, great and effectual doors are opened to our ministers, and were they in circumstances to travel and preach more extensively, I doubt not but many large and flour-ishing churches might be established on the principles of immer-sion and free salvation, where sprinkling is practised by the most of those who preach a free gospel, and predestination is believed by the most of those who practise immersion. I found the people in Sampson county, especially, very desirous to become more ac-quainted with our sentiments. Many of the brethren and friends there have purchased the Review of Butler's Letters and the Chris-tian Melody, the most of whom were well pleased with those books. As two editions of Hymn books of 2000 copies each, have just been published here for the use of the churches, the Christian Melody is not now as saleable in this state as it probably will be a few years hence; but a book combining so many excellencies should be used in all the churches in the Connexion, as soon as circumstances will permit. I send you the names of 15 new subscribers to the Star, and probably 8 or 10 more in Sampson county, who live several miles from the nearest Post Office, will subscribe soon, and take it from the Office by regular turns. Those who read this paper are gener-ally well pleased with it, and I have often wondered why so few of the brethren, compared with the whole Connexion, are subscribers to this useful miscellany.

The brethren here have taken efficient measures to publish a his-tory of the churches in the southern states; and although it will not be a literary work, it will save from oblivion many incidents connected with the rise and progress of the connexion, which, without it, would soon be irrecoverably lost. And if the brethren of the North ever intend to publish a history of this kind, unless it is done soon, many things which would add much to the value of

111

the work will of necessity be omitted. As a Connexion, we have too often been rather slow to commence operations; but when we have undertaken any thing there has generally been something done towards accomplishing it, and I earnestly desire that the time may soon arrive when something more will be done on the subject under consideration, than just to talk about its necessity and utility.

In haste, yours in gospel bonds,

ELIAS HUTCHINS.

The *Morning Star* for April 4, 1833, referenced a letter from Hutchins that was apparently written about the middle of March. It simply sent along to the paper a copy of a letter written to "an aged minister of the gospel" in North Carolina by his adult son, describing in glowing terms his recent conversion and pleading for the conversion of his brothers and sisters. The letter was signed "J. A. F."—perhaps J. A. Fonville, son of Frederick Fonville.

As far as I found, Hutchins wrote just once more from North Carolina, this time from Lenoir County on March 25, 1833[85]—although he did not leave the state until May.

Dear Brethren,

Through the mercy of God, I am still permitted to labor in this part of the gospel field; but I have often regretted, and do still regret, that I have done so little where there is so much to be accomplished.

About the middle of last month I visited the church in Orange Co. in this state, where I spent eight days. This church is situated more than 100 miles from the nearest of the other churches in the Connexion, and by deaths, removals, and exclusions, it is reduced to only 9 members. I attended a few meetings with the people, all

---

85 *Morning Star*, April 18, 1833.

of which were quite interesting; and in some of them saints were quickened and several mourners presented themselves for prayer.

Of late there has been an interesting revival near Kinston in this county, under the labors of Eld. Jesse Vause. A few weeks since, he commenced preaching in the vicinity of the revival, to appearance, with but little prospect of success. But notwithstanding he at first met with but little encouragement, as there were but few professors in the place, and some of them were not prepared to rejoice in a revival unless it was in their own order, the Lord blessed his labors to the awakening and conversion of several precious souls, and he has lately baptized between 25 and 30 persons in that vicinity.

I send you the names of ten new subscribers to the Morning Star, and hope soon to be able to send you a few more. I feel more and more interested in the prosperity of our infant Book Concern, and I do hope an institution so well calculated to promote the interests of the Connexion will be well supported by our brethren and friends. I also hope, that the list of subscribers to the Star will be so much increased as to enable the publishers to enlarge that useful paper in the course of the spring. This step I am persuaded will greatly increase its patronage, and consequently its usefulness.

ELIAS HUTCHINS.

It seems clear that the Free Will Baptists in North Carolina sincerely wanted Hutchins and his wife to remain in the state rather than to return to New England. Graham observes, "They were pressed to make North Carolina their future home. As an inducement to remain, a house and a slave were kindly offered them, together with large promises for the future. Of course, this offer was promptly declined. During this visit, his labors were greatly blessed, but in the spring they returned to Sandwich" in New Hampshire.[86]

---

86 Graham, "Biographical Sketch," 99. Graham used Hutchins's personal journal.

If Hutchins was not writing again from North Carolina, Robert McNab was. In an extract from a letter dated April 20, 1833, at Coxes Store, McNab notes that Calvinistic Baptists in the state were dividing over the question of missions.[87] Of those who supported missions, he noted the following, in conclusion.

> Notwithstanding this they think the Freewill Doctrine a danger-ous one. They do not like us, because we hold to open commu-nion; and, lastly, they think it altogether contrary to Scripture to admit of a possibility of falling from grace. However, notwithstand-ing all these different classes employ so many means to prejudice the minds of persons against our sentiments and practices, I find that no other sect increases much where our preachers labor. And why? Because we preach the truth.
> ROBERT MCNAB.

McNab wrote again on May 21, 1833. His letter advocated for the estab-lishment of an academy "for the benefit of our Connexion."[88] He had felt inadequate to promote the idea but two significant communications had en-couraged him.

> At length I wrote Elder Jesse Heath, (who is at present the oldest preacher belonging to the Bethel or Shiloh conference,) and re-ceived in reply the following answer. I believe his view on the sub-ject, in consequence of his age and long standing as a zealous and useful ambassador of Christ, will have the desired effect. Therefore I shall insert it. It is as follows. "I am, my Brother, in favor of the establishment of an Academy for the benefit of the Connexion, and would freely patronize it. I think it would meet the approbation of our brethren. At least, there would be no impropriety in calling

---

87 *Morning Star*, May 30, 1833.
88 *Morning Star*, June 20, 1833.

their attention to the subject, and if we can get sufficient encouragement, I wish it to go into effect as soon as possible. As it regards a teacher, I should like to get one of our brethren from the north."

At this point in the letter, McNab pointed out that Calvinistic Baptists were working to establish such an academy. And then he described his other communication.

I conversed with brother Hutchins a few months ago on the matter, and his reply was, that he had serious thoughts of suggesting to the brethren of the last conference the propriety of falling on some such plan as our Connexion at the north have.

After citing both Heath and Hutchins, then, McNab noted that there were nearly 3,000 Free Will Baptists in North Carolina, which should be enough to support such an endeavor. He concluded.

We should however make this a matter of fervent prayer, for unless God smiles on all our attempts to do good, we cannot expect to prosper. For though Paul may plant and Apollos water, yet God alone can give the increase.
ROB'T. MCNAB.

Although Hutchins was now back in New England, his "native country" as he called it, thoughts of the visits to North Carolina were still with him. He wrote one last letter to the *Morning Star* about his ministry in the Old North State, dated at Limerick, Maine, on July 8, 1833.[89]

Dear Brethren,
For the information of my friends at a distance, with many of whom I cannot conveniently correspond, I wish you to give this

---

89 *Morning Star*, July 11, 1833.

communication a place in the columns of the Star.

For the space of two or three months after my arrival in N. Carolina last Oct. my health was much better than it had been for some months before I went there. But the unusually wet winter and the fatigue occasioned by my labor, considerably reduced my health before spring, and as the warm weather commenced I became quite billious, since which time I have been no better, than I was before I went to the South. My wife enjoyed very good health through the winter, excepting an attack of the rheumatism. I sailed from Newbern, N. C. the 24th of May and arrived at Sandwich the 6th of June.

During the last six weeks that I spent at the South, nearly 30 persons were added to the churches that I visited during that time, and in several places there were prospects of more additions.

The brethren and friends in N. C. generally treated me very kindly, and as I left them with little or no expectation of ever seeing them again this side the grave, our parting in many instances was extremely painful.

Since my return to Sandwich I have spent the most of my time in travelling and preaching as usual.

About ten days since, I set out with my wife on a visit to New Portland, intending also to visit my friends in several other places in this state.

But again, contrary to my expectations, I am disappointed for the present in visiting the place of my nativity and likewise altogether disappointed in visiting several other places, as I feel bound to spend some time in Limerick.

Many of my christian friends in different and distant parts with whom I have spent many pleasant hours both at the house of God and in the social circle, I shall meet no more in this vale of tears. But O may we meet in that happy state where storms of trouble shall never be known, and when we see the rainbow painted by heaven's never setting sun on the dark clouds of our afflictions, rejoice that they are blown over never more to return.

Elias Hutchins.

Conclusion

I have told the story I wanted to tell. Even so, I think it may be helpful to conclude with three observations about the significance of Elias Hutchins's visits to Jesse Heath and the North Carolina Free Will Baptists in 1829-30 and 1832-33. There are some things, here, that we learn about ourselves.

First, it seems likely that the North Carolina movement we know variously as the Palmer movement or "General Baptists," began to use the name "Free Will Baptist," officially, shortly before Hutchins visited the South, probably about 1828. In the first chapter in this volume, I have dealt with the forms of the name and there I cited Rufus K. Hearn as saying that the "Free Will" (however spelled) was adopted in 1828. I also noted that Hearn was relying on what Elias Hutchins said. Now of course such "word of mouth" testimony falls short of firm proof. Even so, we should keep in mind that Hutchins had no source of information about the North Carolina Free Will Baptists except for what Heath and others told him. And they were so near to 1828 that, as Michael Pelt said, there is no good reason to doubt this information. Furthermore, we have no written evidence of the use of "Free Will Baptist" on "official" documents in North Carolina before about that time.

I do not mind adding one other likely observation to this, even if it involves some speculation. Given that Heath learned about the Free Will Baptists in the North and wrote to editor Buzzell of the *Morning Star* in 1827, it seems likely that this knowledge played a part in the willingness of the North Carolina Free Will Baptists to begin accepting the name officially. Otherwise, the timing would seem too coincidental to be credible.

I do not mean to suggest that they were not *called* "free willers" before this, including "free will Baptists." That this was a name used in England and in the colonies—North and South—for general atonement Baptists, is indisputable. I simply mean to say that it seems likely that the North Carolina Free Will Baptists first began using the name *of themselves* in *official* publications, at that time, and that perhaps they were emboldened in this way when they learned about the larger movement in New England that had done the same thing not many years before. Again, see the first chapter in this volume.

Second, some of the information that has been revealed in the story gives us a candid picture of the state of Free Will Baptists in North Carolina during the first third of the nineteenth century. It is a picture of how they were before they had spread anywhere beyond the eastern part of the state—except for a fledgling branch in South Carolina. Furthermore, it is a picture that may surprise us, in a disappointing sort of way.

I have deliberately included, in referencing the published material that makes up this story, the basic information required for this picture, and now I bring it together.

In about 1807, according to Jesse Heath, when he had entered the Free Will Baptist ministry some twenty years before he wrote the *Morning Star* in 1827, there were five small churches and three ministers. It is almost a shock to realize that this was eighty years after Paul Palmer planted the first church of these sentiments in 1727. True, the original movement had fairly soon grown to at least 16 churches, but the Calvinistic invasion had turned nearly all of them away from the "General Baptist" doctrine and fellowship. What is clear is that the movement had suffered greatly and struggled to survive. And in 1807 there were but five churches.

In 1825, according to the same letter, there were about 800 members, no doubt representing more than five churches.

When Heath wrote in December 1827, after the annual conference in November, he indicated that there were nineteen ministers and about the same number of churches.

In 1828, according to the following, there were about 980 members.

In 1829, the minutes show 26 churches, 27 ministers, and an increase of about 250 members to a total of 1,232.

In 1830, according to Heath's letter of November after the annual conference, there was an increase in membership of about 660, bringing the total to 1,892.

This is enough to substantiate that this period was one of encouraging growth in the movement. The numbers of churches, ministers, and members were steadily growing. Among other things, during the annual conference in 1831, Redding Moore and the churches in South Carolina under his leadership were amicably dismissed to form their own conference. Thus growth was not just numeric but geographic. The weak and struggling movement was becoming stronger and more aggressive.

Third, while we have no way of measuring things like this, it seems likely that Elias Hutchins made some meaningful contributions to the revival spirit among the churches in North Carolina. At the same time, I think an objective appraisal would say that the outreach and growth involved was by no means his doing alone. The correspondence makes clear that the growth had begun before he came to North Carolina, and that it continued during, between, and after his visits. Fundamentally, it was the evangelistic zeal of the North Carolina brethren on which the increase was built.

Even so, there seems to be no doubt that Hutchins and his visits, preaching, and counsel were much appreciated. Apparently, he was well liked and regarded highly as a man of integrity and zeal for evangelism. The friendship was mutual, and he made his mark on the movement in the South.[90]

---

90 As recently as 1916, E. T. Phillips, editor of *The Free Will Baptist*, observed that after the fledgling FWB movement in North Carolina was decimated by the Calvinists' invasion, the few churches that remained "rallied, reorganized, and, being later reinforced by Free Will Baptists from the North, especially from Maine, regained most of the lost ground"—apparently referring to Hutchins' visits. *Census of Religious Bodies 1926: Baptist Bodies: Statistics, Denominational History, Doctrine, and Organization* (Washington: United States Government Printing Office, 1929), 86.

4

Elias Hutchins in North Carolina, 1829-33

This chapter reproduces an article by this title that appeared in The Free-will Baptist Quarterly, X:3 (July, 1862). *I considered weaving some of it into the preceding chapter but finally decided to include the entire article as a separate chapter. Where the previous chapter tells the story from the letters and notices that appeared in the* Morning Star, *the unidentified author of this chapter drew entirely from Hutchins's personal journal.*

Since Hutchins included in his letters some of the things he wrote in his journal, there is some repetition here. As a whole, however, this chapter presents another perspective, and this is the reason I include it. It was written, after all, by one of the Northern Free Will Baptists in 1862, some thirty years after Hutchins's last visit to North Carolina, and in the midst of the Civil War. The reader, therefore, gets the perspective of the Northern Free Will Baptists toward the South and the slavery that was at issue during that terrible, internecine conflict.

The article is interesting, then, for more than one reason. One is for its information about Carolina Free Will Baptists in the years 1829-30 and 1832-33 when Elias Hutchins visited there from New England. His journal provides a unique perspective on that, and this chapter supplements the previous one in that regard. This is a genuine piece of early North Carolina Free Will Baptist history!

Another reason is the insight the journal gives us into Elias Hutchins himself, and into his passion for evangelism.

Yet another reason, as I have just said, is the insight it gives us into the mindset that lay behind the Civil War. In the 1862 author's explanations (not in those of Hutchins himself), we see something of the Yankee attitude of condescension toward the South at the time. While the slavery that was at issue was an evil that needed to be rectified, this Northern Free Will Baptist was unjustifiably hostile toward his Southern Free Will Baptist brethren. In this, he was manifesting the activism of his denomination at the time: the Northern Free Will Baptists were strong in the anti-slavery cause. That activism easily led to intolerance of their first cousins south of the Mason-Dixon. Perhaps one cannot be at war with others without developing hatred of them.

At any rate, this article helps us understand just why the Northern and Southern Free Will Baptists did not establish a union. There had been some efforts in that direction, and a few of the associations of churches in the South had actually joined the Randallite General Conference. But the Civil War made that less practical. Had slavery not been an issue, a broad and permanent union might have been consummated—though whether for good or ill is another matter. Regardless, the 1910-11 merger (see chapter six) brought all such possibilities to an end. The Northern and Southern Free Will Baptists remained two distinct denominations and the Northern one ceased to exist as a denomination.

*I have faithfully copied the original article as it appears, except that I have put most of Hutchins's words in italicized and indented sections as an aid to the reader. Within those sections, any words not italicized are those of the 1862 author of the article. All footnotes are mine. The symbols * * * are original and represent material in Hutchins's journal that the author skipped.*

I can only wish that Hutchins's original journal might yet be found. I have sought it everywhere I can think of to look. What is clear, from reading the following article, is that the journal would add much to the information we have. If any reader has any ideas about where it might be found, I will welcome all suggestions.

Since the outbreak of the slaveholders' rebellion, everything showing the nature of Southern society is invested with peculiar interest. If the great rebellion shall be so overruled by Divine Providence as virtually to overthrow slavery, we shall have another instance in which cannons prove to be great civilizers, another instance in which He who ruleth in heaven and in earth permits horrid war, in some sense to prepare the way for the gospel of peace. Our whole South-land, from which the guilty cause of the present rebellion has for several years excluded the preaching of the full gospel, may thus be opened again, like Madagascar, for the missionary of the cross. When that happy day comes, as come it must, there will be before the church a mission field of vast proportions, and one that can present to every Christian of this nation the most imperative claims for pecuniary outlay and self-sacrificing zeal. The condition of both whites and blacks after this desolating war, and, especially in the changes of society to which the war must inevitably lead, will demand a great amount of philanthropic and missionary labor. The church will need to remember the vast proportions of the war, in order duly to apprehend the proportions of her own work rendered necessary by the war and its cause. In that great work our denomination must undertake her full share.

If Hutchins had lived two or three years longer,[1] who can imagine, much less describe, the feelings with which he would have read of Burnside's capture of Newbern and Washington. In the former place he preached to

---

1 Hutchins died in 1859; see the previous chapter.

crowded and tearful audiences. In the region round about it, he sounded out the gospel. His comings and goings made him familiar with the ground so recently stained by the blood of battle. Had he been with the expedition that captured Washington, he would have passed on his right and left, as he sailed up the Pamlico river, the scenes of some of his most successful labors. He would have remembered the times that eager listeners came to snatch up his words. He would have remembered some of the most intensely interesting baptismal scenes his eyes ever beheld. Had he been a chaplain in the army of Burnside, he might now and then have recognized among the rebel prisoners some of his old converts in a plight that would have suggested to him the propriety of claiming the whole glory of their conversion.

> *The Freewill Baptists of North Carolina, it is supposed,* says Hutchins, *were originally descendants from the General Baptists in England, and their history can be traced back to about 1762. In about 1764, two Baptist preachers from New Jersey succeeded in proselyting the most of the churches in North Carolina to the peculiarities of Calvinism. A mere handful, however, with two or three preachers, retained their former free-will sentiments, and endeavored to maintain their ground, although they had to encounter severe opposition. Their discouragements were very numerous, and, for many years, their prospects were truly of a gloomy character. For nearly sixty years, they stood by themselves, and gained but little ground. But, after passing through various conflicts for the space of time just mentioned, they providentially heard of the Freewill Baptists of the North, with whom they commenced a correspondence in 1825. Since that time, much of their opposition and many of their discouragements have subsided—very interesting revivals have taken place among them.*

Of the few preachers who remained faithful, despite the great defection, Elder Parker seems to have been decidedly the ablest and most abundant in labors. The organization of several of the churches is ascribed to him. Elder William Fulker seems to have been his contemporary. Fulker died after a long pastorate in one of the oldest churches in 1779, a year before Randall became pastor of our first church at New Durham. After him the next prominent preacher was William Winfield, till the conversion of James Roach in 1792. Upon Roach fell the mantle of Parker. Suffice it to say that these men and their colaborers maintained the cause till prosperity came as above intimated. In the years from about 1830 to 1840, and perhaps longer, the Freewill Baptists had quite overtaken in prosperity the Calvinistic Baptists, their boastful and arrogant opposers, not to say persecutors.

Hutchins visited those churches in the autumn of 1829, and itinerated among them about eight months; and, again, in the autumn of 1832, making a stay of about seven months. He witnessed great prosperity among them. Within the last few years they have been twice distracted and divided. First, the defection of preachers and churches to Campbellism was considerable. Next, in 1853, after nearly a full recovery of their former strength and number, the discussion about Masonic and other secret societies, divided them into two nearly equal rival conferences, each, of course, claiming to be the original. These churches never succeeded in establishing any periodical or weekly publication. Owing to the anti-slavery discussion, they dropped the Morning Star, which for a season seemed to infuse new life into them. The old acquaintances of Hutchins, who corresponded with him nearly to the day of his death, often implored him to send them from the North preachers of "the right kind," by which they meant pro-slavery men.[2]

The correspondence between the Freewill Baptists of the North and South, was terminated by the action of our General Conference in 1839.

---

2   The author is making a judgment that seems entirely unjustified. I doubt that this was their meaning and think they more likely meant men like Hutchins who were fervent and evangelistic.

In 1819, the first time we find their statistics, they had a dozen churches, numbering, in the aggregate, 512 members. In 1829, when Hutchins first visited them, there were 26 churches and a membership of 1232, having so increased since 1825, from 19 churches and 730 members. In 1834, there were 46 churches and 2788 members. In 1837, the number of churches remained the same, but the membership was reduced to 2113. From our last accounts from them we judge each of "the original" conferences numbers more than the undivided conferences did in 1847.

We will here mention that there is another association, or rather, as they call it, Conference of Freewill Baptists in correspondence with those of North Carolina, but located in South Carolina. These churches were dismissed from the North Carolina Conference in 1831, for the purpose of forming the new one. In 1849, twenty years after Hutchins visited that region, the South Carolina Conference had, as we shall soon notice; 9 churches and a membership of 305. At first all these churches in the Carolinas were, like the General Baptists of England, close communionists. But in later years they have, we have no doubt, become fully free communionists, for we find in the minutes of a conference, several years ago, they voted to lay aside the restriction for one year, and even a year or two before Hutchins visited them, they had passed at one Conference the following resolution: "Resolved, That the liberty of conscience in communion shall be granted; that is, if any that are in good standing amongst the different denominations shall make application, they may be admitted to eat and drink with us."

In the State of Alabama, Pickens County, an association of General, or Freewill Baptists, was formed about 1850. It was making some progress as late as 1856, and had then left off the "General" part of its name. Their articles of faith are thoroughly free-will and free-communion. Ellis Gore, the preacher who is evidently the leader of this movement, in his circular letter shows by his remarks that he has thought to the bottom of the communion question. "The spirit [logical basis] of close communion," says he, "is the spirit of Popery. Popery makes the Roman Catholic church the only gospel church on earth; close communionists make their church the only gospel church on earth. Popery makes its rules of doctrines and usages the infallible guide to which all must conform; close communionism does the same. Close communionism is illiberal and exclusive in its tendency, and we think it high time that every obstacle to the efficient combination of the entire energies of the whole church of Christ should be removed. We are one body and one bread in Christ; children of the same spiritual Father; and may the fire of God's love be kindled and continue to burn in our hearts until it shall consume and utterly destroy every barrier which separates his children—until the watchmen shall see eye to eye, and lift up their voices together."

In 1856 Hutchins had a letter from Ellis Gore, which is now in our possession. In this letter, which has more force than elegance, he replies to the request for information concerning Freewill Baptists of the South, by mentioning an association in sympathy with his sentiments in Tuscaloosa county, Alabama.

We now propose to give a few pages of the journal, in some instances word for word; in others we shall be obliged to pass more rapidly in our own words. In most cases we shall be obliged, also, for want of space, to omit his interesting reflections suggested by the scenes and events around him.

Tuesday, 6th, [October, 1829,] *I went to Boston, and Friday, 9th, sailed for North Carolina, but on account of a head wind, returned to the harbor. Monday, 12th, we again put to sea, and, the wind being favorable, arrived at Ocrecoke Bar, N. C, Sunday morning, Oct. 18th.*

Soon after we came to anchor, a number of sailors came on board, who, with the pilots and our own crew, amounted to about twenty souls. After praying with them [as he had from time to time with the sailors, by permission of the Captain during the voyage,] *I gave them the parting hand, when some of them were quite moved, and, seizing my hand with both theirs, seemed to feel much interest in my welfare.*

Any one at all acquainted with Hutchins, would expect it of him, to attach the warm-hearted sailors to himself even during so short a voyage. It does not surprise us to find that he is a preacher and a Christian at sea as much as on land. The life and example of Hutchins are a severe rebuke to many, both laymen and preachers, who may be seen in our day at sea. In his short stay at Portsmouth, mentioned in the next extract, the reader will see how interested he always was, even among strangers, to be about the Master's business. After the parting above described, he thus continues the narrative:

> *I was then set ashore at Portsmouth and introduced to a family of Methodists, with whom I tarried five days, and was treated with the greatest kindness. During my stay, I attended* [conducted] *four meetings* [besides] *one funeral.*
>
> *Friday morning, 23d, I sailed from Portsmouth and landed at Newbern, about dark, where I was joyfully received by the brethren. Saturday, Lord's day, Monday and Tuesday, I held meetings in the place, and had much pleasure and freedom in preaching to the large congregations that attended on the word; but I learned with sorrow that there were serious difficulties existing in the church.*
>
> *Wednesday, 28th; I went to Eld. Jesse Heath's. Having held a correspondence with him for nearly two years, and having long anticipated the pleasure of a personal interview, our meeting was peculiarly interesting and productive of much mutual consolation.* * * *
>
> *Saturday, 31st, the Quarterly Meeting commenced, in the meeting house at Core Creek, Craven Co. I attended at that time, but found religion at a rather low ebb; but I had the pleasure of forming an acquaintance with the brethren there.*
>
> *Thursday, Nov. 5th,* [1829,] *the Annual Conference commenced at Bay River meeting house, a few miles below Newbern.* * * * *Great*

union prevailed through the different sessions of the Conference; the business was amicably done; the preaching was evangelical and powerful, and its salutary influences were felt by many in the course of the meeting. It was at that time very sickly at Bay River, and I was informed that three or four men who were able to attend the Conference died in the space of a few days. O! how seldom preachers realize, when addressing their congregations, the uncertainty of life, and how careful they should be to address their hearers in reference to eternity and under a sense of the vast importance of faithfully warning the wicked to turn ere it be forever too late.

His first visit to the interior he thus describes:

The week after the conference I rode in company with Elder Heath and the two [Christian] *preachers from the West, about sixty miles back into the country, where we attended several meetings. On week days, we met from two hundred to three hundred people, and on the Sabbath nearly one thousand. They generally heard with much interest; many were deeply affected, and some rejoiced under the word; some were received as candidates for baptism, who (with others) submitted to that ordinance soon after. We were together on this tour about one week; were favored with much freedom in preaching the word; were kindly received and well entertained by our friends; and, with them, enjoyed much Divine consolation.*

Among other instances of the eagerness of the people to listen to preaching, is the following in his next note:

"Monday, 16th, [Nov.] *after taking an affectionate leave of the brethren who accompanied me, I went home with a brother Hood, of Lenoir Co., with the intention of taking a little rest and doing some writing; but, by the time it was dark, his house was full of people to whom I gladly delivered a discourse instead of resting myself. Some came four miles to visit me that evening. The next night, though*

> *there was no appointment for meeting, the house was again filled,*
> *and another sermon was preached.*

This can but remind the reader of that occasion in our Saviour's earthly pilgrimage, when he said to his disciples, "Come ye yourselves apart, and rest awhile." But the anxious people found the place of the Saviour's retreat, and he preached to them all the day long, and in the evening fed them with miraculous bread. Though he was mourning over the recent death of John the Baptist, and though his weary frame needed rest, yet he would not send the people, hungry for his word, away empty. Hutchins had the spirit of his Master, and though he could not take the needed rest, because it was his meat and drink to do the will of Him that sent him, yet we find his health improving. In the next sentence he says:

> *I now began to hope my visit to the South would be made a bless-*
> *ing to many and a means of improving my health. The harvest is*
> *great, the laborers few, and much help needed. I had meetings al-*
> *most every day, and had I been able to preach three times where I did*
> *but once, I should of necessity have had to deny many who earnestly*
> *requested meetings. The cause of Christ lay near my heart, and I*
> *viewed no sacrifice that I could make too dear for its promotion. I*
> *felt not to ask for the riches, the honors, or the pleasures of this vain*
> *world; neither, for long life; but I could sincerely say, "O, let me*
> *see the benevolent religion of Jesus extending its influence far and*
> *wide, counteracting the baneful effects of sin, and sweetly inclining*
> *the hearts of ungrateful, rebellious sinners to turn to God. Then let*
> *me leave this world in peace, my eyes having seen the salvation of*
> *the Lord!"*

We need not here pause to remark how fully this prayer was granted unto Hutchins, and how each, with a heart like his, can enter into like inheritance. Nor need we stay to say to many a sickly preacher, if he could have

130

such a vacation as this which Hutchins enjoyed, that of giving the heavenly bread to the hungry crowds, his health would improve much faster than it ever did by ordinary vacations.

We find that, between the 16th of November and 5th of December, he had attended "meetings in various parts of Craven and Lenoir counties," and he adds that "generally I had much satisfaction in preaching to the large and attentive congregations that came out to hear the word." On the 5th of December he was preaching to a large and solemn congregation in the meeting house at Luzen Swamp; in the evening at another place he was preaching a funeral sermon; the next day, Sabbath, he was "preaching with unusual freedom to a large and attentive congregation at Wheat Swamp, Lenoir Co. In the evening he preached to another congregation. Monday he was on his way with Bro. Hood to South Carolina, preaching, of course, as he went. Of his meeting Monday evening, he says,

> I met a well-behaved congregation in a place mostly destitute of preaching. * * * The next day I fulfilled an appointment at Indian Spring, Wayne county. This was an interesting time. The saints were made to rejoice and sinners to feel their need of Christ, several of whom were baptized soon after.

On Saturday, 12th, he reached Mount Elon, Darlington District, South Carolina. Here, in company with a Calvinistic Baptist preacher, he held "a two days' meeting."

> The word was feelingly dispensed, Christian friendship prevailed, sinners were affectionately invited to seek the Lord, and many, to appearance, were almost persuaded to be Christians; but, alas, I fear that the most were not altogether persuaded.

The following Wednesday, the 16th of December, he arrived at "Elder Redding Moore's, Marion District," and was kindly received. Mr. Moore had moved several years before from North Carolina; he had for thirteen years been the sole preacher of free salvation in that vicinity; he had suffered much for the cause; at length two other preachers had been raised up to strengthen his hands, and he was greatly encouraged at the time Hutchins visited him. The church of which he was pastor numbered some fifty, but was thirty miles away. Hutchins, though he held several meetings with Mr. Moore in his neighborhood, did not visit his church—meetings "generally interesting, and some signs of revival."

We have already seen that there is a Conference now in that region. Darlington and Marion districts lie on the railroad which leads from Wilmington, North Carolina, to Columbia, South Carolina. Of course there were no railroads there at that time. Hutchins performed all these journeys on horseback. This, we believe, was his only visit to South Carolina, and lasted but a few days, for on Monday, the 21st, he set out to return to Lenoir county, in North Carolina, at which he arrived on Christmas, in the evening, and was the next day at the Quarterly Meeting at Bethel, which is near the Luzen Swamp church. Here we must pass over a very interesting personal incident which is stated at some length in the journal:

> *The Quarterly Meeting was attended with much solemnity and with obvious manifestations of the Divine presence. The neighborhood of Bethel was formerly filled with dissipation of almost every description; consequently, with the most, religion was mentioned only as a subject of ridicule. But a late revival had produced a great change in the morals of the place. The obscene songs of the drunken and lascivious had given place to the sweet music of Zion; prayer had taken the place of swearing and lying; the Sabbath, formerly a day of drinking and gambling, of fighting and horse-racing, was religiously observed; and the salutary influences of pure religion were too obvious to be denied by its most inveterate enemies.*

But we must pass over the ground more rapidly. The next Saturday and Sabbath, the first of the new year, he was at a Quarterly Meeting at Luzen Swamp. Two youths were baptized, increasing the joy of the occasion. Tuesday night he preached at Kingston,[3] the capital of the county, to a very few hearers, yet constituting the largest audience for religious purposes, in that place, for a long time. The circus, however, was largely attended, and even professors of religion, by their presence, encouraged the worthless men and low women that constituted the circus company.

> *Wednesday, 6th,* [Jan., 1830,] *I met a large congregation at Sandhill Chapel. Just as the meeting commenced, a man under the influence of liquor and rage approached the house, raving and swearing in an awful manner, and pouring abuse on all around him. Some were frightened and others irritated at his conduct; for awhile the meeting was broken up. But, in a short time, he was led off and the congregation took seats, after which we had a solemn and peaceable waiting before the Lord. With due deference to the feelings of the drunken man's friends, I took occasion from the circumstance to caution my hearers against the intemperate use of ardent spirits, and against associating with those addicted to that practice.*

This last sentence indicates, perhaps, that Hutchins had not yet taken the ground of total abstinence. It is much like the language of the English pulpit today, a generation later. The next Saturday (9th) he meets troubles, in another form, arising from the intemperate use of liquor. It is at a Quarterly Meeting at Grimsley meeting house in Green county.

> *The first day was a time of much trial and grief, owing to several cases of late intoxication among the members of the church! The*

---

3   The article consistently spells Kinston incorrectly and even includes a footnote opining that Hutchins, who spelled it correctly, must have been spelling it like it was pronounced by the inhabitants!

133

next day a large concourse of people attended; —careless professers were solemnly warned to bear a daily cross, and shun evil practices; the mourners in Zion were comforted; and sinners were entreated to seek the Lord, and prepare for a dying hour.

A few days later, he gives us another glimpse of society in the South, at least as he found it at Little Creek, in the same county:

Religion was at a low ebb; the morals of the place were much corrupted by a store and a set of unprincipled characters who visit it, near the M. H. [meeting house.] People of respectability were often disturbed in their devotions by the almost continual passing in and out of these pests of society, who are frequently found at the grog-shop. Often at the close of worship, the friends of good order were grieved or disgusted at the scenes about the store; after having listened to the sound of the gospel, their ears were frequently saluted with the profane oaths and "the filthy conversation" of tiplers and rakes; and, what was still worse, report said, (and there was too much ground to believe it,[4]) that some professors would disgrace themselves and dishonor the cause of religion by uniting with those shameless mortals and spending hours in drinking and carousing with them. Intemperance was quite common, and its baneful influences were too often extended to some of the members of the church. I endeavored to clear religion of the scandal brought upon it by its professed friends, solemnly warning them to give up their pretensions to religion, or "cease to do evil and learn to do well."

*Saturday and Sabbath * * * the congregation was large, [at Q. M.] and for that place generally well-behaved. But, I had to expose the conduct of a few well-dressed, ill-behaved young men at the water side.*

---

4 I assume Hutchins meant, "*not* to believe it."

After a short visit to Newbern and Stony Creek, he returned to this stronghold of drunkenness, and renewed his exertions for its reformation. At the Quarterly Meeting just mentioned, the keepers of the store, the headquarters of vice, had attempted to hire an impenitent colored man to present himself as a candidate to the church; but he, "having more good breeding" than the liquor sellers, "refused to be guilty of such disgraceful conduct!" Now that Hutchins made remarks which stung some of the guilty company of drinkers, and his persuasive preaching was beginning to win others, they put forward one of their own number as a candidate for baptism. He was refused. At the close of the meeting he "went to his own company," and "set up a laugh at their unsuccessful attempt to deceive us." This visit, despite all these hinderances, proved to be "an awakening time," and "a visible change was seen in the countenance, and conduct of a large majority of the immense auditory that attended the meeting."

> *Feb. 3d, I attended a meeting at Bro. Anderson's on Piney Creek. This place was formerly noted for fiddling and dancing, drinking, &c. But the fiddler was convinced "of the error of his ways," laid aside his violin and began to seek the Lord. A revival commenced; the worship of God took the place of those scenes of mirth and revelry; a church was gathered; the fiddler soon began to blow the gospel's silver trump, and lead his fellow men to the refined pleasures of religion. O, that every fiddler would conduct in such a manner and assist in gathering the people to the glorious Shiloh; for surely their present admirers will have no use for them on their dying beds.*

Having now given what may serve as a specimen of the journal, we must content ourself with giving, without following the order of time further, some of the incidents attending the labors of Hutchins in several of the counties he visited. The counties in which he preached most, with their respective capitals, it may be well to mention at this point: Craven county, capital,

Newbern; Beaufort, Washington; Lenoir, Kingston; Green, Snowhill; and Pitt, Greenville.

CRAVEN COUNTY

Craven county, whose capital has recently come into possession of the Union forces, has an area of about a thousand square miles. In 1850 its population was nearly fifteen thousand, over one-third of whom were slaves. Newbern itself contains just about one-third of the entire population of the county. It is at the confluence of Trent and the Neuse rivers, thirty miles from the mouth of the latter. Its communication with the ocean is through Ocrecoke inlet. Its commerce was, previous to this war, for a Southern place, quite respectable.

We have already noticed the first visit of Hutchins to this town, and the trials in which he found the church. He had left the place with good prospects of a revival. Upon the 20th of January, 1830, he was there again. The good prospects had disappeared. He mourned over the disunion, stubbornness, inordinate ambition and other unholy conduct of church members. At a later time, he visited the church when small pox prevailed in Newbern, but he did not fear that so much as he did that disease with which the church was infected. His spirit was evidently quite depressed.

The time of rejoicing, however, came at length. The dark clouds passed away. The meetinghouse was too small to contain the audiences that assembled to hear him. Of a meeting in May, he says,

> *The power of the Lord was present to heal; on Lord's day morning Elder Pipkin led eight followers of the Lamb into the water in obedience to His command. The hearts of Christians seemed "knit together in love," and it appeared that peace and harmony were about to be restored to this confused and tried church.*

His eyes had now seen tokens from the Lord, and the time to take the parting hand had come. He preached a farewell sermon. "A scene more solemn and deeply affecting for such an occasion," says the preacher, "I never before witnessed." But he witnessed similar scenes soon after at several places as he went to them to take leave of his friends. "My sensations," he remarks, "were of such a nature that it would be in vain for me to attempt a description of them; many around me wept aloud, and signs of sorrow and grief were visible on almost every countenance." It recalled Luke's description of a parting scene. "They all wept sore, and fell on Paul's neck and kissed him, sorrowing most of all for the words which he spake, that they should see his face no more."

Core Creek, Stony Branch, Spring Creek, Little Swift Creek, Bay River, Goose Creek, and Post Oak, are among the other places visited in this county. It was probably at Core Creek that Hutchins met Jesse Heath, his correspondent for many years, and some of whose letters are in our possession. Here, too, he first attended a Quarterly Meeting, which is so different from ours that we must explain in a few words. It is the custom among those churches to hold each four business meetings a year, that is, one quarterly. One of these is called the Yearly Meeting, and the others Quarterly Meetings. These terms, therefore, do not, as among us, refer to the action of associated churches. These meetings are occasions of importance in the individual church. Then the roll is called, and each member answers to his or her name; each member must be present, or afterwards assign a reasonable excuse; the church difficulties are adjusted in open meeting, a proceeding which attracts crowds of curious spectators; the Lord's supper and feet washing are observed, usually in the evening. It is then "a door is opened into the church," that is, an opportunity is given for candidates to present themselves for membership. The candidates arise and walk to a place near the pulpit, the men taking their position on the one side, and the women on the other. The minister says, as he calls the candidates by name, one after another, "Is there any objection to this person?" Many of the church respond, "No objection!" After the candidate relates experience, the minister, taking him by the hand, says, "Brother, I give you the right hand of fellowship, and receive you as a member of the Baptist church, hoping the Lord will bless and save you for his name's sake."

Bay River is the name of a church which seemed to be the central point around which others above named are situated. It is either at a place now called Milton, or Milton Park, on the maps, or near it, north-east from Newbern. Here it was that our brother first met with the North Carolina Freewill Baptists in Annual Conference, or, as we would say, Yearly Meeting. It was a few days after his first arrival in the South, and, by their request, he preached the opening discourse, from the very words, we believe, which Mr. Goadby used as his text on a like occasion at our General Conference in 1847. "Then tidings of these things came unto the ears of the church which was in Jerusalem; and they sent forth Barnabas, that he should go as far as Antioch: who, when he came and had seen the grace of God, was glad, and exhorted them all, that with purpose of heart they would cleave unto the Lord." The Conference gave him a very cordial reception, appointing him to preach on the Sabbath, voting him money from the general funds, and requesting him to address a circular letter to the churches, to be published with the minutes. On the Sabbath his text was, "Is there no balm in Gilead ?" &c. The published minutes say, "A large congregation attended, and the word of salvation was dispensed with zeal and faithfulness, and, we trust, a blessing will ensue."

Hutchins preached in this region the following spring with considerable success. He mentions something like forty baptisms.

> *This was a glorious time to many souls,* [says he in speaking of one of his visits]; *Zion began to enlarge her borders,—to lengthen her cords and strengthen her stakes. * * * Elder Pipkin baptized*

eight happy converts, which had a solemn effect on the minds of the unconverted, and revived the drooping spirits of the almost discouraged saints.

At a meeting at another place, a day or two before this occasion, he mentions that the service was disturbed by a drunken man, who was soon after indicted for the offence. At Little Swift River was his last meeting in this region, of which we find the following note:

*I was enabled to speak with a good degree of freedom. * * * Here, likewise, I bade many of my friends adieu; and, the next day, I was with my horse carried over the Neuse river on a raft, two miles above Newbern.*

BEAUFORT COUNTY

The several churches in this county were quite separated from the rest in the State. They were very destitute of preachers, and heartily welcomed our diligent and laborious evangelist, whose labors here met with signal success. Pungo river church seemed to be the central and chief church; with it Pantego, Beaver Dam, Beaver Creek, North Creek and others, were in intimate association. They had suffered much together for the cause of free salvation. Hutchins became warmly attached to this people. "I was cordially received," says he, "by my brethren and friends generally, (for my Master's sake, I trust,) but in no place more so than in Beaufort county, and especially at Pungo river." His meetings among this people were sometimes so large that their meeting houses would with difficulty contain the women alone. Not less than twenty would sometimes come forward for prayer at the close of a meeting. At Shiloh, forty came forward on one occasion. Baptismal scenes were frequent. On one baptismal occasion he officiated himself, baptizing eight candidates. But usually Elder Henry Smith administered the ordinance.

This was a time, [to give an example in the words of the journal,] *that will long be remembered by many in that place. On Lord's day. Eld. Smith baptized twenty persons, and among this number was his oldest daughter. The candidates were of different ages, from nearly eighty years down to about eighteen. On the shore they joined hands and marched into the river, led by brother Smith. After reaching a suitable depth, they all stood still and the administrator commenced baptizing on the right hand—went on, to the left. They then turned about and marched back to the shore. Three were baptized a few minutes afterward. The scene was solemn and impressive, well calculated to animate the Christian and fill the minds of dear sinners with awe, as much of the Divine presence was felt on the occasion. The large congregation that witnessed the performance, evinced, by a commendable decorum, great respect for this too much neglected ordinance.*

The mode here described, of "marching into the water," hand in hand, is usual in that country, when the place of baptism is favorable to it. The labors of our brother in this region were attended usually by solemn congregations, but, as in other places, they were sometimes disturbed by drunkenness.

During the time of his labors in Beaufort county, he made a visit to Martin county on the north. In like manner from Craven county he made excursions southward to Jones county, preaching at Trenton, the capital, and one or two other places. Among the places where he preached in Beaufort county, we must make particular mention of Bath, a few miles below Washington. Through both of these places he was probably accustomed to pass in his journeys from Pungo River to Pitt and Green counties, but makes mention of them only in connection with his second tour to North Carolina. In Bath he found the highest kind of Episcopalians, but no encouragements in his spiritual labors. We give here another extract from the journal:

Bath is pleasantly situated on a navigable creek, not far from the mouth of Pamlico river. It is said that it was the residence of one of the colonial or provincial governors. It contains but few houses, and is a place of but little business. Some say that there is a curse on the place for the abuse which the celebrated Whitefield received there on one of his tours through this country. The Episcopalian meeting house was shut against him, and he was otherwise disrespectfully treated; and, when he departed, he shook off the dust of his feet against them. And it is a saying that neither religion or business has since prospered on these accounts.

Some years since, a negro was burnt here for killing his master, this being formerly the awful punishment for that crime in the Southern States. I was informed that a forked post was set in the ground with the prongs upward. In these forks, the negro was set, his feet reaching nearly to the ground, where they were bound. A chain was put around his body, and likewise around the forks, in such a manner as to confine him between them. Dry and combustible materials were put around him, among which, and especially near the criminal, were large quantities of pitch-wood shavings. When the time of execution arrived, the sheriff with tears approached the awful pile, to which he applied the fatal torch, and, instantly, the negro was enveloped in the devouring element. With an awful exertion, he gave two hideous screeches, the flames at the same time issuing from his mouth nearly half a yard; then all was still, while his body was consumed.

Take the following glimpse of Washington, to which Burnside, as we read this morning, has sent an officer to enlist a regiment of loyal troops:

I passed through the town of Washington, a large village on the Pamlico river. In an old field near this village, a pit, about twenty feet in length and six or eight in depth and width, was found in the night the preceding October [1832]; *from it, some persons, supposed to be negroes, ran as it was approached. This circumstance*

141

> *for a short time considerably alarmed the inhabitants of the place,*
> *as it was thought by some that it was dug by the run-away negroes,*
> *and others concerned with them, as a place of deposit for weapons*
> *intended to be used in killing the whites. However, nothing serious*
> *followed. But fear is among the many evils of slavery.*

We shall not have space in this article for further notice of his observations about slavery. Here is another view of Washington in relation to another evil that greatly afflicts the South:

> *During Monday, it being the day before Christmas, [1832] I saw*
> *in Washington, on the way to and from it, some fifty or a hundred*
> *horse-carts from different parts of the country; and of all that I saw*
> *on that day, there was not one without a jug, or some other vessel*
> *for carrying liquor, each cart having from one to six jugs, either*
> *full of ardent spirits, or to be filled for Christmas. So indispens-*
> *ably necessary for that day was this diabolical article in that part*
> *of the country, that those who could not themselves go for it sent by*
> *their neighbors. * * * North Carolina is the worst place I ever saw*
> *for the use of ardent spirits among respectable people. It is gener-*
> *ally presented two or three times a day, and all are urged to drink.*
> *With many religious people there, the first thing in the morning*
> *is prayer; the next, one or two drams; and the third, breakfast. O,*
> *when will this curse become unfashionable and disgraceful, and be*
> *laid aside as foolish and sinful!"*

Hutchins had now, if not before, reached the doctrine of total abstinence.

> *It is surprising to me,* [he continues,] *that on Christmas, more*
> *than any other day, in the Southern States and many other places,*
> *spirits must be plentifully used. Was Christ a drunkard, a glutton,*
> *a rioter, or a warrior, that the day kept in remembrance of his birth*
> *should be kept by drinking, firing, swearing, fighting, gambling,*
> *horse-racing, fiddling, dancing, and the commission of crimes*

142

which modesty blushes to name? Let a heathen come into almost any part of Christendom on that day, and he would think it a day set apart for the service of the devil.

The next day after this Christmas, he went to preach the funeral sermon for a slave woman of his friend, the Rev. Jesse Heath. On that occasion, had Hutchins been like many Northern and Southern Doctors of Divinity, he would have proved, in effect, that Christ was a slaveholder, and then railed against infidels for not adoring him.

Not more than a day or two later, he went to Post Oak, in Craven county, to which we refer for the purpose of having here the statement of Hutchins in reference to an evil till lately peculiar to the slave States alone;

Many in the place were given to drink, and among them some professors of religion. Saturday, I observed that several ladies went out during preaching, for the purpose of "rubbing snuff." This is a practice [snuff-rubbing] *that prevails among all classes of ladies at the South, whether high or low, rich or poor, black or white, bond or free, old or young. They take a piece of twig three or four inches long, chew one end of it to a brush, which they dip into a box of snuff, then put it into their mouths and rub their teeth.* * * * *Before I commenced preaching on Sabbath morning, I told the people that when I saw ladies going out of meeting unnecessarily, I was inclined to think that they had something in their snuff-boxes that they loved more than they did the gospel. This hint had the desired effect, and there was but little going out to use the box that day.*

GREEN COUNTY

This lies directly west of Beaufort county. Grimsley meeting house, Harts, Little Creek, and Hookerton are the places of principal mention in this county. Of two of them we have already spoken. Hutchins enjoyed considerable success in this county which he visited, like most others, three or four times. Here he speaks of large numbers of inquirers, and interesting baptisms; as well as of some discouragements.

PITT COUNTY

—Is still west of Green, and shared considerably in the labors of our evangelist, who twice visited the churches at Green Swamp and other places. He did not remain to see so much of the fruit of the labor in this county, as in Beaufort, Craven, Green and Lenoir. Yet some fruit he saw, and in after days he heard of more.

LENOIR COUNTY

In this county, which lies west of Craven, he preached much more than in any other named or to be named. Repeatedly he preached at Luzen Swamp, Wheat Swamp, Bethel, Kingston, Sand Hill Chapel, and less frequently at Woodenton and other places. At Kingston, so unpromising at first, by reason of the circus, he at length had large audiences, among whom were Universalists, who admitted his candor while he dealt severely with their doctrine. In the other places the joy of the reaper often lightened the toil of the sower.

We have already seen that this was the first county he visited in the interior. Here we find him the following June, on the fifth day of which he remarks:

> *Completed twenty-nine years of my unprofitable life—bade my dear brother Heath, brother Bond and several others farewell— was quite low in health—went to Hookerton and preached to nearly three hundred people.*
>
> *Lord's day, 6th, Elder Braxton baptized eight persons at Wheat Swamp, after which I preached to nearly one thousand people. Here I left most of my acquaintances in North Carolina. O, how hard to*

*part with kind and affectionate friends—many friends in tears—
my heart full of sorrow. * * * Our minds were alive to sensations
impossible to describe, and a profusion of tears attested the reluctance with which we took the parting hand. I had a journey of over
600 miles to perform on horseback, in a low state of health and in
the heat of summer. I raised my heart to God, committed myself to
his protection, and mentally implored the light of his countenance,
and the aid of his Spirit to attend me on my lonesome way.*

He had preached at nearly fifty places, not to mention numerous funeral
sermons, during the last eight months; at most of them repeatedly, and not
unfrequently holding two and three days' meetings; these places widely dis-
persed throughout seven or eight large counties; his conversations in private were often more exhausting than his public labors; his health most of
the time feeble; his labors, peculiarly blessed nearly all the time, afforded
no rest, and, yet he unaffectedly writes down at the close of this period of
wonderful activity and usefulness, "My unprofitable life." We may well call
to mind the significant language of the Bible, "If the righteous scarcely be
saved, where shall the ungodly and sinner appear!"

Hutchins had now set his face northward. Passing through Wake county,
in which is the capital of the State, he had reached the residence of Elder
Fonville, in Orange county. Fonville received him with open arms. Here
the two days' meeting, previously appointed by letter, was attended, with
little apparent results. The wife of Fonville, however, was baptized by the
evangelist, who, after resting a week in that "hilly country," pursued his
journey. The next Sabbath [June 27] he preached at "a brother Davis' tav-
ern in Wythe county in Virginia." The next three days, he travelled "in company with the President of the college at Columbia, Tennessee." July 1st,
in the evening, he preached at Tazwell, in that State. Pursuing his journey,
he passed through Cumberland Gap, and spent the following Saturday and

Sabbath in a "meeting with the United. Baptists, near Barbourville, Knox Co., Kentucky."

> *Thursday, July 8th,* [1830] *I crossed the Ohio river at Fredericksburg, Kentucky, and was soon among my dear friends, in Indiana, by whom I was kindly received, having been absent from them nearly two years.*

He resumed his labors among the churches in Indiana and Ohio. He did not, however, forget his friends in North Carolina. His labors and successes had now become a part of the history of the Freewill Baptist cause in that State. Their annual Conference held its session that autumn at Grimsley meeting house, Green county. Hutchins, though absent in body, was present by a letter, which the Conference ordered to be published with its minutes. In this letter, after a mention of the kindness he had received among the churches, he enters upon a historical sketch, encouraging them to renewed exertion, as already, by God's blessing, they had so wonderfully prospered the last five years. From the time of the great defection, they had gained, in sixty years, a membership of only 800.

"But O, my brethren," said he, "what has God done for you in the course of five years!" They then numbered 1900. But their Northern friend was too faithful to them not to suggest improvements, especially in the practice of temperance.

> *Permit me, with a due sense of my unworthiness,* [said he,] *to point out some evils which have done much harm, and from which I pray God ever to keep us. In some places, it is often the case that professors are at sales, elections, courts, shows, stores, &c., with little or no business to call them there; and some, on week days, have left the house of God to loiter about places where little else was to be seen but wickedness and revelry. At such places always may be found, those who are not friendly to religion, and who delight in drawing its professors into a*

146

snare. Some, by such characters, have been prevailed upon to drink, a little at first; this created a desire for more; and, being now less able to resist their inclination to drink, many have become intoxicated. Their conduct has brought shame and remorse on their own minds, grief and anguish of soul on their brethren and friends, and a reproach on the cause of God.

So much evil has resulted from the practice of drinking before going to meeting and after returning from it, that the church at Pungo river, as well as many respectable individuals in that part of the country have laid it aside; the bottle is now no longer seen among the things with which friends are entertained. I should rejoice that this laudable effort to suppress intemperance was well seconded by the other churches composing your Conference; and I do hope that an example so well worthy of imitation, will be copied by all the friends of morality and religion.

Two years later, we find in the minutes of one of the Conferences[5] into which the one was divided at the session just noticed, that two motions were made by Rev. Jesse Heath touching the subject Hutchins had pressed upon the attention of his friends. The first was, "that no brother should keep a grog or tippling shop, under the penalty of excommunication;" and, the second, "that no member shall treat with ardent spirits, for any candidate for a post of profit." They were both referred to "the General Committee," and that, so far as the minutes show, was the last of them.

This was a few days before Hutchins arrived in North Carolina on his second tour. He was, however, at the session of the other Conference,[6] held at Luzon Swamp, Nov. 8, 1832. Among the proceedings of this session, it will interest some to read the following:

---

5   The Shiloh Conference, apparently, meeting in October, 1832.
6   The Bethel Conference.

On motion, Elders Jesse Heath and E. Hutchins were appointed to publish a history of our connection in this and the adjoining States.

Agreed, that we recommend the brethren of our connection to patronize the Morning Star, published by the Freewill Baptists at the North.

Voted, that ten dollars, out of the general fund, be given to Elder E. Hutchins.

Lord's day, Nov. 12, Elder R. McNab introduced the services and preached on Mark 15:34. Elder E. Hutchins followed, from Deut. 32:1, 2; and, with gratitude to God, we can say that the close of this day's meeting was solemn and very interesting. The congregation was mostly in a flood of tears; saints rejoiced, sinners mourned and cried for mercy, while large numbers of people crowded around the stage and united in singing, and, in shaking the friendly parting hand.

Bro. Hutchins gave an invitation to mourners, and it was thought about fifty came forward, and desired the prayers of the people of God. As many were desirous, and the prospect very encouraging, another meeting was appointed for the next day. * * * In the close of this meeting, [next day after a sermon by Hutchins,] a door was opened for the reception of members, when six happy converts came forward and were joyfully received.

A few months more, and it will be thirty years since that meeting. It is stated in the minutes that 3500 people were present. The shaking of hands during singing, is a common practice, as the journal notices, in that country. The preachers sometimes came down from the pulpit to participate in it. It is often mentioned in the journal, that the weeping was general and profuse under preaching. How dear must a man of such unaffected and devout emotions as was Hutchins have been to such a people! It is no wonder they offered him houses and lands and slaves, if he would make his home with them. In this tour his wife was with him, and she was received with an interest not inferior to that shown everywhere to him. Probably slavery alone prevented them from spending their days in that inviting land.[7]

Hutchins, in his second tour, went over nearly all his former fields of labor. He also extended his acquaintance into new fields, in Sampson and Duplin counties, in which, as in his old fields, he met with great encouragement in his ministry to souls. Everywhere the people parted with him with reluctance and in tears. But evils that he could not cure, nor even be permitted to try to cure, he would not voluntarily endure. He turned from a land so congenial to his health, and a people, in many things, so dear to his heart, to visit them no more. On the 24th of May, 1832, he sailed from Newbern.

It is remarked in "The History of the Freewill Baptists for Half a Century," that not only churches, but Quarterly Meetings and Yearly Meetings have sprung up along the track which John Colby pursued in his unaccountable missionary journey to Ohio. The opinion is intimated that the Divine Spirit in sending forth the missionary foreshadowed those manifestations of grace, from which those churches sprung into life. There are persons who believe that the impulse which sent John Brown forth, almost single handed, to capture the great State of Virginia and release her bondmen, was designed to foreshadow the events now transpiring by Divine permission on "the sacred soil." When another generation has passed, perhaps the historian may have the data for a similar remark concerning these wonderful missionary tours of Elias Hutchins. It may be then that flourishing Freewill Baptist churches, untainted by slavery, may be numerous in those counties so often traversed by this laborious evangelist, under an impulse as peculiar as that experienced by Colby.

In the coming day of freedom, we trust our denomination may at least watch for the providential openings in North Carolina. We believe that State

---

7   This is another of the author's unjustified opinions; the "probably" tends to indicate that Hutchins himself said no such thing.

furnishes us the best prospects of a glorious field of extension, far beyond what Kentucky or any other part of the South promises. Slavery only hindereth for a season. It may be, its work of division is about completed. The separation of 1839 may be superseded by a holy and perpetual union. Let us be ready for our part. Let us wait in hope.

5

Thomas E. Peden and the "National" that Might Have Been, 1892-1910

Most contemporary Free Will Baptists are unaware that there was a "national association" of Free Will Baptists before the 1935 organization we know now, one that included the Free Will Baptists of the South. Both Michael Pelt and William F. Davidson have given this brief attention, but neither had the complete information that is available now.[1] The organization lasted from 1895 to 1910, and it came about on this wise.

By way of background: in 1827, the Northern Freewill Baptists had organized their own national body, the General Conference. It met annually 1827-1833, biennially 1835-1841, and triennially from 1844 until it merged with the Northern Baptists in 1910-11. My story is not about that body, but it grows out of it.

---

1   Michael R. Pelt, *A History of Original Free Will Baptists* (Mount Olive: Mount Olive College Press, 1996), 182-186; William F. Davidson, *The Free Will Baptists in America 1727-1984* (Nashville: Randall House Publications, 1985), 337-339.

By the twenty-ninth session of the General Conference in 1895, at least one man was becoming seriously dissatisfied with the direction it was taking. His name was Thomas E. Peden, a minister from Ohio—and sometimes West Virginia. He was active in the General Conference and had served in various capacities in that organization. At the twenty-eighth session in Lowell, Massachusetts, October 5-11, 1892, Peden was present, representing West Virginia Free Will Baptists. He was on the Church Polity Board and led prayer at least twice.[2]

The General Conference was in transition in 1892, which included becoming incorporated and rewriting its charter and constitution. Among other things, this entailed changing the name from the General Conference of Freewill Baptists to the General Conference of Free Baptists. When the new constitution was up for consideration, an Ohio delegate named Davis made a motion that would require ratification of the new constitution by the Yearly Meetings and other representing bodies. The influential George Ball offered a substitute motion that would bypass that requirement and simply urge the representative bodies to accept the new constitution and "cordially unite" behind it. Peden was among those who spoke in favor of Davis's original. Ultimately, Ball's motion was ruled out of order, but another substitute motion was passed, providing for the representative bodies to express their approval or disapproval in writing and that, when enough of them to represent three-fourths of the resident members of the Conference had approved, the change would become final and all bodies would be expected to transfer their funds and merge their interests into the newly constituted organization.[3]

We have no way of knowing precisely what bothered Peden about this. Some have suggested he was opposed to the incorporation. Norman Baxter

2 *Minutes of the General Conference of Freewill Baptists*, 1892, 8, 16.
3 *Minutes of the General Conference of Freewill Baptists*, 1892, 66-67.

said, "We do not have the express objections to incorporation, but since the 'Pedenites' declared themselves as the legitimate successors of the founding fathers who remained unincorporated we may assume that they felt incorporation was a departure from the founders' position."[4] One could speculate, as Davidson does,[5] that Peden saw the merger with Northern Baptists coming down the road and this was the reason he resisted incorporation, but that is speculation. Perhaps he objected to the name change; he would at least use that fact in pressing his own claims. Regardless, the only thing we know for sure is what we find in the minutes of the next triennial session of the General Conference.

Peden Begins a Rival Conference

The 1895 session met in Winnebago, Minnesota. Peden was not there in person, but he sent a letter that the Conference took note of, saying "A communication was received from Rev. Thos. E. Peden of Ohio, protesting against the adoption of the new constitution and making the following demand."[6] The minutes then reproduce Peden's entire letter:

> Sciotoville, O., Sept. 20, 1895
> *To the Free Baptist General Conference and Conference Board:*
> By means which we will not here discuss you are in control of the permanent funds of the Home Mission, Foreign Mission, and Education societies, and as these funds were given by Freewill Baptists to promote the cause of Christ through their own chosen denomination, and would not have been given, as we have strong reasons to believe, to any "Free Baptist" society or organization,

4 Norman Allen Baxter, *History of the Freewill Baptists: A Study in New England Separatism* (Rochester: American Baptist Historical Society, 1957), 164, n. 39.

5 William F. Davidson, *The Free Will Baptists in History* (Nashville: Randall House, 2001), 258.

6 *Minutes of the General Conference of Free Baptists,* 1895, 47.

we request you as honest men to turn said funds over to Bro. O. Eakins, treasurer, or to his successor in office, to be used as intended by the donors for the advancement of the Freewill Baptist denomination through these respective channels. We also ask you to give possession of all mission property in India, the Freewill Baptist Printing Establishment (See Art. 7 of the Constitution, found in the Treatise), and all other moneys and properties belonging to the General Conference or any of its Boards; also, so far as under your control, the property and endowments of all colleges and other schools under our denominational control. We are asking simply for what is honestly ours, and hope that litigation will not be necessary among men professing Christianity.

As the clerk failed to give notice of the meeting of the Freewill Baptist General Conference at Winnegabo, Minn., as per adjournment was expected, a committee appointed by a called conference announced at a late date that it will meet in Coalton, O. Only a small delegation, enough to adjourn at least, is expected. They will transact some necessary business, and probably adjourn until some time in next year. Boards will be appointed, or those appointed last year will hold over, to attend to the denominational interests.

Respectfully submitted in behalf of the executive committee appointed at the called session of the Freewill Baptist General Conference.

Thos. E. Peden, *Clerk*[7]

The General Conference responded as follows: "On motion of Ball of New York it was voted that the communication of Bro. Peden be referred to a Special Committee of five, to report a suitable reply to be returned. The

---

7 *Minutes of the General Conference of Free Baptists*, 1895, 47-48.

chair appointed as such committee, Ball of New York, Webb of Maine, Mrs. Cheney of Maine, Fulton and Patch of Ohio."[8]

What Peden was doing seems reasonably clear. According to the old constitution, the 1895 meeting of the General Conference of *Freewill* Baptists had not been announced; only a meeting of the General Conference of *Free* Baptists (as newly constituted) had been announced. Consequently, and apparently at his behest, an 1895 meeting of the General Conference of *Freewill* Baptists (as named in the old constitution) had been scheduled for Coalton, Ohio, by a group he represented, a group claiming to be the true "General Conference of *Freewill* Baptists" and to be entitled to all funds and properties of that organization (as named under the old constitution). This was a bold move, one that did not really work out.

What did work was that, from that point on, there was an alternate version of the General Conference sponsored by Peden and his associates. Before providing more information about that, however, it seems appropriate to finish the story of the General Conference response to Peden's effort. As just noted, it was determined in 1895 that a letter of response should be sent to Peden. The 1895 minutes, consequently, also include the following at a point later in the proceedings.

> Ball of New York, for the special committee to prepare a reply to Rev. T. E. Peden of Ohio, submitted the following communication, which was adopted as read, and the clerk was directed to forward the same to the brother in the name of the Conference:
>
> *Thomas E. Peden and Others:*
> Dear Brethren:—The Free Baptist General Conference acknowledges the receipt of your favor of Sept. 30, 1895, dated at Sciotoville, O., and has carefully considered the points of interest

---

8 *Minutes of the General Conference of Free Baptists*, 1895, 48.

presented. In response the Conference is glad to express endless confidence in your sincerity, yet it deeply regrets the attitude you have assumed. In changing some of the methods of the work of the Freewill Baptist denomination it was expected that some diversity of views would be entertained. The experience of other denominations, while making such changes, led to expectations of this kind, but to the credit of Freewill Baptists it can be truly said that their forbearance and kindness in the premises have exceeded that of any other denomination in like circumstances. Out of a resident membership of 58,847 the large number of 49,565 voted in favor of the changes proposed before said changes were made. And since that vote was taken, and the changes put into operation, the expressed feeling in favor of the new order of things is warm and almost unanimous. The reports which have come up to this General Conference from the Yearly Meetings and Associations are most cheering, indicating new life and courage in all our borders.

We devoutly wish that you especially, dear Bro. Peden, could have been with us, both to feel and increase this new inspiration. The Conference writes you to express its warm and most fraternal interest in you personally, and the unanimous wish of the brotherhood that you will reconsider your attitude and fully resume your walk with the people who always have highly esteemed you, and with whom you have labored many years with significant success.

Geo. H. Ball,
L. M. Webb,
Mrs. E. B. Cheney,
W. J. Fulton,
O. D. Patch[9]

---

9 *Minutes of the General Conference of Free Baptists*, 1895, 70.

This was not quite the end of it in the records of the General Conference. In the minutes of the next session at Ocean Park, Maine, in 1898, the following appears.

The report of the committee on troubles in southern Ohio was made and is briefly as follows:

1. Mr. Peden continues his opposition to General Conference, is misleading brethren and churches as to the polity and purpose of our organization under our present constitution.

2. That the Peden Conference held at Coulton [sic], Ohio, in October, 1895, was very small, no ministers attending from a distance, and only the neighbors in the immediate vicinity attending, and the only business transacted was to adjourn to meet at Coffers [sic] Chapel, Nashville, Tenn.

3. That the small following Mr. Peden has is steadily weakening, and that all southern Ohio is substantially in accord with General Conference.[10]

After this, there are a few references back to the matter. The 1907 General Conference minutes report that there had been some communication "with that section of our own denomination, which in 1892 severed itself from our present General Conference and has called itself the original Free Will Baptist Conference of North America."[11] In 1917, in a descriptive history, after relating how the General Conference had been incorporated in 1892 in Maine, the following appears:

This centralization of functions and powers was not acceptable to all of the denomination, although ordered by an overwhelming majority. A fraction, under the leadership of Rev. Thomas E. Peden, then of Ohio, declared themselves as independent of the incorpo-

---

10 *Minutes of the General Conference of Free Baptists*, 1898, 24.
11 *Minutes of the General Conference of Free Baptists*, 1907, 104.

rated body and as the sole and legitimate successors of the "fathers" who had founded the denomination and had remained unincorporated. Unsuccessful appeals to the courts were made to secure title to some of the property in Ohio and adjacent states; and since that time those who followed Mr. Peden, sometimes termed "Pedenites", have remained separate and distinct from the General Conference of Free Baptists, professing themselves to be the original Free Will Baptists. They have established fellowship with a branch of Free Will Baptists, centering in North Carolina, who became separated from their northern brethren in ante-bellum days over war-issues.[12]

Response to Peden in the Ohio River Yearly Meeting

Peden's efforts were also rejected by many of his brethren of the Ohio River Yearly Meeting, where he had been clerk since 1859.[13] Indeed, he was clerk there in 1892, when he attended that years' triennial session of the General Conference (above), and again in 1893. But there was more involved than his displeasure with the course of the General Conference.

When the Ohio River Yearly Meeting met in 1893, Peden and others who had attended the 1892 General Conference gave their report and presented the new constitution for ratification as had been decided there in 1892. The minutes include this resolution, which was adopted:

> Whereas the contemplated new constitution of General Conference proposes radical changes in our church polity, changes

---

12 *Minutes of the General Conference of Free Baptists*, 1917, 62. The comment is somewhat disingenuous; there was apparently never an organic connection between the Randall movement and the North Carolina Free Will Baptists, even though some publications in the North listed them. The North deliberately ceased listing them because some of those in the South were slaveholders.

13 He was also clerk of the Ministers Conference of the Ohio River Yearly Meeting from its organization in 1862 until 1879.

regarding the propriety of which the membership of this Y. M. differ in opinion considering that such changes should be intelligently and prayerfully considered and whereas there is not now time for a free and full discussion of this subject, such as would be desired by parties of either side before submitting to an opposite decision: Resolved, That a vote on the ratifying of the new constitution shall be postponed for one more year of prayerful, careful consideration.

What part Peden might have played in this is not mentioned.

The 1894 minutes are missing, but the minutes of the years following appear to indicate that the Ohio River Y. M. (Yearly Meeting) ratified the new constitution. It is clear that the Gallia Q. M. (Quarterly Meeting), at its meeting of June 8, 1894, in anticipation of this Y. M., instructed its delegates to the Y. M. to vote to ratify the new constitution.[14] Peden, who was still clerk of the Y. M. in 1894, might have objected to this, but we have no way of knowing unless minutes for that year can be found; apparently, Peden never entered them in the record book.

We do have the minutes for 1895, however, and these reveal that there was something more afoot. Peden had been ministering in West Virginia, as president of West Virginia College, and had become involved in what could be called "the Powell-Peden case." He and a fellow minister, David Powell, had made accusations against each other, but we do not know their nature. The Ohio River Y. M. had appointed, at the annual meeting in August 1894, a committee to investigate this matter, given that the West Virginia Quarterly Meeting reported to it.

The 1895 Ohio River minutes contain the committee's lengthy report. Previously, the West Virginia Quarterly Meeting had "deposed" Powell from the ministry and excluded the Flemington, West Virginia, church—

---

14   Minutes, Gallia Q. M., June 8, 1894 (p. 92 of handwritten record book).

perhaps Powell's pastorate—from its membership, siding with Peden. The
Y. M. committee found differently, however, saying that all the actions in
West Virginia had been "irregular, consequently illegal." The Ohio River
Y. M. approved the committee report and sent a communication to the West
Virginia Q. M. asking them to rescind their actions regarding Powell and the
Flemington church. This meant that Peden had lost the battle, whatever it
was. (Powell would later be highly praised in an obituary in the Ohio River
Y. M. Ministers Conference minutes in 1905.)

As a result, Peden immediately resigned as clerk and the Y. M. elected
his successor—and proceeded to elect delegates to the next General Conference, which would meet in Winnebago, Minnesota, later in the same year.
This was August 9, 1895; in September Peden would write the letter to the
General Conference quoted above.

It would seem more than accidental that these events transpired so closely
together, but it would also be presumptuous to say, at this date and without
more information, whether Peden was justified in his quarrel with Powell
and the Ohio River Y. M.

After this point, Peden played no further role in the proceedings of the
(original) Ohio River Y. M.—he had read a paper on "Ministerial Qualifica-
tions" at the Ministers Conference that had preceded the annual meeting.[15]
The affair is briefly mentioned, however. The 1896 minutes record a resolution adopted, to this effect:

> Resolved, that, as a Yearly Meeting we disapprove of the conduct
> of Rev. T. E. Peden and Rev. Peter Williams in opposition to our
> denominational unity and work, and, while they continue in such
> course, we do not hold them as in good standing as ministers in our
> Yearly Meeting. Resolved, that the clerk be instructed to place the

15 Minutes, Ministers Conference of the Ohio River Y. M. for August 8-9, 1895 (p. 28 in record
book).

above resolution on the Y. M. record, send a copy to each of our denominational papers, and to each of the named brethren, and forward a copy to each Q. M. clerk in the Yearly Meeting.

The 1898 minutes record the following:

> As to the request of Bro. Reisinger, clerk of Jackson Q. M., that this Y. M. consider the action of T. E. Peden against the denomination: Your committee recommends that this Conference reaffirm their action of 1896, that we still disapprove of his conduct in opposition of our denominational unity and work, and request all members of this Y. M. whenever the opportunity presents itself to do all in their power to inform those who have been misled in regard to our church work and denomination.

The 1899 minutes of the Ministers Conference of the Yearly Meeting include this:

> C. O. Clark offered a resolution to the effect that the Ex. Com. do not consider any application for Certificate of standing from T. E. Peden. Amended by J. M. Davis to read: "Unless T. E. Peden gives satisfactory evidence that he has laid aside all hostility to the denomination." Amendment accepted and resolution passed.

And there the matter rested, except that in 1906 the minutes reveal that one Brother Glover of Buchtel, "has seen his mistake in following the Peden element, and desires earnestly to come back to us and be recognized in good standing with us." The committee investigating this recommended that he be granted a certificate of good standing—as a minister, apparently—and the recommendation was adopted.

In actuality, there was considerable turmoil in Southern Ohio, but it goes beyond the purpose of this chapter to attempt to tell that story in detail. In summary, the "Peden defection"—if I may call it that—involved the fracturing of conferences (Y. M.s and Q. M.s) and churches. Where there was one Ohio River Y. M. previously, there were now two of them, for example. Where there had been one Gallia Q. M. reporting to the Ohio River Y. M., there were now two by that name. In both cases, the ones following Peden were in the minority. We have no records of these organizations from that period.

In at least one local church there were rival groups claiming to be the true church. This was the Sciotoville Free Will Baptist Church, and the two groups went to court: first in 1899 and again in 1906. In the 1899 suit, Peden's group—he was apparently the pastor, at least of the faction—lost the right to use the property. The 1906 suit was to "quiet title," and those who had won the 1899 suit were successful in retaining title. That church is now the Beacon Baptist Church of Sciotoville.

In the end, some of the churches remained Free Will Baptist, disconnected from the (Randall) General Conference and ultimately became part of the National Association of Free Will Baptists. Others of the Ohio River Y. M. churches, probably the majority, stayed loyal to the Randallites, subsequently participated in the merger, and became Baptist churches. Yet others are extinct and some are independent of any denominational affiliation. And it may be that some of the churches that ultimately became part of the National Association of Free Will Baptists did not follow Peden but waited until the merger to break with the Randallites. All of this needs more research and cannot be detailed now.

But by 1895—and this was fifteen years before the 1910-11 merger—there was a (Peden) version of the "Ohio River Yearly Meeting," claiming to be the "original." Its minutes are not available. Even so, its participation in the newly formed General Conference (Peden version) makes its existence clear, and that takes us back to the main thread of the story.

The New Triennial General Conference

For the purposes of this story, then, a new organization had come into existence, under Peden's leadership, billing itself as the General Conference of Freewill Baptists and in effect claiming to be the true successor to the General Conference of the Randall movement Freewill Baptists. Its first "regular" session, therefore, was in 1895 at Coalton, Ohio; but in keeping with its claim, it was identified as the twenty-ninth session. The reason for this was that the 1895 session in Winnebago, Minnesota, to which Peden sent the letter quoted above, was indeed the twenty-ninth session of the (Randall) General Conference.

According to Peden's letter, there had been a "called" meeting of his group, self-identified as the "General Conference of Freewill Baptists," shortly before. As will be seen, this took place in Sciotoville, Ohio (date unknown), and although minutes were recorded they have apparently not survived. According to the letter this "called meeting" must have done two things: (1) appoint an executive committee, which included Peden as clerk; (2) name a committee (perhaps the same?) to set a time and place for its 1895 meeting in competition with the meeting in Winnebago, Minnesota.

That committee, as noted, set Coalton, Ohio, as the place and October as the date. We do not have minutes of the 1895 meeting in their original form, but we do have a report, which amounts to the same thing, found in the pages of *The Free Will Baptist*, published in Ayden, North Carolina, December 4, 1895.[16] I include here some excerpts from that report.

---

16 Special thanks to Gary Barefoot, Curator of the FWB Historical Collection at the University of Mount Olive in North Carolina, for providing a photocopy of the page with this report.

GENERAL CONFERENCE

The Free Will Baptist[17] General Conference began its 29th session with a prayer and praise meeting, at Coalton, Ohio, Oct. 2, 1895, at 10 a.m. Met at 2 p.m. and spent an hour in prayer service. Adjourned until 7 p.m. Night session. Prayer was offered by Rev. Robert L. Farmer. The election of officers resulted in the choice of Rev. R. L. Farmer, Moderator; Rev. John A. Oliver [sic],[18] assistant; Minerva Bennett, clerk. Minutes of last session, held at Lowell, were presented in pamphlet form. Minutes of called session, held at Sciotoville, O., read and approved. Letters were read from the Ohio and Kentucky Y. M., Ohio River Y. M., and W. Va. State Convention. Voted to allow all loyal Free Will Baptists present to represent the non-reporting Yearly Meetings. ...

Morning Session, Oct. 3.

.... Declared the office of clerk vacant. Per Constitution, proceeded to election by ballot. Appointed Bro. Alonzo Lacey and Bro. Samuel Shumate tellers. Four votes were cast for Rev. John A. Oiler, and 10 for T. E. Peden, who was declared elected.

Appointed Bro. Sam'l Shumate, Revs. John Mullen, John A. Oiler, T. E. Peden and K. R. Davis, an Executive Committee with full power to act for Conference until its next meeting. ...

Afternoon Session.

.... [In report of the Education committee:] We are, as ever, strongly in favor of a sanctified education, and urge our people to continue establishing schools, until every State has at least one Free Will Baptist institution of learning. The major part of the professors and teachers in each college or other school, should be loyal to the Constitution of General Conference adopted in 1841.

---

17 I suspect that Peden would have written "Freewill Baptist." Perhaps the editor at Ayden made the change to "Free Will Baptist" in accord with his usual practice. (See chapter one in this volume.)

18 As the rest of the minutes show, this should be Oiler, not Oliver.

... [In report of the Publications committee:] We commend the
Free Will Baptist, published at Ayden, N. C., and the Church
Watchman, published at South New Lynne, Ohio, to our people
as worthy of their confidence and support. ...

Adjourned to meet in the city of Nashville, Tenn., the first
Wednesday in Oct., 1896, at 10 a.m., to finish the business of this
session of our triennial Conference.

Thos. E. Peden, Cl'k.

R. L. Farmer, Mod.

Sessions of the New General Conference

Here, then, is a complete list of the meetings of this "Triennial Free Will
Baptist General Conference," as it was called by its next regular session in
1898.[19]

1895 (date unknown)—called session, Sciotoville, Ohio, in advance of first meeting; no record.

October 2-3, 1895—regular session, Coalton, Ohio, as described
above. Letters from the Ohio and Kentucky Y. M., Ohio River Y.
M., and W. Va. State Convention. Officers: Moderator, Robert L.
Farmer; Assistant Moderator, John A. Oiler; Clerk, Minerva Bennett, replaced by Thomas E. Peden.

October 7, 1896—adjourned session, Cofer's Chapel, Nashville,
Tennessee; no record. But we do possess an advance announce-
ment of this session, authored by Peden and published in *The Free
Will Baptist* paper, in Ayden, North Carolina, on May 27, 1896.[20]

---

19 For the 1901 and 1904 sessions the wording was "Free Will Baptist Triennial General Conference," and for 1907 and 1910 "Free Will Baptist General Conference."

20 Again, thanks to Gary Barefoot, Curator of the FWB Historical Collection at the University
of Mount Olive, for a scan of this announcement, which I have transcribed.

Among other things, Peden gives a list of the "objects" of the General Conference:

1. Mutual acquaintance.
2. Union of our different organizations.
3. To promote uniformity of practice.
4. To encourage the publication of denominational books, papers, tracts, &c.
5. To promote Home Mission work.
6. To sustain Foreign Mission work.
7. To build and sustain Schools and Colleges.
8. Anything that Providence indicates for the glory of God and the good of humanity.
9. All these without infringing on the independence of the churches, or the local bodies composing it.

After providing information about how easy it was to join the organization, Peden's announcement observed: "It is hoped that all the Free Will Baptist organizations in the United States will be represented without fail, in the coming session at Nashville, Tenn., Oct. 7, 1896, at 10 A.M. The writer believes it the most important General Conference ever held, and is very anxious to see all the Southern organizations fully represented."

October 5-8, 1898—regular session, Ayden, NC. Letters from the Ohio and Kentucky Y. M. and the Ohio River Y. M.; other delegates representing the Eastern Conference (NC), the Central Conference (NC), the Cape Fear Conference (NC), and the Western Conference (NC). Officers: Moderator, S. J. Halstead (NC), Assistant Moderator, W. H. Lathinghouse (NC); Clerk, Thomas E. Peden (OH); Assistant Clerk, Mrs. Lovie Harrison (NC). Included G. W. Binkley (TN) and Wm. Dyke (AR) on boards.

The Committee on the State of the Denomination, chaired by Peden, expressed "regret that some of our Conferences, Associations, and Yearly Meetings are not connected in our grand Union of work." Interestingly, the traditional statistical table in the back wishfully includes a full listing of all the bodies that had made up the roll of the Randall General Conference.

The Committee on Education took note of the near completion of "a building for a Theological School at Ayden, N. C.," soon to open, and heartily commended it as worthy of support and students. They also recommended, for those unable to attend, "the Correspondence School of Theology conducted by Eld. T. E. Peden." Young people in the churches were urged to form A. C. F. Societies.[21] The Committee on Publications urged the "publishing house in Ayden" to "publish a full supply of Sabbath school literature."

The report of the Committee on Free Will Baptist Union, adopted, said, "We desire a Union of all Free Will Baptists" for the "betterment of the cause of Christ," in which "All shall hold their original faith and practice, and the co-operation shall in no wise interfere or conflict with church government, usage, or practice."

October 1-7, 1901—regular session, Cofer's Chapel, Nashville, TN. Letters of representation (in the minutes) from the following associations: Cumberland (TN), North Dakota, Horry (SC), Cape Fear (NC), Hamburg (AR), Mt. Moriah (NC/SC), Stone (TN), Ohio River, Western (NC). (Again, the statistical table in the back lists all the bodies of the northern General Conference.) Officers: Moderator, P. T. Lucas (NC); Assistant Moderator, G. V. Frey (TN)[22]; Clerk-Treasurer, Thomas E. Peden (OH/NC); Assistant Clerk, J. E. Hudgens (TN).

---

21 A. C. F. = Advocates of Christian Fidelity, for young people in the northern Free Will Baptist churches.

22 It is ironic that G. V. Frey subsequently went from Tennessee to minister among the original Ohio River YM Free Baptists that remained loyal to the Randall General Conference; see the minutes of the Ohio River YM for August 12, 1904, when he was assistant moderator and preached.

A "Historical Sketch" in the front includes the following, referring to conferences, associations, or yearly meetings: "These are all advisory bodies for mutual consultation and the promotion of general interests. All ecclesiastical power is in the individual, or local church."

Minutes include: "Accepted by unanimous vote, the Charter of incorporation, granted by the Secretary of State of Ohio and passed a vote of thanks to the committee for obtaining it." (This may indicate that Peden's original objection was not to the incorporation of the northern General Conference, as such, but to some features of it, including the name change.)

Peden is identified, in the minutes, as "Prof. T. E. Peden, A. M., Principal of the Free Will Baptist Theological Seminary, Ayden, N. C." He preached the "Conference sermon" on the theme, "Principles and Influence of the Free Will Baptist denomination."

The Committee on Education again commended the Seminary at Ayden, *The Free Will Baptist* paper, and "our new hymn book, Zion's Free Will Baptist Gospel Voices" (published at Ayden).

The Committee on Necrology took note of the death of Prof. Ransom Dunn (of the Randall movement) as "one of the greatest losses the Denomination has ever sustained."

October 5-11, 1904—regular session, Dunn, North Carolina. This session was strongly promoted in the pages of *The Free Will Baptist*. One 1904 issue has at least five references to the upcoming meetings, including: a note from the well-known blind evangelist E. L. StClaire of Georgia, urging that many associations were making plans to attend and "it seems that we will have a fair representation from the different states." Another, apparently by the editor, urged, "The Free Will Baptist Triennial General Conference" is "just what we need. It has been doing good work, under

God, for seventy seven years [!] and has a brighter prospect before it than ever before."[23]

Letters of representation (in the minutes) from the following associations: Alabama State Line, Central (NC), Horry (SC); Mt. Moriah (NC/SC), Pee Dee (NC), North Dakota, Georgia Union, South Carolina, South Georgia, Western (NC), Scioto (OH), Chattahoochee (GA), Ohio River, and Eastern (NC). (The statistical table in the back continues to list all bodies of the northern General Conference.)

Officers: Moderator, W. P. Gause (SC); Assistant Moderators, H. F. Wogan (ND) and J. J. Baggett (SC); Clerk-Treasurer, Thomas E. Peden (OH/NC).

The Temperance Committee included, in its report: "We advise our Theological Schools to receive no one as a ministerial student who smokes cigarettes."

The Committee on Education commended the Seminary in Ayden, Beulah High School (NC), and North Dakota University, and instructed the trustees "to secure sites and found schools in W. Va., Ky., S. C., Ga., Texas, Ala., Ark., Ind., Ty.,[24] Mo., and other States and Territories as the Lord opens the way. Interestingly, the report includes this: "Having what we consider as credible evidence that Hillsdale College [in Michigan, of the Randall movement] will be conducted in accordance with its charter and constitution, giving the Free Will Baptist [sic] a good majority of the faculty and trustees. Therefore, Resolved, That we commend it, as in the past to the favorable consideration of our people." (Peden was the committee chairman.) The minutes also include, apparently, a brief statement about Hillsdale from J. W. Mauck, its president.

---

23 *The Free Will Baptist*, June 1, 1904, p. 2. One notes the persistence in claiming the conference as seventy-seven years old to identify it with the original General Conference of the Randallites.

24 Apparently an abbreviation for the Tyronza Association in Arkansas.

October 2-10, 1907—regular session, Cofer's Chapel, Nashville, TN. Letters of representation (in the minutes) from the following associations: Ohio River, Scioto (OH), Liberty (AL), South Carolina, Flat Creek (TN), Georgia Union, South Georgia, Tennessee River, State Line (FL), Central (NC), Cape Fear (NC), Alabama State, Chattahoochee (GA), Cumberland (TN), West Virginia, Western (NC), Denton's Creek (TX), and Midway (GA). (The statistical table in the back continues to list all the bodies that made up the northern General Conference.)

Officers: Moderator, Dell Upton (WV); Assistant Moderators, J. M. Emmanuel (GA) and Woods Springfield (AL); Clerk-Treasurer, Thomas E. Peden (OH/NC); Assistant Clerks, Earnest Poston (SC) and E. B. Joyner (GA).

The Conference appointed Thomas E. Peden as "a committee of one to employ counsel and test in the courts the eligibility of the acting trustees of Rio Grande College, located in Gallia Co., Ohio, and we will sustain him in the effort."

This appears: "Resolved, that we elect Eld. Dell Upton, D. D., Financial Evangelist and general agent for the Theological Seminary at Ayden, N. C. That his duties shall be to travel through our denomination, present the general interests of our church to the people and raise funds for their support." The resolution went on to provide that what he collected would be divided equally between the Seminary and the Executive Committee of the General Conference, and that he would be compensated in the way he and the Executive Committee agreed.

October 5-14, 1910—regular session, Florence, AL FWB Church. Letters of representation (in the minutes) from the following associations: Salem (FL), Canadian (OK), Western (NC), Eastern (NC), Flat Creek (TN), State Line (AL/FL), Liberty No. 1 (AL), Liberty No. 2 (AL), Georgia Union, Tennessee River, Southern Oklahoma, Scioto (OH), North Florida, West Virginia, Midway

170

(GA), and Ohio River; the Cumberland (TN) and Piedmont (NC) gave verbal reports. Elder Charles Elmer Furman, of Brooklyn, NY, was present and participated.

Officers: Moderator, Jefferson D. Stephens (FL); Assistant Moderators, W. L. Hooper (OH) and W. A. Poole (TN); Clerk-Treasurer, Thomas E. Peden (OH/NC); Assistant Clerks, J. G. Harris (GA) and W. T. Kendrick (FL).

Peden "reported that he had not commenced suit for possession of Rio Grande College for lack of money to pay the attorneys a reasonable retaining fee." Subsequently, the Conference "voted to continue the committee on Rio Grande College" and asked them "to investigate the legality of the Free Will Baptist General Conference held in Cleveland, Ohio in 1907." Still later, the following: "Committee on the Cleveland Pseudo General Conference: Whereas, the meeting at Cleveland, Ohio, in 1907, claiming to be a General Conference was composed mainly of delegates from yearly meetings that belong to this General Conference [!], had not asked for dismission and were in no way authorized to hold such meeting, therefore Resolved, That it was an illegal body and all its acts null and void and have no binding force upon any of our people." (Peden chaired this committee.)

The Committee on Education commended again the Seminary in Ayden, North Carolina, and urged the trustees "to secure and keep a well qualified consecrated man for president and professor of Theology"—reflecting the fact that Peden had retired from the presidency. The Committee also advised the trustees of "the Free Will Baptist University at Nashville, Tenn." to retain the charter and begin operation "at the earliest possible time." (This "University" had been charted by Dell Upton during his stint as pastor at Cofer's Chapel, but never materialized.)

Interestingly, on Sunday the ninth the Conference supplied preachers for a number of churches in Florence, in addition to the Free Will Baptist Church, including: First Missionary Baptist,

Missionary Baptist of East Florence, Methodist, Church of God, and First Presbyterian.

The Conference selected the Midway Association in Georgia to host the next meeting.

That meeting did not take place; nor did any other meeting of this short-lived Triennial General Conference. The reasons for this failure are not recorded. Pelt says, "Interest in continuing the organization seems to have waned after the session in 1910. The following year, without stating any grounds for its action, the Central Conference in North Carolina voted to withdraw. ... For whatever reason the General Conference seems to have expired."[25] John L. Welch said that, after 1910, "no other meetings were held because the people were unable to attend."[26] He added, "Dr. Peden, his wife, and a girl that was raised in their home came back from Florence, Alabama, through Nashville and spent a Sunday with us and preached for me. I was pastor of the church [Cofer's Chapel] at that time, and they left here and went on back home and that was the last session of that General Conference. They didn't disband. They just didn't meet, because nobody was interested enough to keep it going."[27]

It seems likely that Peden's age, coupled with his retirement from the Ayden Seminary (see below) in 1910, and his death in 1913—when the next session was to take place—contributed heavily. It may even be that the merger of the Randall movement General Conference with Northern Baptists, consummated in 1910-11, added some discouragement about the possibility of rescuing resources from that organization for the rival conference in the South. At least the chances of enlisting many of the Yearly Meetings and agencies of the northern group grew dimmer.

---

25 Pelt, *History*, 186.

26 John L. Welch, transcription of interview conducted by Robert E. Picirilli, dated April 25, 1971, 11.

27 Welch, 12-13.

In spite of the demise of this "national" that didn't succeed, however, in one possible sense it lived on. Both Welch and Pelt, in the material just cited, regarded the General Conference of the Southeast, which began in 1921, as a "revival" of the organization Peden "headed" (to use Welch's word). And, of course, that revived General Conference was one of the two primary bodies, the other being the Co-operative General Association,[28] that merged in 1935 to form the National Association of Free Will Baptists, the "national" that did survive.

Who Was Thomas Peden?

Except for the brief attention given to this man by Pelt and Davidson, Peden has not received much attention in Free Will Baptist history. He deserves better, and my intention is to provide, now, the information that is available.[29]

Thomas Ewing Peden, the oldest of ten children, was the son of John and Elizabeth (Ewing) Peden, born near Ewington in Gallia County, Ohio, September 13, 1832, in a

Rev. Thomas E. Peden.

log house. His great-grandfather, William ("Oswego Bill") Ewing, had been a captive of the Oswego Indians. He was named for his grandfather on his mother's side, Thomas Ewing. He attended first the Adny School, near his

---

28 For that organization, see chapter six in this volume.

29 The biographical information to follow is mostly from three sources: (1) *Free Baptist Cyclopaedia* [hereafter *Cyclopaedia*], eds. G. A. Burgess and J. T. Ward (Free Baptist Cyclopaedia Co., 1889), 514; (2) Mabel Scott Himebrook [a niece of Peden's], "Biographical Sketch of Dr. Peden," *The Free Will Baptist*, May 13, 1942, 4-5; (3) Abby Gail Goodnite and Ivan M. Tribe, "Ira Z. Haning and His Free-will Baptist Brethren: The Spiritual Rocks in the Rio Grande College Foundation" (unpublished), 5. My thanks to Jim McComas for pointing me to the Himebrook article and to Alton Loveless for providing me with the third document.

173

home, and then the Academy at Ewington—walking the two miles back and forth. Subsequent studies were at Albany, Ohio.[30]

He was converted and joined the church in 1850, married Louisa Martin in 1858, was licensed to preach that same year, and was ordained the following year by the Athens Quarterly Meeting. His early ministry was primarily with the churches of the Ohio River Yearly Meeting, "the care of three or four churches being usually his work."[31] During his years in the ministry he baptized 595 converts.[32] He served as pastor at various churches, including Downington, Cheshire, Kyger, Harrisburg, Gilboa, Ewington, Mt. Tabor, Huntington, and another in Huntington Township—the last perhaps an African-American congregation which he founded. Apparently, he also planted and, according to his niece, at one time "owned" (!) the Free Will Baptist Church in Ewington.[33] He also assisted in organizing several other churches.

Peden enlisted in the Union Army (the 173rd Ohio Valley Infantry) in 1864, following the prior example of his two brothers, Henry and Jerdon, both of whom were seriously wounded at Missionary Ridge near Lookout Mountain, Tennessee.[34] All three served until the end of the war. His niece said Peden was a Chaplain, but that is highly improbable in any way other than informally. She told about one occasion when he allowed a Rebel soldier who had been taken prisoner to sneak away and visit his sick child, only two miles away, after promising to return to confinement at a certain

---

30 Pelt, *History*, 186, adds that he was a graduate of Albany Manual Labor University, "a type of institution which emphasized labor as an essential part of the total educational experience."

31 *Cyclopaedia*, 514.

32 Himebrook, 4, said his ministry lasted sixty-one years, but the time from licensing to preach to death is but fifty-five years.

33 Himebrook, 4.

34 Himebrook, 4, says it was the 153rd Regiment Co. I, in which he enlisted in 1861, and that Peden had three brothers in the War. I have not attempted to determine which source is correct.

time—a promise kept. Peden mustered out of the Union Army at Nashville, Tennessee.

Peden was from early adulthood very involved in educational work, much of this in the Free Will Baptist cause. Apparently, he taught his first term of school at the age of sixteen. Immediately after his Civil War service, in 1866 he taught school and kept a diary which still exists.[35] Among Free Will Baptists, he began as principal of Randall Academy at Berlin Cross Roads in Jackson County. He was one of the members of the original Board of Trustees of Rio Grande College in Ohio when it opened for business in 1876 under the leadership of its first president, Ransom Dunn. He was on the board for twelve years and taught there for five, during which he was associate pastor of the Calvary Church nearby. The Rio Grande catalogs listed him as instructor in English and librarian.[36] In 1885-86, he was principal of Cheshire Academy, a Free Will Baptist school in Cheshire, Ohio—and was in his third year of publishing a newspaper entitled *The Central Freewill Baptist*.[37]

By 1887, Peden moved to Flemington, West Virginia, to be president of West Virginia College, "a fledgling Freewill Baptist school."[38] One denominational periodical published this related note: "Bro. Thomas E. Peden has moved to Flemington, West Virginia, and become connected with West Virginia College. He is a man of ability and push—one of the sort that makes

---

35 The diary is in the Free Will Baptist Historical Collection at the University of Mount Olive in North Carolina.

36 Goodnite and Tribe, 5.

37 This is clear from an advertisement for the Cheshire Academy in *The Central Freewill Baptist*, vol. III, no. 2 (Feb 1886), 4. Thanks to Gary Barefoot for a scan of the page with the advertisement, from this single issue of the publication in the Free Will Baptist Historical Collection at Mount Olive, North Carolina.

38 Goodnite and Tribe, 5. They give 1884 as the date for Peden's move to West Virginia, but in light of their own summary of his twelve years on the board at Rio Grande, the 1887 date seems more likely correct; of course, it is possible that he continued to serve on the Rio Grande Board while he was president at West Virginia College.

things go, and is a valuable accession in that quarter."[39] The editor, A. D. Williams, who had also been active in the Ohio River Yearly Meeting, with Peden, while serving in West Virginia, apparently wrote this.

How long Peden stayed at West Virginia College is not entirely clear from these accounts, but it seems likely that he left at about the same time his struggles there led to his separation from the Ohio River Y. M. in 1895, as described above. Indeed, his niece reported that he came back to Portsmouth, Ohio, to teach in 1894.[40] She also related an anecdote to the effect that Peden, while attending a church conference in Nashville (perhaps one of the General Conference sessions mentioned above), visited a Greek class in the "College of Nashville," and demonstrated his superior knowledge of the subject.

Long before his break with the northern General Conference, related above, Peden was very active in denominational affairs, at both the local and national level. He was clerk of the Ohio River Yearly Meeting from 1859 to 1895. As the *Free Baptist Cyclopaedia* put it, he was "a recognized leader among the Freewill Baptists of the vicinity."[41] That entry was published in 1889, well before Peden's decision to bolt the Conference and begin a rival organization. His niece's summary was that "he was well educated and spoke with a definite accent, and did a wonderful work in the promotion of the Free Will Baptist Faith, being dearly loved by all the church folks everywhere."[42]

---

39 *The Western Free Baptist* (Kenesaw, Neb.), III:4 (July 1887), 5.

40 Himebrook, 4.

41 *Cyclopaedia*, 514. The article includes an engraved portrait of Peden, used in this article. Pelt, *History*, 217, also has a photograph. The Free Will Baptist Historical Collection in Nashville, Tennessee, has a photograph of Peden and his wife and several associates in Ayden, North Carolina.

42 Himebrook, 5.

As already noted, Peden sent a report of the 1895 session he led in Coalton, Ohio, to *The Free Will Baptist* in Ayden, North Carolina. He also sent an advance announcement of the 1896 "adjourned" session in Nashville, Tennessee, to the same paper, also noted above. Pelt suggests that "Peden had become known to Free Will Baptists in North Carolina through the pages of the [*Free Will*] *Baptist*," and wonders whether he visited Ayden in person before employment there.[43] Perhaps some North Carolina Free Will Baptist leaders attended the 1896 session in Nashville and were acquainted with him there; but we do not have minutes of that session and cannot confirm their presence. At any rate, Peden became head of the Free Will Baptist Seminary in Ayden, serving in that capacity from 1898, "soon after its opening,"[44] to 1910, when he "resigned his post ... because of his age (seventy-seven years) and declining health. He had served long enough to set the tone of the institution and to provide theological training for a number of men who were serving as pastors of churches."[45] Among other things, he had proposed that the Seminary "should be placed under the direct control of the Triennial General Conference," which would give it a larger constituency.[46] That proposal did not come to fruition, and perhaps Peden's vision for the Seminary became dimmed. Interestingly, the *Free Will Baptist Record*, for December 1908, published by Dell Upton,[47] at the time pastor of Cofer's Chapel in Nashville, included this somewhat emotional plea:

> There is something pathetic in the affair of the Seminary in that they can't find some one to take the chair of mathematics. Dr. Peden

---

43 Michael Pelt, *A History of Ayden Seminary and Eureka College* (undated paper), 4.
44 Pelt, *History*, 181.
45 Pelt, *History*, 224.
46 Pelt, *Seminary*, 5-6.
47 Upton, from West Virginia, had no doubt labored with Peden in the work in Ohio and West Virginia and considered himself a friend.

has given his whole life to the cause, and has held on nearly twenty years beyond the limits for retired life, and is now required to do two men's work that he may sustain the life of an institution that ought to be strong with age and rich with friends.

Dear brethren of the East, do you not know that if you work Dr. Peden to death, no man of sense will ever take his place? The Doctor should have rest instead of overwork, and to whom shall he look for rest except those whom he has served? YOU must rally.

In its issue for February 5, 1913, *The Free Will Baptist* carried an announcement of Peden's death at the age of eighty. Pelt reports, "His contribution as a minister and educator among Free Will Baptists had assured him a place in the memory of all friends of Christian education in the denomination. His funeral was conducted by R. F. Pittman, a graduate of the seminary, and now a member of its faculty, and his body was laid to rest in the Ayden cemetery."[48]

Goodnite and Tribe conclude their biographical sketch of Peden by saying, "In old age, he led a conservative faction of the denomination that refused to merge with the Northern Baptist Convention, initially known as 'the Peden Baptists' that eventually joined forces with the southern wing of the Free-Will Baptist movement."[49] They apparently did not know about his ministry at Ayden or his rival General Conference. Another Rio Grande historian makes similar observations: "Peden was of a fiery disposition and he and others were able to influence a number of the Free Baptist churches in Ohio against the merger."[50] This article shows awareness of Peden's role

48 Pelt, *History*, 226.

49 Goodnite and Tribe, 5-6.

50 James Sherman Porter, *Lamp of the Hills: The Authorized Centennial History of Rio Grande College* (Rio Grande College? 1976?), 122-23. I thank Dr. Alton Loveless for providing me with this reference.

at Ayden, although it incorrectly names him as "president" of the southern Free Will Baptists' General Conference; Peden was always its Clerk.

Conclusion

One wonders just how all the Southern brothers took Thomas Peden and his determined efforts to supplant the General Conference of the North. Did they think there really was a chance of winning some of the resources of that body for their cause? Did they simply tolerate him for their own ends? Having no record of their thoughts on the matter, we cannot say. What seems clear is that Peden won for himself a level of appreciation in the South, especially for his work at the Ayden Seminary, and that his leadership kept the (Southern) Triennial General Conference going until his own energies failed.

There is at least one significant piece of information in this that contributes to seeing ourselves correctly. Perhaps previously unknown to us, the fact is that the Free Will Baptists of Southern Ohio—and apparently of West Virginia and Kentucky—came out of the Randall General Conference *before* the 1910-11 merger of that body with the Northern Baptists. I have always assumed they left as a result of the merger and simply resisted amalgamation into the Northern Baptists—and some of them might have. But what is clear, now, is that at least some of them—and perhaps all—had withdrawn more than a decade earlier, and that they had other reasons for doing so. Also clear is the fact that *whole* organizations, like the Ohio River Yearly Meeting or any of its member Quarterly Meetings, did not resist the merger. Instead, those who followed Peden were only part of those larger organizations, resulting in competing organizations.

Postscript

As a concluding aside, there were many organizations named "General Conference" in our history, and it is easy to get them confused. Here is the way I identify them by subject-headings in cataloging the Free Will Baptist Historical Collection:

1. *General Conference of Free Will Baptists (Southeastern U. S.)*—the body begun in 1921 which merged with the Co-operative General Association in 1935 to form the National Association of Free Will Baptists.

2. *General FWB Conference (Triennial, 1895-1910)*—the one Peden led and which is the subject of this chapter.

3. *General Conference of Freewill Baptists (Randall movement)*—the Northern organization.

4. *General Conference of Original Free Will Baptists*—organized (1965), as a broader association, by the brethren of the North Carolina State Convention after it separated from the National Association of Free Will Baptists.

5. *General Conference of Original Free Will Baptists of North Carolina*—the old organization within North Carolina (in the 1800s) that later (before 1900) divided into the Eastern, Western, and Central Conferences.

6. *General FWB Conference, Revived (N. C.)*—one begun by those loyal to the National Association after the North Carolina State Convention separated from the National Association, with the idea of "reviving" the one listed above as number 5. This organization was later replaced, amiably, by other associations in the state.

6

John H. Wolfe, the Lost Churches of Kansas and Nebraska, and the Co-operative General Association, 1910-1935

When I entered Free Will Baptist Bible College in the fall of 1949, I soon encountered the name of John H. Wolfe, on labels in some of the books in the college library. Later I learned that the 1948-49 yearbook had been dedicated to him and that a picture of the man, reproduced here, was used on the dedicatory page. There is much more to the story than is found in the dedication inscription, but that seems a good place to begin.

Last year our hearts were thrilled one day in Chapel as Brother Johnson read to us a letter from Rev. and Mrs. John H. Wolfe. The letter stated that this couple had sold their home and were sending the receipts to the Free Will Baptist Bible College. This very generous and sacrificial gift made possible our present library. Rev. Wolfe has also donated some four hundred volumes to our library.

He has served this denomination long and faithfully, having joined the Pleasant Hill, Iowa, Free Will Baptist Church on February 27, 1877. He entered College and the Theological Seminary in Hillsdale, Michigan, graduating in the class of 1897 with the degree of Bachelor of Divinity. He was ordained to the Gospel Ministry in Jackson, Michigan, January 10, 1897. After graduation, he accepted the call as pastor of the First Free Will Baptist Church at Lincoln, Nebraska. He has served as President of the Tecumseh (Oklahoma) College and for fifty years was Chairman of the Executive Board of Free Will Baptists [of Nebraska].

For his love and loyalty to the cause of Christ and for his interest and great generosity to the Free Will Baptist Bible College, we gratefully dedicate this the 1949 volume of THE LUMEN to Rev. John H. Wolfe, B.D.

This dedicatory tribute falls far short of telling the full story of a faithful and active Free Will Baptist minister. The story is about much more than the man and touches on many significant events in Free Will Baptist history, many of them not well known.

Wolfe was born to German immigrants near Olin, Iowa, on January 7, 1863, the only son of John and Barbara (Pferseke) Wolfe. His father died while serving the Union Army in the Civil War in 1864, but his mother stayed on to keep the land they had homesteaded. In 1877, at the age of fourteen, Wolfe and two of his five sisters were converted during a revival meeting at the Pleasant Hill Free Will Baptist Church in Olin. They and their mother, formerly a German Lutheran, joined the church at the time.

After high school, Wolfe married Delia Scriven in 1884, in Marshall, Iowa. Both of them enrolled in Hillsdale College, a Free Will Baptist institution in Michigan, in 1889. Both took the same course of study in preparation for the ministry. Both also worked their way through the program, he as assistant librarian five hours a day (1891-97) and she in various jobs. During their senior year, he was assistant pastor at the Free Will Baptist church in Jackson, Michigan. Both were ordained to the ministry at Jackson on January 10, 1897. They completed their studies that year and received Bachelors of Divinity degrees. Their names appear in the *Hillsdale Collegian* for July 1, 1897, as having completed the "full theological" program—that included classical and biblical Greek, Hebrew, and Latin.

There are other references to Wolfe in Hillsdale publications. The *Hillsdale Collegian* for January 26, 1894, reported that he was chosen "to publish next year's hand-book" for the Young Men's Christian Association on campus. The *Hillsdale Herald* for September 16, 1896, listed the results of "society elections," showing that he was elected vice-president of the Theadelphic Literary Society.

After graduation, the Wolfes relocated to Lincoln, Nebraska, where they served the local Free Will Baptist church. The *Hillsdale Collegian* for November 4, 1897, includes a letter from him in Lincoln, discussing the work of the assistant librarian. The spring 1900 manual of the Theadelphic Literary Society reports,

> After graduation, he went to Nebraska, and was assistant pastor at Lincoln two years. He was President of the city Union C. E.[1] for one year, and has been Chairman of the Nebraska Y. M. Executive Board since 1898. He is now pastor of the Free Baptist church near Adams, Neb. While in College, Mr. Wolfe proved himself a faithful worker, a man of good business judgment and executive ability.

---

1 Christian Endeavor (Society), the FWB young people's organization.

From the time they took up residence in Nebraska until their deaths, the Wolfes were active ministers among Free Will Baptists, and this chapter will relate some of the details of that ministry. Among other things, Wolfe was "state agent" (on behalf of the General Conference of the Northern Free Will Baptists) for the work in Kansas and Nebraska from 1898 to 1903. Beginning in 1903, he relinquished his pastoral work to serve full time as field superintendent for the Northern Kansas and Nebraska Yearly Meetings—a position he held for many years.[2] There is no list of the churches he served as pastor, but some of his letters make clear that he was serving the Grandview church until January 1922, the Long Branch church near Elk Creek, Nebraska, in late 1922, and the Hickory Grove church near Haddam, Kansas, beginning in early 1923. The Reverend Mrs. Wolfe died in 1949 and the Reverend Mr. Wolfe in 1954, just eight days short of his ninety-second birthday. Both were buried in the Pawnee City Cemetery in Pawnee City, Nebraska.[3]

The 1910-11 Merger of the Northern Free Will Baptists

The first thing of special importance to our story of John H. Wolfe is the fact that he led some of the Free Will Baptists in Kansas and Nebraska—all the fruit of the Randall movement—to resist the merger of the Northern Free Will Baptists with the Northern Baptists (now American Baptists) in 1910-

---

2　John H. Wolfe, "Freewill Baptists in Nebraska," in Albert Watkins, Volume 3, *History of Nebraska: A History of Nebraska from the Earliest Explorations to the Present Time* (Lincoln: Western Publishing and Engraving Co., 1913), 413-414.

3　For most of the biographical information in these paragraphs I have relied on several sources: (1) the findagrave.com website, which includes basic information (much of it supplied by Winnie Yandell) and an obituary (as well as a picture of the Wolfes' gravestone); (2) Damon C. Dodd, "God's Man of Great Faith: the Story of Rev. John H. Wolfe," *Contact* 1:2 (Dec. 1953), 4, 6; (3) information supplied to me by Hillsdale College. I am especially indebted to Ms. Linda Moore, Public Services Librarian of the Mossey Library at Hillsdale, for going beyond the call of duty to send me copies of the information I have cited from Hillsdale publications.

11. Everything else in this story grows out of that.

Since most readers of this account will already know about that merger, I will only survey the events. The movement begun by Benjamin Randall in 1780, in New Durham, New Hampshire, had grown rapidly and extensively, and from humble beginnings into a position of considerable respect in the religious milieu of the times, especially in New England and spreading westward across the upper Midwest. By 1908, the denomination could report that it included 1,292 churches with some 87,015 members.[4] There were a number of educational institutions, including some still in existence, like Bates College in Maine, Hillsdale College in Michigan, and Rio Grande College in Southern Ohio.[5] The original Randallites had already absorbed some other groups with similar views, including the Free Communion Baptists in 1841, also known as Free Baptists. In 1892 the General Conference officially became "Free Baptists." Ecumenical tendencies continued to grow, and most of the Free Baptists were open to the prospect of union with Northern Baptists.

Only some small pockets of resistance were encountered.[6] John H. Wolfe, in Kansas and Nebraska, was one of those who resisted the merger. Before describing his personal involvement, I will briefly outline the events in the General Conference (of the Northern Free Will Baptists), which met every three years, that culminated in the merger. This summary is based on the official minutes of that organization.

---

4 Minutes of the General Conference of Free Baptists for 1910, 95. The numbers were somewhat overstated, although not greatly, and would be corrected in 1910.

5 The minutes of the General Conference for 1910, 95, name three institutions "of academic grade," six colleges, and two seminaries.

6 Chapter five in this volume relates the story of Thomas Peden in Southern Ohio, who was able to lead a relatively small number of churches in that state, and in Kentucky and West Virginia, to bolt from the triennial General Conference of Freewill/Free Baptists. But that departure occurred several years before the merger took place, so we cannot be certain that the prospects of the merger were involved.

Before 1904, official discussion about union with other bodies was limited to denominations with similar doctrine and practice. The 1898 minutes, for example, include these words as part of H. M. Ford's report as Field Secretary of the Conference:

> We need to seek a closer union with all liberal Baptists.[7] That resolution favoring and inviting union with the Free Baptists of Nova Scotia and the Free Christian Baptists of New Brunswick passed by the executive committee of Conference Board should include the Freewill Baptists of the south and the General Baptists of the west, and the Church of God.[8] All these bodies substantially agreeing in polity and doctrine, no compromise and the surrender of no conviction being needed, there is no reason why the separation should longer continue to the detriment of the cause. Let the union come, the sooner the better, and let us be one people, and let the marriage ceremony proceed at once. It would be something to remember.[9]

At the 1904 session, the first official movement toward union with denominations other than those named in 1898 began to be seriously considered. A couple of resolutions about union with Baptists were referred to the Committee on the Denomination, and that Committee recommended that twelve persons be named to confer with similar committees appointed by other denominations to "consult respecting doctrinal and other grounds of union" and report to the next General Conference. This had been, at least in part, precipitated by overtures from the Disciples of Christ.[10] This Commit-

---

7 As used here, "liberal Baptists" means those of Arminian persuasion.

8 I assume this means the Winebrennarians.

9 Minutes of the General Conference of Free Baptists for 1898, 39-40.

10 Minutes of the General Conference of Free Baptists for 1904, 93, 130, 136, 139.

tee would be known as the "Committee on Conference with Other Christian People" and played a leading role in the merger.

At the 1907 session of the General Conference, this Committee reported extensive conversations with representatives of the Disciples of Christ, the Congregationalists, and the Northern Baptists. The report made clear that the possibility of union with the last of these three seemed the most promising. It offered a resolution affirming essential unity between the Baptists and the Free Baptists and recommended that the talks toward union continue. The Committee also made clear that they were seeking nothing short of "organic union."[11] The subsequent report of the Committee on the Denomination supported the idea and made clear that any form of union would require approval of at least two-thirds of the Yearly Meetings and other associations composing the General Conference, and that the approving bodies must represent at least three-fourths of the resident church membership of the denomination.[12]

In 1910, then, the Committee brought to the General Conference (at Ocean Park, Maine), the "Basis of Union" for approval. The full report of the Committee included the provision that "Differences [in faith and practice], if still existing, may be left, where the New Testament leaves them, to the teaching of the Scriptures under the guidance of the Holy Spirit."[13]

Actually, the Committee's recommended Basis of Union had been drafted and presented to the Conference *Board* in 1908. The Board had approved and ordered that it be presented to the Yearly Meetings and Associations comprising the General Conference for approval or rejection. So when the matter came before the General Conference in 1910, it had for all practical

---

11 Minutes of the General Conference of Free Baptists for 1907, 113. The report is on pp. 102-113.

12 Minutes of the General Conference of Free Baptists for 1907, 172.

13 Minutes of the General Conference of Free Baptists for 1910, 92.

purposes already received the needed ratification by the constituent bodies, as defined above.

The report at the 1910 session included a chart showing just how that voting had gone. Twenty-eight bodies representing a total of 44,481 resident members had approved the union. Five bodies representing 1,721 resident members had voted against it, including the Ohio and Kentucky, Illinois, Nebraska, Northern Kansas, and Southeast Missouri Yearly Meetings, all with relatively small numbers. Several other Yearly Meetings or Associations had not reported any action at all: Southern Ohio, West Virginia, Big Sandy, Kentucky, Louisiana, Western Missouri, Northeast Missouri, Southwest Missouri, Northwest Missouri, Mississippi, Union of Tennessee, Unicoi of Tennessee, Western Texas, and Central Texas.[14] These also represented small numbers of resident members.

At the 1910 General Conference, the vote on the first recommendation, for approval of the "Basis of Union," was carried, 61-15.[15] This was the key vote; regarding the rest of the report, the minutes simply indicate that "The report was taken up item by item and adopted. Finally the report was adopted as a whole."[16]

And now to Wolfe's perspective. We would not have any information about his views of the merger (other than knowing that he did not participate in it) if it were not for a 1953 interview of Wolfe by Damon Dodd, reported in the December 1953 issue of *Contact* magazine, the second issue of that periodical. In the following paragraphs, I will include information from

---

14 Minutes of the General Conference of Free Baptists for 1910, 102, 104. Those approving were 58 % of the bodies and 84% of resident members. But by not counting the bodies that took no action at all, those approving made 85% of the bodies *that voted*, and so could be represented as more than the required two-thirds.

15 Minutes of the General Conference of Free Baptists for 1910, 119-20.

16 Minutes of the General Conference of Free Baptists for 1910, 121.

that interview in this part of the story.[17]

At the time of the interview in 1953, Wolfe was 90 years old. It is not surprising, therefore, that his memory was sometimes faulty, especially as to dates—assuming that Dodd reported him accurately. From what has been related above, we gather that the committee to explore possibilities with Northern Baptists was appointed in 1904, not 1898; and the "Basis of Union" (which Wolfe or Dodd called "Articles of Merger") was presented in 1910, not 1907. Otherwise, I think we may trust Dodd's article as accurately reflecting Wolfe's perceptions of what transpired.

According to Dodd, Wolfe first heard talk about the possibility of a merger with Northern Baptists while he was assistant pastor at Jackson, Michigan, during his senior year at Hillsdale in 1896-97. Wolfe regarded Henry M. Ford and Harry S. Meyers as two of the Free Baptist leaders who pushed the idea. He thought "they believed that a merger would enhance their possibilities for personal prestige."[18]

Wolfe was present and active, as a delegate from the Nebraska Yearly Meeting, at all the crucial sessions of the General Conference: in 1901 (Harper's Ferry, WV), 1904 (Hillsdale, MI), 1907 (Cleveland, OH), and 1910 (Ocean Park, ME). Some of that time, he was "agent" of the Conference on behalf of the work in Nebraska and reported as such. He served on several committees. Twice (1901, 1904) he was nominated for, but not elected to, the Conference Board.[19]

---

17 See note 3, above, for bibliographic information. I see no need to continue to provide formal citations from this article; the information following that comes from it will be obvious.

18 Ford was field secretary for the Conference and Myers secretary for the youth work.

19 For references to Wolfe during these sessions, see Minutes of the General Conference of Free Baptists for 1901, 5, 46, 71, 77-78, 99-100; Minutes of the General Conference of Free Baptists for 1904, 7, 9, 12, 62, 92, 118; Minutes of the General Conference of Free Baptists for 1907, 7, 9, 16, 27-28, 36-37, 150-51, 157-58; Minutes of the General Conference of Free Baptists for 1910, 8, 12, 36, 119.

According to Dodd, reporting his interview with Wolfe, the Basis of Union presented to the Conference included the idea that all questions of doctrinal difference would be left to "strict Biblical interpretation." This perception seems justified in light of the information given above. To this, Wolfe and some other Western leaders objected: "They asked who was to do the interpreting—the Free Will Baptists or Northern Baptists. Said Brother Wolfe, 'We feared that the old Northern Baptist doctrine of predestination and eternal security would become the official doctrine'."

Wolfe reported that, before the voting, the influential Professor A. W. Anthony of Bates College stated publicly that this was not a vote on organic union but for fellowship.[20] Wolfe apparently felt this was a misrepresentation that swayed some to vote in favor of the merger.[21]

When the General Conference proceeded to act on approval of the Committee recommendations, the minutes show that speakers included "Ferguson of Texas" and that prayer was offered by "Wolfe of Nebraska."

After the key vote had carried, the next question related to the funds, asking, "Can we rightfully spend it for something else?" meaning something other than Free Will Baptists had given it for. "Professor Anthony waved his hand aloft and shouted, 'Away with the old dead hand of the past'." Even so, as each proposal for appropriating the various funds came up, the Reverend T. C. Ferguson of Missouri[22] repeatedly cast a lone dissenting vote. After a bit, Ferguson turned to Wolfe and urged him, "Come on, brother, let's ex-

---

20 Perhaps this reflected the statement in the "Basis of Union" that it was a "plan for co-operation in missionary and denominational work"; see Minutes of the General Conference of Free Baptists for 1910, 93. But organic union was certainly the intended and realized outcome.

21 There is evidence that some of the constituent bodies voted for the basis of union with an understanding that "organic union" was *not* intended. The minutes of the Ohio River Y. M. in 1909 show that they changed from voting No to voting Yes with the idea that the basis of union meant "cooperation in Mission work and not an organic union of the two bodies."

22 As noted, Ferguson was actually representing Texas at the time.

press ourselves against them." To this Wolfe replied, "Inasmuch as they've already decided to hang us, I don't care what kind of rope they use."

After the Merger

Dodd indicates that others joined Wolfe in resistance to the merger, including Marcus L. Morse, a Nebraska layman who played a leading role on the Executive Committee of the Nebraska Yearly Meeting with Wolfe, along with Ferguson of Missouri and Mawhorter of Indiana.[23] But the cause was mostly lost. Dodd says: "Soon after the merger, court action forced the Free Will Baptist churches in Nebraska to go to the Northern Baptist movement. Only a few churches contested the action and they were soon defeated. This action was upheld by the Supreme Court of the state of Nebraska." This representation appears to be misleading. The courts had nothing to do with the churches' decisions to join the Baptists; but they upheld the churches' rights to their property when they did.

What is surprising is that the Nebraska Yearly Meeting and its Executive Board continued to function—uninvolved in the General Conference of Free Baptists or the Northern Baptists—as legal entities for many years.[24] They went on almost as though nothing had happened. But the minutes of the Yearly Meeting, and of its Executive Board, provide a candid picture of the struggles that were involved in attempting to keep the work together. Wolfe was the leading figure, most of the time being chairman of the Executive Board and moderator of the Yearly Meeting. His wife, Delia Wolfe, was clerk of the latter. Morse was clerk, then treasurer, of the Executive Board.

---

23 T. J. Mawhorter of Indiana was elected to the General Conference Board at the 1901 and 1904 sessions. See Minutes of the General Conference of Free Baptists for 1901, 133; Minutes of the General Conference of Free Baptists for 1904, 131. Apparently, Mawhorter ultimately accepted the merger.

24 Dodd quoted Wolfe to say, in 1953: "In reality, the Nebraska Yearly Meeting of Free Will Baptists was never dissolved. It still exists officially."

Without attempting a church-by-church account, I will describe the discouraging course of events more broadly, focusing primarily on Nebraska. But what transpired there was also generally true in Kansas.

My starting point is 1910, when the General Conference voted for union with the Northern Baptists. The Free Will Baptist work in Kansas and Nebraska was already weak. The denominational yearbook published in 1911 listed all the churches that had reported in recent years, as follows[25] (Y. M. = Yearly Meeting; Q. M. = Quarterly Meeting; members are sometimes *resident* members).

The Nebraska Y. M.

    Clearview Q. M.: 4 churches, 52 members;

    Custer County Q. M.: 2 churches, 16 members;

    Hastings Q. M.: 6 churches, 81 members;

    Nemeha River Q. M.: 3 churches, 115 members.

The Northern Kansas Y. M.

    Cloud and Republic Q. M.: 2 churches, 86 members;

    Horton Q. M.: 3 churches, 35 members;

    Washington County Q M.: 1 church, 93 members.

The Southern Kansas Y. M.

    Row Valley Q. M.: 5 churches, 63 members

    Sumner and Cowley Q. M.: 1 church, 39 members.

This represents a total of 27 churches, most very small (averaging 21 or 22 members), with which John H. Wolfe and his companions had to work. All of them were ultimately lost to a continuing Free Will Baptist identity; but this was not an overnight happening.

Losses had begun even before the vote for merger in 1910. In his August 1908 report to the Executive Board, Wolfe noted,

---

25 *Free Baptist Register and Year Book 1911* (Hillsdale: General Conference Free Baptists, 1911), 46-48.

A few of our pastors have felt that they could not wait the prospects of a denominational union with the Baptists so have packed baggage and moved over into the Baptist camp. This has weakened our forces, scattered our flocks, and brought discouragement into our otherwise courageous churches. To rally our forces, man our churches, and bring back hope, are the problems we face today and must solve.[26]

He went on to report that the Copp Memorial church of Adams was without a pastor because Brother Walcott, its pastor, had gone over to the Baptists. So had Brother Willisford, another minister. Furthermore, the Lincoln church had disbanded—not necessarily related to the merger. During this session, the Yearly Meeting minutes recorded, "After reading of 'basis of union,' followed by some discussion, the vote was taken by ballot — 26 votes against, 3 in favor."[27]

This 1908 vote of the Yearly Meeting against union with the Baptists did not lay the matter to rest. In his August 1909 report to the Executive Board (as Field Secretary for both the Northern Kansas Y. M. and the Nebraska Y. M.), Wolfe echoed this again: "The unsettled condition of the denomination at large upon the union question has hindered our work here in the West to no little extent." He went on to report that the Long Branch church "has united with the Baptist church at Johnson, employing one of their pastors, Rev. M. R. Holt."[28] Furthermore, "the Copp Memorial church has preaching every two weeks by the pastor of the Baptist church at Sterling." For

---

26 Minutes, the Executive Board of the Nebraska Yearly Meeting of Freewill Baptists, for August 14, 1908. The pages of this manuscript journal are not numbered and I will not continue to provide footnotes to excerpts from these minutes; they may in each case be located by the dates of the meetings, which will be indicated.

27 Minutes of the Nebraska Yearly Meeting of Free Baptists (hereafter NYMFB, 38. (In this manuscript journal, the pages are numbered.)

28 Since the Long Branch church continued to show up in the minutes, I assume that a remnant of its membership remained loyal to the Nebraska Y. M. for some time to follow.

that matter, both in 1910 and 1911, the Nebraska Y. M. minutes show that "visiting delegates" were sent to the Baptist Association. In 1911, these delegates included Wolfe himself.[29]

The March 1911 minutes of the Executive Board include, "Talked over the present and future prospect of our church work which didn't seem to be very encouraging for us as a denomination. And all on account of the so much talked of union with the so-called Regular Baptists." In the annual August meeting, this notation appears, "Absent Rev. Powers, whose resignation is in the hands of the chairman and later will be presented to conference for action as it is now in session and will no doubt be accepted as he has left the denomination and taken work with the regular Baptists." Wolfe's report added, "Elm Island has been supplied by the Baptists. Bro. Powers, a member of the Board, has gone to Loup City to become pastor of a Baptist church, and Kenesaw has settled Rev. F. M. Sturdevant, a former Baptist brother, as their pastor."

William D. Myers was chairman of the Executive Board during the August 1912 meeting. His report concluded with the recommendation "That we still stand loyal to the Nebraska Yearly Meeting of Free Will Baptists,[30] thus keeping a united front for work for Christ and the Church."

This selection of excerpts may tend to imply that there was nothing but defeat in prospect. That would be too strong. Wolfe and others continued to labor in hope. But the slow depletion of the ranks pointed toward an apparently inevitable conclusion.

Property disputes were sure to arise, given the structure of the Yearly Meeting. A "System of Cooperation" had been adopted a number of years earlier, and it included the requirement that if aid had been provided for

---

29 NYMFB, 56, 74.

30 This is the spelling in the minutes. All forms of the name—*Freewill, Free-will, Free Will,* and *Free* occur frequently throughout. See the first chapter in this volume.

the erection of a local church building, then the Executive Board would hold the deed in trust.[31] Indeed, the Board acted without hesitation to construct buildings, oversee pastoral supply, and give other directions to the churches. In that light, then, one is not surprised to read the following in the minutes of the April 1914 meeting of the Executive Board.

> In as much as the union with the Missionary Baptists has been presented to our yearly meeting at two former sessions and voted almost unanimously in the negative, there seems to have been some agency at work in our churches to change sentiment, as evidenced by the number of requests received of late, wanting the Board to give them a deed of their church property. But notwithstanding how willingly [sic] we might be to comply with their requests it's evident legally we cannot do so. That's a matter for the yearly meeting to decide.

The minutes go on to provide a copy of one such letter, from the Copp Memorial Church at Adams, requesting the Board "to return to us the deed of the church property, so as to enable this church to come into closer relation with the Nebraska Baptist State Convention, which is assisting this church in sustaining the services." The Board's lengthy reply follows, affirming that "after due deliberation and close study again of the Co-operative System, incorporated under the laws of the State of Nebraska," and after consulting "eminent lawyers," the request could not be granted. Three long paragraphs of reasons are attached. Subsequently, the August 1914 minutes record that "Prof. A. W. Anthony of the State of Maine was present in behalf of the Copp Memorial church at Adams in regard to having the Board deed to them their church property, which the Board cannot legally

---

31 See pamphlet, *System of Co-operation of the Nebraska Yearly Meeting of Freewill Baptists,* dated May 1, 1906, and carrying Wolfe's name. According to Wolfe, "Freewill Baptists," the system had existed since 1883.

do."[32] Ultimately, the Copp Memorial Church, as "The Baptist Church of Adams," took the Executive Board of the Nebraska Yearly Meeting to court and won the property.[33]

Other cases also wound up in court. The first one apparently involved the Kenesaw church, which had been planted by the Rev. A. D. Williams in 1883. It was served by the Rev. Lizzie McAdams as recently as 1913, who was succeeded by the Rev. W. F Davis in 1914—apparently its pastor at the time of the suit. In his report to the Executive Board in August 1916, Wolfe observed, "The only dark cloud hanging over [our] beloved work and field today is the suit in court brought by our Kenesaw brethren asking for the title to the church at that place."[34] The May 1917 minutes of the Executive Board contain this further report by Wolfe: "The trial came off in district court of Hastings May 11 and 12, 1917, and at this date, May 24th, no decision has been handed down by the judge."

In fact, the decision—in the matter of "Kenesaw Free Baptist Church vs. Lattimer, et al"[35]—went against the Nebraska Yearly Meeting and in favor of the local church in Kenesaw.[36] The decision was appealed to the Nebraska Supreme Court, which upheld the judgment of the district court. Among other things, the Supreme Court said that "every member of the present

---

32 According to NYMFB, 87, Anthony was called on to lead the opening prayer of the Yearly Meeting on this occasion. As will be noted below, Anthony returned later to testify in court.

33 Extensive correspondence and legal documents regarding this lawsuit are in the FWB Historical Collection.

34 At the annual meeting of the Y. M. in 1915, the credentials committee, with M. L. Morse as chairman, had reported that the Kenesaw church had united with the South Central Association of Baptists and had thereby "severed their connection with the Nebraska Yearly Meeting of Free-will Baptists." NYMFB, 96.

35 G. S. Latimer (as his name is properly spelled) was Chairman of the Executive Board in Nebraska at the time the suit was filed in 1916.

36 Hugh LaMaster, attorney-at-law in Tecumseh, Nebraska, representing the Kenesaw congregation, on January 3, 1920, sent to M. L. Morse a bill for the District Court costs, totaling $167.90; he included a receipt for the same from the clerk of the court, dated January 2, 1920.

congregation at Kenesaw" was in agreement with the church's wishes, so that "what might be considered as the individual right of a member of the church is not involved."

The Court also noted that the defendants—the Nebraska Yearly Meeting—"contend that differences exist between the old organization and the union touching freedom of the will, general atonement, open communion, and perseverance of the saints," but it refused to involve itself in those differences and ruled that they were not of such a nature as to show that the local church had violated its implied trust or abandoned the purposes for which it was organized. The conclusion was that "the Kenesaw Freewill Baptist Church are entitled to have their property in the hands of those who are in accord with their purposes and who do not deny them the right to take the step which they have taken in their church affiliations."[37]

The situation continued to deteriorate. At one point there were some fifteen churches identified with the Nebraska Yearly Meeting. By April 1917 the minutes of the Executive Board show eight churches in the Hastings Q. M. (including the six listed in 1911, above) and three in the Nemeha River Q. M. (the same three as in 1911, above). The Clearwater and Custer County Q. M.s had surely been entirely lost by that date, so the number of churches was reduced to eleven. By 1922, the Hastings Q. M. reported only five churches and the Nemeha River Q. M. two, although there was then a Union Center Q. M. with apparently one church—making a total of eight churches and five ministers (of whom the Wolfes were two).[38]

---

37 The information in this paragraph comes from two documents printed from the internet and found in the FWB Historical Collection at Welch College, Nashville, TN. One is a brief history of the church entitled "Free Will Baptist Church"; the other is "Kenesaw Free Baptist Church v. Lattimer et al." My thanks to George C. Lee for uncovering these documents.

38 Minutes of the Nebraska Yearly Meeting of Free-Will Baptists, August 16-20, 1922. These printed minutes are the last we have; I am not sure how long the Y. M. continued to meet.

The M. L. Morse papers include many letters and legal documents that mark the decline, especially during the years leading up to 1929. Examples include the disbanding of the Thompson church in 1918; deeding the Smithfield church to "The Baptist Church of Smithfield" in 1923; the Elwood suit settled in 1925; the disbanding of the Geneva church in 1929; and deeding the Grandview property to its local trustees in 1929.

By the time of Dodd's interview with Wolfe in 1953, only the Elm Island Church (originally in the Hastings Q. M.) remained in the Free Will Baptist fold in Nebraska. This church was ten miles north of Kenesaw, and Wolfe's membership was there. There are now no Free Will Baptist churches in Nebraska or Kansas that came from this background.[39]

It seems a fitting conclusion to this part of this chapter to cite, at length, from the report of A. W. Anthony given to the General Conference of Free Baptists in 1917.[40]

> The one exception [to the smooth union of Free Baptists and Baptists] is in the state of Nebraska. Under the leadership of one family [!][41] the Nebraska Yearly Meeting of Free Baptists,—which, in the first canvass of the question of approving the Basis of Union, voted against approval,—has persisted in opposition to union, has withheld property of local churches, where possible, from the control of churches which wished to join Baptist organizations, and has sought in various ways to hinder and thwart the General

---

39 Up until the middle 1950s, a few Kansas churches maintained membership in two associations rooted in Missouri: the Central Western Missouri and Southeastern Kansas Association and the Northwestern Missouri and Northeastern Kansas Association. But Kansas churches dropped from these associations and from the associations' names. The Hickory Grove Church near Haddam, Kansas, which will be mentioned at the end of this chapter, was one of these and perhaps the last surviving one, in the second of the two associations named.

40 In spite of the merger, for legal purposes the General Conference of Free Baptists continued to meet at intervals.

41 Obviously, Anthony was referring to the Wolfes.

Conference and its plans. This faction in opposition, centering in Nebraska, has sought to gather about itself the discontented in any part of the country, but has failed save in the south west. ...

With these brethren, in sympathy at least, and in partial correspondence, are the brethren who call themselves Freewill Baptists in the South, with headquarters at Ayden, North Carolina, who represent in part the successors of the Freewill Baptists, who broke from the General Conference over the question of slavery before the war,[42] and in part the survivors of the followers of Rev. Thomas E. Peden, who severed their connection with General Conference in 1892, because of the incorporation of our body.[43] Whether this movement, spread through a wide territory, chiefly through the southern-middle belt of states, can succeed or not, remains to be demonstrated. ...

The most unfortunate aspect of this movement is the condition in which it leaves the Free Baptist churches of Nebraska. These churches, which have steadily decreased in numbers and in strength, are surrounded with Baptist churches, as like them as are Baptist churches throughout the north, ready in the equipment of a strong state convention to give fellowship, sympathy and aid, which this mistaken leadership forbids. One test case is now before the courts, upon which judgment is awaited, to determine whether the Executive Committee of the Nebraska Yearly Meeting of Free Baptists, which holds in trust title to most of the surviving Free Baptist churches of that state, can successfully restrain the Kenesaw Free Baptist church from joining a Baptist Association, by withholding from it its property. In June last I made a visit to Hastings, Nebraska, to give testimony before the court upon this

---

42 Anthony's observation was either ignorant or disingenuous. It was the General Conference that decided to sever relations with the North Carolina Free Will Baptists in 1839 because some in the South were slaveholders.

43 See the chapter about Peden in this volume.

issue.[44]

A New Outlook for the Work

Anthony's report, just cited, also indicated that in 1917 Wolfe and his co-workers were undertaking new ventures. They had good reason to be discouraged with the state of the work in Kansas and Nebraska, but they did not allow this to dampen all enthusiasm for the future. Wolfe, for one, had begun to look abroad and to nurture hopes for a wider fellowship of Free Will Baptists, and for new endeavors that would strengthen and revive the work. Perhaps he came to realize that the work in the two states he cared deeply about could not be saved apart from the help of other Free Will Baptists.

By 1916, then, new projects were taking root in Wolfe's thinking, apparently fertilized by increasing contacts with others from outside Nebraska and Kansas. Two of these were H. M. and Lizzie McAdams, who came to Kansas and Nebraska primarily as evangelists and poured a great deal of effort for many years into strengthening the churches in the two states and to assisting in many aspects of the work. The August 1915 minutes of the Executive Committee of the Nebraska Y. M. record that they had written from Texas about their desire to return to Nebraska "and engage in evangelistic work" if the Y. M. would cover their railroad fare.[45] The Committee voted to do this, and from this point on the forward-looking McAdamses were busy in preaching to revive the various local churches and in promoting the various projects that developed.

---

44 Minutes of the General Conference of Free Baptists for 1917, 50-52. (This was four years after the 1913 session, during which the conference provided that it need not meet every third year.)

45 The 1914 minutes of the Southwestern Convention of Freewill Baptists, 31-32, show that the McAdamses were officially evangelists for that organization at the time and so immediately prior to returning to Kansas and Nebraska.

Among the most important of Wolfe's contacts from out of state were Free Will Baptist brothers in the neighboring state of Missouri. One of these was the Rev. T. C. Ferguson, who with Wolfe had voted against the union at the 1910 General Conference. No doubt, the two men had kept in touch. As early as 1912, Ferguson was present for the Nebraska Yearly Meeting and preached.[46] The year before that, in 1911, the Rev. G. S. Latimer, from the Northwest Missouri Yearly Meeting of Free Baptists, had visited and preached.[47] Apparently Latimer came to stay: the 1912 minutes of the Yearly Meeting identify him as pastor of the Grandview church in Nebraska.[48] In 1914, he was elected moderator,[49] and he continued to be active in the Yearly Meeting until March 1916, when the minutes of the Executive Board show that he resigned "to take a work in another state the first of April." He was headed for the Hickory Grove church near Haddam, Kansas.[50]

Interaction with the Missouri brethren flowed in both directions. The minutes of a November 1914 decision show that Latimer was sent as a "corresponding messenger" to the Missouri State Conference, with "his traveling expenses only" to be paid from the general fund. Pinned to this page is a letter of appreciation dated January 25, 1915, from C. E. Mann, clerk of the Missouri body. Among other things the letter expressed pleasure that the Free Will Baptists in Nebraska were "standing true" and reported that there were "about 10,000 Free Baptists in Missouri." Obviously, whether those numbers were accurate or not,[51] this represented the kind of strength on

---

46 NYMFB, 78. (It is possible that I missed earlier visits by Ferguson.)

47 NYMFB, 69. Latimer is also said to be from Oklahoma City; whether he was a pastor there at the time is not clear.

48 NYMFB, 72, 79.

49 NYMFB, 88. The Yearly Meeting did not convene in 1913.

50 The minutes of that church for February 16, 1916, report: "Bro. G. S. Latimer was called for $550.00 per year and parsonage free."

51 Such numbers were often carelessly exaggerated. In a number of places in the documents I examined I found estimates that there were 300,000 Free Will Baptists that were potential

which the weak work in Nebraska and Kansas could draw. The August 1915 minutes of the Executive Board show that Latimer had "urged closer affiliation between" the Free Baptists of Missouri, Kansas, and Nebraska. At the same session, in his annual report, Latimer also made this recommendation:

> In view of the fact that General Conference has taken itself out of the denomination against the wish and vote of the Nebraska Yearly Meeting and have endeavored by all the means within their power to force the Nebraska Yearly Meeting to accept their action and leave the old land marks established by our fathers in the year 1780, and believe that we are no longer morally bound to what remains of General Conference,
>
> Therefore, I recommend that we, the Nebraska Yearly Meeting of Freewill Baptists, take the legal steps necessary to dissolve any relations that may exist between the Nebraska Yearly Meeting of Freewill Baptists and General Conference of Freewill Baptists.[52]

It is not clear what motivated this, or whether there was in fact still any tie to the General Conference to be dissolved.[53] The 1913 session of the General Conference had adopted a provision that any organization not desiring to continue to be a member need only file an application for dismissal and that the responsibilities of membership would be regarded as ceasing when the application was approved by the Conference Board.[54] Apparently that had not been done. At any rate, a letter from A. W. Anthony (on a Federal

---

members of a united body.

52 NYMFB, 98.

53 Technically, the "General Conference of Freewill Baptists" no longer existed, having changed its name long before the merger to "General Conference of Free Baptists." See the chapter on Thomas Peden in this volume.

54 Minutes of the General Conference of Free Baptists for 1913, 97. That such approvals were granted is clear from a 1917 action of the General Conference: "The requests for dismissal of the Western Missouri Association and the Southern Illinois Yearly Meeting were by vote granted." Minutes of the General Conference of Free Baptists for 1917, 41.

Council of Churches letterhead) dated August 23, 1915, addressed to Joseph Mauck, President of Hillsdale College, had this to report.

> I received a telegram last evening from Nebraska saying that the Neb.Yearly Meeting had voted to withdraw from the General Conference and take steps for establishing a new General Conference. I do not think that this movement can amount to much, ... But it will be disquieting in several sections of the country, particularly in the Southwest, where T. C. Ferguson and some others have been waiting for, and fomenting, this thing. There are, too, in other sections, Ohio, for example, some churches which will welcome this revolt.

The September 1915 minutes of the Executive Board of the Nebraska Y. M. indicate that Wolfe himself would be the corresponding messenger to that year's Missouri State Conference. It comes as no surprise, then, to find that Wolfe reported back to the Executive Board in March of 1916 and submitted a glowing and ambitious report, as follows:

> To the Executive Board:
> The undersigned delegate to the Missouri State Association would respectively submit his report at this your semi-annual meeting. He attended the said meeting held at Hannon, Mo., in November and was cordially received. Bro. Latimer, the delegate from the Y. M. and myself were given an whole half day in which to set before them the actions of the Nebraska Yearly Meeting, viz.:
> 1 That we, with other bodies of Free Baptists, organize a co-operative association for larger work.
> 2 That we start a denominational paper jointly with other bodies.
> 3 That we start a college.
> 4 That we, with other like bodies, establish a Biblical Correspondence School.

All of which after due consideration were unanimously adopted.

After which the newly elected Board of the Missouri State Association and Bro. Latimer and myself met to consider the carrying out as far as possible the vote taken.

Voted that Bro. Latimer visit the Tecumseh, Okla., field and investigate the offer of a building and 120 acres of land.

Voted that we accept the offer of Bro. Morris[55] to sell us the Freewill Baptist News plant for $350 dollars and that we ask Bro. Morris to continue its editor and publisher until after the Dec. 1916 meeting at Pattonsburg, Mo., when the Co-operative Association will be asked to take over the plant.

Bro. Morris to have all money above the remaining expenses.

Voted that we change the name of the News to that of the New Morning Star and that we give Bro. Morris four associate editors.

Signed John H. Wolfe

The contrast between this plan and the real situation in Kansas and Nebraska at the time is almost breathtaking. The Wolfes and Latimer were obviously people of vision. In the midst of their weakness, they saw a new and promising day ahead, and they proceeded to share their vision with others in a convincing fashion. Dodd says, reflecting Wolfe's memories,

Brother Wolfe was instrumental in the reorganizing of Western Free Will Baptist forces. One day while in conversation with Mrs. Wolfe and the Rev. G. S. Latimer ... the question arose, "Why can't we have a Conference of Free Will Baptists of the West?" The three of them planned it all out and the following fall met with the Missouri State Association and laid the proposal before them.

The grand plan concisely laid out in Wolfe's report included a number of significant proposals. Since each of them has its own place in the story being told here, I will single out the major features of it for individual treatment in the following pages.

The Co-operative General Association of Free Will Baptists

The linchpin of Wolfe's and Latimer's vision was the formation of a broader association of churches in the West. Only in that way could the weak work in Kansas and Nebraska draw strength from the work in other places like their neighbors to the East and South, Missouri and Oklahoma. Everything else in the program would depend on such an organization.

When William Fuller, the clerk of the Executive Board of the Nebraska Yearly Meeting, wrote in the minutes of their September 1915 meeting that they had voted to send John H. Wolfe as a corresponding messenger to the Missouri State Conference, he added a note of explanation: "The object of sending the above messenger to Mo. State Conference was to (endeavor to) organize a General Association of all Free Baptists."

When the Board met again in March 1916, Wolfe reported that the idea had met with approval in Missouri and that a meeting had been set for December 1916, near Pattonsburg, Missouri, "to effect a permanent organization." Consequently, during its August 1916 session, the Nebraska Yearly Meeting named six delegates to represent at Pattonsburg. They were John H. Wolfe, M. L. Morse, W. E. Dearmore, Alva Hall, Clay McPherson, and R. V. Whitaker.[56]

There was already in existence a broader organization of Free Will Baptist associations, and one wonders why Wolfe and Latimer and others did not regard that as the needed one. This was the Southwestern Convention of Freewill Baptists, and it included associations in Texas, Oklahoma, and

---

56 NYMFB, 112.

Missouri.[57] Indeed, the Wolfes were "visiting messengers" to that organization in 1912, in Earlsboro, Oklahoma, representing the Nebraska Y. M. Latimer had been a part of it; Ferguson was then a part of it.[58] Perhaps the reason for beginning a new organization lay in the fact that the Southwestern was continuing to participate in the Northern General Conference activities.

At any rate, Dodd's interview article reports that

> representatives from Kansas, Nebraska, Missouri, Oklahoma, and Texas met at the Old Philadelphia (Muddy) Church near Plattsburg [sic], Missouri, and perfected the organization. ... The name "Cooperative General Association of Free Will Baptists" was chosen and Brother Wolfe was elected moderator. This first meeting lasted three days, coming to a grand climax on the closing day, December 31, 1916.

Actually, the meeting lasted five days, December 27-31. There were no representatives from Oklahoma, and there was a representative from North Carolina. When moderator Wolfe—who continued in that office for at least the first three years—called for the "credentials of all delegates who desired to go into the proposed Co-operative General Association of Freewill Baptists," delegates were seated from nine bodies, as follows:

Nebraska Y. M.: Rev. John H. Wolfe, Rev. W. E. Dearmore, Rev. H. M. McAdams, Rev. Leona Mack, Ellis Reger, M. L. Morse;

Northwest Missouri Y. M.: Rev. J. A. Bethel, Rev. S. B. Lewis, Rev. C. E. Mann, Rev. Cora Mann, Rev. G. W. Hensley, Rev. W. H. McKown, Charley Guillman;

---

57 We have minutes only for 1912 ("the twelfth annual session"), 1914, and 1915.
58 Minutes of the Southwestern Convention of Freewill Baptists for 1912, 19.

Northeast Missouri Y. M.:[59] Rev. J. F. Duckworth, James Hardin,
     P. S. Paterson;
Central Western Missouri and Southeastern Kansas Association:
     Rev. T. C. Ferguson, F. L. Parson;
Northern Kansas Y. M.: Rev. G. S. Lattimer, W. L. Bastow;
Laclede County (Mo.) Association: Rev. Ira Waterman;
Niangua (Mo.) Association: Rev. N. J. Breshears;
Central Brazos Association of Texas: Rev. R. A. Roberts;
North Carolina State Convention: Rev. R. F. Pittman.

Subsequently, Rev. S. L. Morris, Rev. Z. B. Dally and wife, and Rev. J. J.
Tatum, all of Texas (Tatum from Bryan, the others from Weatherford) were
welcomed as visitors from their respective associations.[60]

In addition to necessary business like adopting a constitution and bylaws,
the Co-operative General Association acted to purchase the *New Morning
Star* and to elect S. L. Morris as its editor; to adopt the Biblical Correspondence School conducted by Wolfe, Latimer, and J. J. Wood; to adopt the foreign missions work of the Rev. Miss S. A. Esterbook in Barbados; to adopt
the Freewill Baptist Treatise as revised at Harper's Ferry in 1899; and to
establish a denominational school with John H. Wolfe as its president. Many
of these ventures will be discussed more fully in the following sections of this
chapter. All of them became the official programs of the new association.[61]

The association also set aside an afternoon session for Pittman from North
Carolina to present the work there. As a result, the delegates recommended

---

59 The minutes mistakenly say "Northwest" for this Y. M. also.

60 As late as 1917, Dally and Tatum were still involved with the General Conference in the
    North, representing the Southwestern FWB Convention, and were publishing a monthly pa-
    per called the *Free Will Baptist Sentinel*. Tatum was receiving a stipend as a home missionary.
    See Minutes of the General Conference of Free Baptists for 1917 (pages 15, 21, 28, 34, 60).

61 The information in these paragraphs is from the Minutes of the Co-operative General Asso-
    ciation of Freewill Baptists for 1916.

the Ayden, North Carolina, literature to all its Sunday schools and endorsed the Freewill Baptist Seminary there and the orphanage at Middlesex, North Carolina.

There is not space in this chapter to tell the full story of the Co-operative General Association, but a summary account seems appropriate. The organization was constituted to meet in regular session every three years, with provision that "adjourned sessions" could be scheduled when needed during the years in between. At the "first adjourned session" in 1917, meeting in Tecumseh, Oklahoma, the new college was dedicated and R. F. Pittman of North Carolina preached the dedicatory sermon.[62]

Membership in the Association grew, especially during 1917 and 1918, with the addition of several associations in Oklahoma, another in Texas, and one association each in Kentucky, West Virginia, and Ohio (ultimately these three represented through the Tri-State Association).[63] In a letter to Wolfe dated January 24, 1917, M. L. Morse noted that he had subscribed to the *Free Will Baptist* published in Ayden, North Carolina, and that there were Free Will Baptists in Georgia also, observing, "I suppose that in due time they will unite with us." The Illinois Y. M. (later the Southern Illinois Y. M.), the Michigan Y. M., and the Cumberland Association of Tennessee joined in 1918. The 1918 and 1919 sessions met in Paintsville, Kentucky, and Nashville, Tennessee, respectively. There were also some expressions of interest from Georgia and Alabama.

---

62 The FWB Historical Collection has minutes of the Co-operative General Association for 1916-1918, 1922-23, 1934, and 1937-38. It is an embarrassment that this is not a complete set!

63 Interestingly, most of the associations in Texas and Oklahoma that joined the new Co-operative General Association had been members as late as 1915 of the Southwestern Convention of Free Will Baptists, which had continued to represent at the Randall General Conference. Perhaps this movement represented the end of the Southwestern Convention. (We do not have minutes after 1915.)

By 1921, however, any hope of involving the associations in the Southeast was gone. One of the disagreements was about feet washing; see the discussion of this matter below. As a result, the brethren in the Southeast formed the General Conference of Free Will Baptists in 1921, meeting at Cofer's Chapel in Nashville, Tennessee. Thus, Free Will Baptists came to be aligned in two larger, regional organizations. The Co-operative General Association represented the denomination in Texas (Central Brazos and West Fork Associations only), Oklahoma, Kansas, Nebraska, Missouri, Illinois, Ohio, Kentucky, and West Virginia. The General Conference served churches in North and South Carolina, Virginia, Georgia, Florida, Alabama, Mississippi, and Tennessee. Beginning in 1930, the Texas State Convention also participated in the General Conference; so did the Ohio River Y. M. for about the same period of time.

It was not long before these two bodies began to explore the possibility of uniting in one national organization. Ultimately, committees from the two associations began to meet.[64] Interestingly, M. L. Morse represented the Nebraska and Northern Kansas Y. M. at the General Conference in 1932 and was appointed to a committee of that Conference to explore the possibility of union with the Co-operative General Association![65] By 1934, a basis for union had been hammered out, and in 1935, delegates met at Cofer's Chapel Free Will Baptist Church in Nashville, Tennessee, and organized the National Association of Free Will Baptists. The picture nearby shows the

---

64 A December 18, 1971, letter from the Rev. E. C. Morris to the editor of "The History Corner" in *Contact*, relates Morris' role as pastor at Bryan, Texas (beginning in 1929), in attending the 1931 session of the General Conference in South Carolina and inviting that body to meet in Bryan in 1932. He also went to the Co-operative General Association later in 1931 and invited that body to send representatives to the 1932 meeting in Bryan. Both invitations were accepted, which ultimately led to the committee talks that laid the groundwork for the union of the two bodies in 1935.

65 See the minutes of the General Conference for 1932, pages 5 and 16. From minutes of the succeeding years, it appears that Morse continued to represent at General Conference until 1935.

Treatise Committee at this 1935 meeting; the shorter man in the light suit, front right, was M. L. Morse of Nebraska![66]

The National Association was constituted to meet every three years, and so its second session was not until 1938. Meanwhile, the two regional associations were to be renamed and meet annually. The Co-operative General Association became the Western General Association, and the General Conference became the Eastern General Association. Both of these continued to meet until 1938, when all agreed that the National Association should meet annually and the two regional bodies ceased to exist.

---

66 The others, left to right, were J. C. Griffin (NC), C. B. Thompson (TX), Ralph Staten (AR), E. B. Joyner (GA), E. E. Morris (OK), Winford Davis (MO), W. B. Davenport (TN), and M. T. VanHoose (KY).

As for Wolfe, by 1922 he was apparently no longer personally active in the Co-operative General Association meetings.[67] In the 1922 minutes, his name appears only in connection with the Correspondence School. The 1923 minutes include a report from B. F. Brown, now president of the college, who indicated that Wolfe had been offered the presidency in August 1922, and had declined. In the same minutes, Wolfe was again listed as on the faculty of the Correspondence School and his address was given as Haddam, Kansas. Marcus L. Morse represented the Nebraska Y. M. in 1922, but it is not clear how much longer, if any, that body continued to participate—or to function at all.

Indeed, Wolfe and Morse set about to form an entirely different organization, to be known as "The Inter-State Conference of Free Will Baptists." In a letter to Morse dated November 4, 1927, Wolfe reported having developed a plan to unite the Kansas and Nebraska Yearly Meetings, and that the new organization would be open to others as a "national organization." A constitution was drawn up[68] and on December 6, 1927, the Executive Boards of the two Yearly Meetings met and voted to organize and adopt the constitution. Some efforts were made to bring other associations into the organization, but apparently all such efforts were unsuccessful. (See, below, reference to the attempt to bring in the Southern Illinois Y. M.)

Why would Wolfe want to form an organization that would compete with the Co-operative General Association? We simply do not have enough information to provide an answer. It would appear he had grown to feel that the earlier organization did not offer positive prospects. At any rate, he seemed contemptuous of the Oklahoma—or at least of the Tecumseh College—leadership. In the same 1927 letter Wolfe said,

---

67 Since we do not have the minutes for 1919-21, it is not possible to tell just when he ceased to be active.

68 A copy is in the FWB Historical Collection.

The Tecumseh brethren are now trying to raise the money to finish the building so that they may be able to get more out of it for other purposes. I saw by the Mission World that Fields had been up to Cushing to see the Mission World folks about turning over the College property to them. They act as tho' the property would burn their fingers if they held it much longer for a College. Poor folks. I pity their ignorance.

The New Morning Star (and *Free Will Baptist Quarterly*)

From the start in 1915-1916, Wolfe and his associates apparently recognized that it would be essential to their plan for a broader organization and advancement in the work to have a print organ that could be used to rally and inform. They were most certainly aware of the important ministry of the Northern publishing house and its well-known weekly publication, *The Morning Star*. Something similar was needed for the new organization. Even before the Co-operative General Association was organized in December 1916, then, they took deliberate steps to implement the second proposal in the grand plan reported above.

This first information about this appears in Wolfe's report to the Executive Board in March 1916, as follows. Obviously, negotiations had already taken place.

Report of Board's delegate, J. H. Wolfe, to the Missouri State Association held at Hannon in Nov., pertaining to the paper deal, is as follows, viz.:

That in the purchase of the Freewill Baptist News of Weatherford, Texas, for three hundred and fifty dollars—$350. Obligating in no sense the Y. M. for the original purchase price, the same to be raised outside the Y. M. as a body.

And that the present editor and publisher, Rev. S. L. Morris, agrees to edit and publish the same until after the meeting of the co-operative association at Pattonsburg, Missouri, over the 5th Sunday in Dec. next, without any cost to the purchasers.

Receiving for remuneration all money over and above that which takes for paper—printing, mailing, and all necessary expenses of said paper.

Also understood by clerk the same to be held in trust by the Ex. Board of the Neb. Y. M. until after the Dec. 1916 meeting at Pattonsburg, Missouri, when the co-operative association of Freewill Baptists plan to affect [sic] a permanent organization, the same to be turned over to that body when legally organized.

And in case a failure to affect the above permanent organization the property to be at the disposal of the donors.

That negotiations had already taken place is confirmed by a letter dated November 8, 1915, from S. L. Morris to Wolfe,[69] answering questions Wolfe had written to ask following the 1915 meeting of the Missouri State Association. Morris indicated that (1) he supported the formation of the Co-operative General Association and would sell his paper to it; (2) that he would take $350 in cash; (3) that he would remain as editor for a few months, provided he could maintain the publishing schedule he already followed; and (4) that he had no objection to changing the name to the *New Morning Star*. He lamented "the confusion that has been going on for the last seven years"—referring seemingly to the efforts toward merger. He even recommended, if a new editor must be found when the press was moved, that the Reverend Charles T. Rogers of Homeland, Georgia, might be a

---

69 The letter is in the FWB Historical Collection, among the M. L. Morse papers.

good candidate.

The August 1916 minutes of the Executive Board therefore include, in the treasurer's report of Morse, that $2 had been received from Missouri to apply to this, $25.84 had come from Kansas,[70] and $240 from Nebraska. The total, $267.84, had been paid to Wolfe to apply to the purchase.

These minutes further indicate that the Board accepted Wolfe's report that the purchase had been made, and they include a copy of the lengthy "bill of sale" signed by S. L. Morris. It includes an itemized list of the assets conveyed and the estimated value of each, totaling $913. In addition to the press and other typesetting materials, the assets included a "mailing book with something like 1,000 names and addresses of persons who have at one time been subscribers, which would be worth $200 to one starting a paper." Morris conveyed ownership to the Nebraska Executive Board "in trust for the Co-operative Association of Freewill Baptists until the said Co-operative Association shall have become fully organized." He also committed himself to "run the said Freewill Baptist News under its new name, viz: The New Morning Star, until Dec. 21st, 1916," publishing it twice a month in Weatherford, Texas, "unless sooner terminated by mutual consent."

Indeed, at the same meeting, Wolfe's annual report indicated, with obvious pleasure, "We have been able to look into the pages of the New Morning Star as belonging to the denomination." He added, "We need a little more money, some $90 to place the printing plant out of debt and on a foundation to enable it to do a larger work, and just as soon as possible enlarge it so as to print or reprint our books and Sunday School supplies."

Clearly, the printing establishment played a key role in Wolfe's plans for advancement of the work. One of the recommendations attached to his an-

---

70 The minutes of the Hickory Grove church in Kansas for February 16, 1916, report: "A total of $11.00 was raised for purchasing of the Free Baptist News to make it a paper held mutually by the Free Baptists of the United States."

nual report was, "That we attempt to place the New Morning Star into every Free Baptist home in our state." He also recommended that the churches order their Sunday School supplies "through our New Morning Star Publishing House."

The minutes of the 1917 Yearly Meeting included this report from the Committee on Publications:

> In view of the fact that our Publishing House, the New Morning Star, has been nicely located and established in one of the College buildings in Tecumseh, Oklahoma, with a large increase in its number of subscribers; with the addition of about $20.00 worth of new type; and with its good supply of stock and equipment to do all kinds of job and minute work, besides its stock of good books, leaflets, blanks, etc., we recommend that our Yearly Meeting stand by it by faithfully patronizing and supporting it in every way possible, realizing its value in sustaining the Free-will Baptist denomination and advancing the cause of Christ. We also recommend that our Sunday Schools use our own literature, published in Ayden, N.C., which may be purchased through the New Morning Star.
>
> Signed, H. M. McAdams, Chas. Lewis, M. L. Morse[71]

The 1917 Co-operative General Association minutes indicate that a "cylinder press" was purchased and that the balance of $100 pledged to editor Morris the previous year was paid. Wolfe's report, as president of Tecumseh, was that the first work done, after he and his wife moved to Tecumseh on April 15, 1917, was to repair the secondary building on the property—a frame house, 30 by 40 feet—and move the printing press from Weatherford, Texas, into it. Editor Morris reported that the Rev. Samra Smith (a North Carolina native) had merged his publication, the *Biblical Beacon*, into the

---

71 Minutes of the Nebraska Y. M. of Freewill Baptists for 1917 (typewritten), 3.

Star, and that the Rev. W. C. Austin had likewise merged his, the *Gospel Pruning Hook*, "making one paper of the three." The number of subscribers had grown from 500 to nearly double that number. In addition to issues of the periodical, they had also published a new edition of the *Free Will Baptist Treatise*.

The 1918 minutes include a report from the "editors and publishers," S. L. Morris and Samra Smith, indicating that the number of subscribers had nearly doubled again. Plans included publishing the *Star* weekly "instead of semi-monthly, as here-to-fore," beginning in January 1919, and the plan was realized. The issue for November 15, 1918, indicated that the necessary equipment, at a cost of $6,000, had been purchased, and that "dear Bro. Wolfe ... mortgaged his farm, representing his savings of a life-time, to make the purchase possible." The issue for February 1, 1919, included this by Samra Smith:

> And who can measure the mighty influence and power that goes out each week in the NEW MORNING STAR as it reaches its thousands of readers? It goes carrying its sunshine and cheer as your Assistant Pastor, my brother minister. So don't forget to treat your helper kindly by opening more homes for its visits.

But optimism was soon tempered by reality. In 1922, the Committee on Publications recommended "a special effort" toward placing the paper in every Free Will Baptist home and that the paper be "enlarged." In 1923, B. F. Brown's report as president of the college included information that because of the illness of W. H. York, who had been named editor in August of 1922, there had been no issue published from then until November, when the Rev. W. A. Herron[72] was chosen as editor. Taking over as editor in 1924

---

72 I think Hearron is the correct spelling.

after another apparent lapse in publication, Brown[73] wrote:

> Yes, the paper will be published: we are here to stay, at least a year.
>
> It will be mailed out on the first and third Wednesdays of each mo. until we can do better. Things are badly in need of repair; the linotype won't work at all, and it is hand type or no paper, but by working 12 to 16 hours a day, we hope to do as we say above.
>
> It was promised by the Ass'n and by the Ex. board that our publishing house should be repaired and some needed equipment added but it can't be done unless some one sends in some money. ... Now, my friends, how many of you will make an effort to raise some money to send in for the Star fund, to be used by the board to improve the condition of our publishing house?

We have only a little more than two dozen issues of the *New Morning Star*, widely scattered from May 1, 1918 (pictured above)[74] to June 1, 1927.[75] It was issued twice a month in 1918, then weekly beginning in 1919, then back to semi-monthly by 1924 under Brown. I assume, but am not certain, that it continued to be published until 1927, when the college burned and (as will be noted below) the assets of the publishing house were transferred to another (weekly) paper entitled *The Mission World*, published at Cushing, Oklahoma. We have just one (incomplete) issue of that publication, for November 12, 1927, in which it is identified as "Official Organ of the Co-operative General Association in the interest of the Free Will Baptist Church."

---

73 Brown served only a short stint as Tecumseh College president and was no longer in that office.

74 This issue is identified as volume 13, which apparently picks up the numbering of the *Star's* predecessor publication, the *Free Will Baptist News*, thus taking that paper back to about 1906.

75 The number of issues represents the combined total of those held in the FWB Historical Collections at Welch College (7) and the University of Mount Olive, North Carolina (22). I thank Gary Barefoot for scans of the latter.

Subsequently, the *Free Will Baptist Gem*, published in Missouri beginning in 1929, became the official organ of the Co-operative General Association.

The Wolfes personally undertook another regular publication. Beginning perhaps as early as 1918 or 1919, Mrs. Delia S. Wolfe edited a quarterly report known as the *Free Will Baptist Quarterly*. Its purpose, as indicated by its contents, was to provide news on denominational meetings and events. It was small in size, being one 7.5 by 9 inch sheet folded into four narrow pages.[76] We have just nine issues of this publication, scattered from 1923 to 1935.[77] A letter from Delia Wolfe to M. L. Morse, dated February 4, 1927, gives some idea of the costs involved: Printing, $4.50; Envelopes, .25; Stamps, $3.00; Total: $7.75.

The paper contains reports and announcements of denominational meetings in various places, including Kansas and Nebraska, Missouri, Oklahoma, Texas, Illinois, Kentucky, Ohio, and West Virginia. By the 1935 issue, there is also information from Mississippi, Alabama, Arkansas, Tennessee, and North Carolina. What is probably significant is that information about the work in Kansas and Nebraska becomes less and less over this period of time. By 1930, only a few churches in these two states are mentioned, and the 1935 issue has nothing about any work in them.

Tecumseh College

The third element in Wolfe's grand plan for the new future was that they should establish a college. Again, the Wolfes and Latimer were following the pattern they were already familiar with in the old Randall movement. Matching the Northern General Conference was the new Co-operative General Association. Answering to the *Morning Star* and its prolific publish-

---

76 In mid-1928 it became larger with four 7 by 9 pages.

77 The 1923 issue is "vol. 6," which would make 1918 the first year, but the 1927 issue is "vol. 9," which would indicate 1919.

ing house was the *New Morning Star*. And corresponding to the influential educational institutions of the North—including Wolfe's own alma mater, Hillsdale College in Michigan—was to be a new college. Most certainly, the three planners and their associates realized that the future success of the denomination depended greatly on having an effective institution of higher education, especially to prepare the ministers.

Movement in this direction was already afoot when Wolfe and Latimer presented their plan to the Missouri State Conference in November 1915. As noted above, Wolfe's report in March of 1916 included the information that immediately following the session in Missouri he and Latimer had met with the Missouri State Board and they had "Voted that Bro. Latimer visit the Tecumseh, Okla., field and investigate the offer of a building and 120 acres of land." Apparently, such an offer was in prospect, one that Wolfe or Latimer or someone privy to their plans had cultivated. When the Co-operative General Association was formed at the end of 1916, a motion was adopted "to establish a denominational school," and the next action was to place the matter "in the hands of the Executive Board."[78] A subsequent resolution named Wolfe as president and pledged "support to every requirement to carry this school to success."[79]

Tecumseh was a small Oklahoma town, just south of Shawnee and about forty miles east of Oklahoma City. According to Dodd, reporting his interview with Wolfe in 1953, the people of the town gave a building and land, along with $1,000, to the Co-operative General Association for the founding of a college. This was apparently not the real estate mentioned in the previous paragraph. Instead, it was a three-story brick building (forty by sixty feet) that had been erected for Indianola Business College, incorporated in 1904, and five acres "just outside the city limits on the east side of the city of

---

78 Minutes of the Co-operative General Association of Freewill Baptists for 1916, 4.
79 Minutes of the Co-operative General Association of Freewill Baptists for 1916, 5.

Tecumseh."[80] That institution had default-
ed on its mortgage and in 1912 the property
was sold to E. L. Rosebush, president of the
Tecumseh National Bank.[81]

> On March 19, 1917, E. L. and Sue
> Rosebush conveyed the Indianola Col-
> lege property to the Executive board of
> the Co-Operative General Association
> of Free Will Baptists, with a recital in the deed that "…it is expressly
> agreed by and between the parties hereto that this property cannot be
> sold and must be maintained as a college continuously for a period of
> ten (10) years. (WDB 75, p. 192.)[82]

Wolfe was chosen president and asked to move to Tecumseh to take
charge, no salary specified. Accordingly, the Wolfes relocated there and received $33 a month for their administrative duties and teaching. As noted
in the preceding section, the *New Morning Star* publishing was likewise
brought there from Weatherford, Texas. At the adjourned session of the
Co-operative General Association in 1917, the college was dedicated. R. F.
Pittman of North Carolina preached the sermon on the occasion.

---

80 *Tecumseh College Catalog and Announcements, Tenth Session 1926-27)*, 7 (not numbered).
    The picture shown here was donated to the FWB Historical Collection by Mrs. Minnie Har-
    toon, a member of the Tecumseh College Church in 1919. The group in the picture, accord-
    ing to her, was a monthly, Saturday "Covenant meeting" of the church. The picture of early
    faculty members, below, was also donated by her, as was the College Church Hand Book
    referenced below.

81 Some of the information here is from the President's Report in the Minutes of the Co-opera-
    tive General Association of Freewill Baptists for 1917, 12 (unnumbered).

82 Winnie Vance Yandell, *The Family, Life, and Ministry of Isaac Wilson Yandell, M.D., 1876-
    1959* (Oklahoma City: Duplicated, 2008), 17.

Wolfe and his board (in 1917 the others were Charles Mann, Ira Water-man, T. C. Ferguson, and James Hardin) envisioned an ambitious program. The first catalog, for 1917-18, lists the following faculty:

John H. Wolfe, Theology and Philosophy,

S. L. Morris, Sacred History and Apologetics,

Delia S. Wolfe, History and Languages,

Grace I. Morris, Mathematics and Physics,

Samra Smith, Chemistry and Biology,

Pearl Smith, Preparatory Work,

W. E. Dearmore, United States History and Mathematics.

The Reverend Ellen A. Copp of Wisconsin and Professor George W. and Mrs. Angelia Lawrence of Unicoi, Tennessee, were expected to join the faculty soon. The picture nearby shows (left to right) the Morrises, the Lawrences, the Smiths, Dearmore, and the Wolfes.

Five courses of study (most with three years preparatory—as needed, one assumes—and four years of college) were to be offered:

(1) The Classical Course, leading to the B. A. degree and focusing in classical liberal arts studies, including Greek, Latin, Mathematics, Literature, History, Science, and Philosophy.

221

(2) The Philosophical and Scientific Course, leading to the B. S. degree, with Modern Languages and Science replacing Greek "and a few other culture subjects."

(3) The Literary Course, emphasizing Literature and Languages and requiring Latin, French, and German as well as "the thorough study of the English language each year."

(4) The Normal Course, a three-year program preparing teachers for schools by thorough training in the subjects one would have to teach, and requiring "frequent developmental lessons given by the student."

(5) The Classical Theological Course, leading to the B. D. degree and requiring Greek, Hebrew, English Bible, Systematic Theology, Church History, Homiletics, and Pastoral and Practical Theology. A shorter "English Theological Course" was also available that omitted the Greek and Hebrew.

At its 1917 session, the Co-operative General Association voted to add a Business Department. According to the 1918 minutes, this was not immediately done, but a school of music had been added and boasted twenty-two students.[83]

The table of expenses in the first catalog indicates that tuition was $10 per term (three courses each term; three terms each year), and that room and board at the Dearmore home was $4.50 per week or in other private homes "at reasonable rates." The library provided access to 1,000 volumes and was open daily except Sunday. The dates of the three terms that first year were September 12-December 20; January 2-March 21; March 27-June 6. The rules of deportment were brief and to the point:

> The government of the College is based on those rules of conduct which ought to be observed by young gentlemen and ladies assembled for study. Intellectual, moral, and spiritual culture are

---

83 Minutes of the Co-operative General Association for 1918, 7 (unnumbered).

held to be the first and paramount object, and whatever is inconsistent with it, such as habitual absence from church and chapel, social visits between students in study hours, students of opposite sex rooming in the same house, idleness, the use of tobacco in the College buildings or on the grounds, intoxicating drinks, or whatever is believed to be hostile to studious habits and the formation of right character, will not be permitted and will be just cause for the student's dismissal.

All students were required to attend chapel daily and church services on Sunday, either at the College church or at another church selected by the student at the opening of each term.

A Tecumseh College Church was organized in May of 1917, with S. L. Morris as the first pastor. Samra Smith took over as pastor on September 1, 1917. We have a *Tecumseh College Church Hand Book*, prepared by Smith in December 1919, listing more than ninety members and reporting that Sunday School attendance had recently been more than two hundred.

The second catalog, for 1918-19, includes a list of students: I assume they had been enrolled in the first year. Of fifteen named, ten were from Tecumseh—at least residing there at the time; three others were from Non and Macomb, Oklahoma; and two were from Zulch, Texas. In October, Wolfe would report that Mr. and Mrs. William Fuller of Nebraska had visited and given the first $500 endowment and were "delighted with the College and the bright and intelligent lot of students"; and that the Reverend A. B. Talbert of Drumright, Oklahoma, had started a Beneficiary Fund for the theological students.[84] In the same issue of the paper, Samra Smith wrote a challenging article entitled "The Christian College," decrying much of public education and insisting on the importance of a truly Christian education. He

---

84 *The New Morning Star*, October 15, 1918, 2.

reported that six theological students had enrolled the second year, as well as "several in the other departments."[85]

Wolfe apparently continued as president for two years—or perhaps through the fall term of 1919.[86] At least by January 1920, Samra Smith was identified as president in the issue of the *New Morning Star* for that date.[87] The minutes of the Executive Committee of the Nebraska Yearly Meeting for August 13, 1920, show that Wolfe was back in Nebraska then and was once again on the committee and serving as its chair.

The 1921-22 catalog[88] still lists Samra Smith as president. It reports that during the 1920-21 year there were students from eight different states and that even more were expected for the new year. Furthermore, the library had grown to about 3,000 volumes and an athletics program included tennis, basketball, and baseball. Tuition was now $25 per semester, but ordained ministers were charged only half this. The five courses of study were essentially the same as above except that the ministerial program had become the Christian Workers Course.

The 1922 minutes of the Co-operative General Association show that the financial situation was not good. One committee reported that several things were needed: a new roof on the building, plastering on the second and third floors, and "new and sanitary toilets." Another committee found the college to be "showered with claims of indebtedness" and "no money on hand to settle them"—as well as no way of knowing which claims were justified. This

---

85 *The New Morning Star*, October 15, 1918, 4.

86 The gaps in our holdings of the various publications (Co-operative General Association minutes; Tecumseh College catalogs; issues of the *New Morning Star*) make it impossible to be any more precise.

87 Smith was also Moderator of the Co-operative General Association at this date, and the issue indicates that there had been many changes in officers made at the December 1919, meeting in Nashville.

88 We do not have catalogs between the second issue for 1918-19 and this fifth one, which is not complete.

led to yet another committee that considered the various claims and listed the ones rejected and the ones to be paid.[89]

I do not know exactly how long Smith served as president, evidently not more than two years. A used letterhead, dated December, 1921, names Homer Stuart as "Acting President." The letter itself was from W. G. Fields, the college's secretary-treasurer, and it appeared to question Smith's handling of financial affairs. He was writing to M. L. Morse about the interest on Morse's note and said, "I am of the opinion Smith has put it [the note] away somewhere and got money on it." Another sheet—dated December 9, 1921, with probably the same handwriting—says "we have received numerous complaints of bad checks signed Tecumseh College by Samra Smith." It seems clear from these documents that Smith's dealings were being questioned—at least in Nebraska. In a letter to Morse dated December 14, 1922, Wolfe seems to indicate that a note against the College had been "made over to us" and that he would report to the Board of the Co-operative General Association as follows:

> It is being transferred to the Nebraska Yearly Meeting, (The mortgage) until such time when all those Smith creditors are either paid or settlement made so that we shall feel sure that the plant is safe from attachments after which it is the intention of the Nebraska Board to cancel or transfer over to the National Board.

He went on to say, "The thing is to safeguard it to the Denomination. If we who do not practice foot-washing are crowded out, it will be up to our Board to say whether it is to be canceled or demand payment. ...If not foreclosed or forced to sell, then it remains as a gift of the $403." He also joked with Morse about the latter's personal note, saying, "I trust you won't buy any boat to navigate up Salt Creek after your $500 note, but plant a few more

---

89 Minutes of the Co-operative General Association of Freewill Baptists for 1922, 7-8.

potatoes to help Bro. Smith as he no doubt knows where it is and it may turn up some day for collection."

As noted above in the discussion about the Co-operative General Association, in 1922-23 B. F. Brown was president. The faculty were Brown, Mrs. S. L. (Grace I.) Morris for the high school department, and Cora Lamar for the business department. There were twenty-one students enrolled from January to June. Brown would say,

> One of the main things needed to make Tecumseh College a real school is finance. With sufficient finance to pay expenses and make the needed repairs and improvements, Tecumseh College could be made an attractive place; and there would be no lack of students. All the students enrolled last year were residents of Tecumseh.[90]

In November 1924, Mrs. Grace I. Morris held the office of president.[91] In the issue of the paper under this date, Brown (as editor) wrote to promote the success of the college. He said that "a number of noble young people are enrolled" and "getting an education under Christian influence," adding that "If we allow our work at Tecumseh to fail can you measure the loss? If we give it proper support can you tell what our gain will be?" The institution's support had increased some, but more was needed to "pay present operating expenses for carrying on the school work." Still, he expected that "enough is, or will be, raised so that suit on the note will be dropped."[92]

The next (and last) catalog we have was for the 1926-27 term (the tenth session) and named T. A. Sercy—Searcy, I think—as president. In a letter to M. L. Morse dated July 2, 1926, Wolfe said, "They have a new president

---

90 Minutes of the Co-operative General Association of Freewill Baptists for 1923, 2, 11.

91 *The New Morning Star*, November 8, 1924, 4.

92 *The New Morning Star*, November 8, 1924, 5.

again at Tecumseh, a brother Searcy from Iowa but originally from Texas. I don't see how they could do it, as he had gone to the Baptists when he went to Iowa." The faculty had been reduced to five persons, including the president who taught in the theology department. The others were T. B. Mellette (of South Carolina and Georgia) as principal of the high school department; Clyde A. Shults, instructor in the high school department; Cora B. Lamar, shorthand and typewriting; and an unnamed teacher yet "to be supplied" for grades seven and eight.

It seems obvious that the college was struggling. The "Historical Sketch" in the catalog includes the following.

> Our College was formally opened for students September 12, 1917. We have had school every year since, so nine years of the ten are already fulfilled and one more year will give us the property absolutely our own.
>
> Plans were already made and steps taken to make this year the best year of the ten for Tecumseh College. In past years, we were not able to meet the demands of the state law to make our school accredited, but now we are meeting the demands of the law, and the last great objection is removed. Students will now get credits at Tecumseh College the same as they would get in other High-schools of the state, and it will cost less to get an education at Tecumseh College than any other school where students have to live away from home, and under Christian influence too. ...
>
> It is true that, during our nine years at Tecumseh, there have been times when we had a struggle for existence, but both the school and the paper have endured the struggles, and are still alive. Only a few of our people really know the real worth of Tecumseh College, and a smaller number know the price that a few have paid to keep our school and paper going.

At this point, the library was said to contain "at least fifteen hundred volumes." The rules of conduct were essentially the same as before, with a few items added to the things prohibited and grounds for dismissal. These included students visiting in town or the country without proper permission, girls leaving school grounds without a chaperon, and profanity.

The courses of study were basically reduced to three: the Theological Course, the High School Course, and the Commercial Course. The catalog does not describe the required courses in detail but observes that the faculty would arrange the programs to meet the needs. Missing from the list of subjects in the Theological Course were most of the ambitious courses required earlier, including ancient and modern languages. Tuition had increased to $4 per month and ministerial students could attend tuition free.

This was destined to be the last catalog for the college, as well as its last year of operation. On Wednesday, February 23, 1927, the building burned. The *Tecumseh County Democrat* for Friday, February 25, included the following.

TECUMSEH COLLEGE DESTROYED BY FIRE

Fire of unknown origin completely destroyed the Free Will Baptist College here at 5:30 o'clock Wednesday afternoon. ... Since 1911, the school had been under the supervision of the Free Will Baptist denomination. Only a small portion of the furniture was saved. The loss was partially covered by insurance. The college print shop adjoining the administration building was unharmed.[93]

The *Shawnee Morning News* for Thursday, February 24, reported, "the fire, believed caused by defective wiring, started in the roof. ... Low water pressure made it impossible to check the flames."[94]

---

93 Yandell, 18. The year 1911 appears to be an error made by the newspaper reporter.
94 Yandell, 18.

There were supposedly some good intentions to rebuild. Delia Wolfe, in Nebraska, wrote: "It was a great shock when we learned of the loss of Tecumseh College, Tecumseh, Okla., by fire, February 5. But were glad to learn of the spirit to rise and build."[95] John H. Wolfe, however, was skeptical about one of the plans involved: in a letter to M. L. Morse dated November 28, 1927, he wrote:

> Not much going on at Tecumseh, only that the paper gave out a plan for raising $10,000 to go on with finishing the building. ... The GREAT PLAN was for each Free Will Baptist wife to prepare a good Thanksgiving Dinner and charge "the old man" 50 cts. for it and send same to make up this $10,000. I am looking with interest to see this GREAT PLAN worked out. I am just a little fearful that the originator will be sick so he can't ... eat the dinner prepared by the wife after such a strain in evolving such a tremendous plan. Well, well, maybe I should not have so written, for many a BIG THING has come from smaller things than even a Thanksgiving Dinner at 50 cts. per.

In the *New Morning Star* issue for June 1, 1927, W. L. Bean, as foreman of the building committee, reported that "Everything is moving along fine. ... We are planning to have the auditorium ready for the school exercises on the night of May the 23rd."[96] In a letter to M. L. Morse dated September 17, 1927, Wolfe wrote the following:

> He [Bro. Reger, father of Luster Reger] went down with Bro. McAdams to that called meeting at Tecumseh. They were all agreed to stop the College so discontinued it and left the matter of disposal of the property in the hands of the Board. The STAR

95 *Free Will Baptist Quarterly*, 9:2 (April-June, 1927), 3. The date of February 5 is apparently in error.

96 *The New Morning Star*, June 1, 1927, 2-3. See also a report from A. B. Epperson on p. 5.

fixtures are turned over to the MISSION WORLD, or at least that is about the status of things. They could not agree as to how to let loose as some wanted to sell it out-right while others wanted to turn it over into an Old Ministers Home, but all were a unit as to discontinuing the College. Chapel or rather church 40 x 40 is practically finished and the four-foot high foundation for the College proper is done. Another case of not sitting down and counting the cost. But in reality a case of lack of ability. I have written to Bro. Epperson asking that my books be returned. I am afraid most of them are ruined as Sauley Reger who was there when the College burned said that they left the books right out doors for days piled up and in the rain, not caring enough to take them in the shelter of the STAR office.

On February 14, 1928, Delia Wolfe would write, in a letter to M. L. Morse, "Sister Myers … is specially anxious about changing her will. … She has $5,000 left to the Tecumseh College. … Of course since they have no College building and are not trying to keep up any school, she feels she must change it."

Ultimately, any hope of rebuilding the college was not to be realized. President Searcy's appeal was poignant and (unintentionally) prophetic: "If we have a denomination, we must have a School; if we have a School our pastors must favor it. If the pastors fail in this duty, the School fails; if the School fails, our denomination fails; if our denomination fails, then who will bear the blame?"[97]

The college was never reopened.

The Correspondence School of the Bible

The fourth plank in the platform on which to build for the future, offered

---

97 *The New Morning Star,* June 1, 1927, 6.

by the Wolfes and Latimer in 1915-16, was a correspondence school. In this too, as in the three previous parts of the grand plan, they were following the pattern already established in the Randall denomination. Indeed, Wolfe had begun such a program even before he made his pitch to the Missouri State Association that led to the founding of the Co-operative General Association. A 1930 publication indicates that the Correspondence School of the Bible had been in existence for 31 years, dating it back to about 1900.

When the Co-operative General Association was formed in December 1916, one of the actions was as follows:

> Motion carried to adopt the Freewill Baptist Biblical Correspondence School, formerly conducted by Rev. John Wolfe, G. S. Lattimer and J. J. Wood under the auspices of the Nebraska Yearly Meeting and the Missouri State Association.
> Motion carried to elect the following faculty for the Correspondence School: Rev. J. H. Wolfe, Pawnee City, Neb.; Rev. G. S. Lattimer, Hadam, Kansas; and Rev. Ira Waterman, Eldridge, Mo.[98]

Wolfe was responsible for Systematic Theology; Latimer for Church History and Evidence of Christianity; and Waterman for Pastoral and Practical Theology.[99]

The following year's report by Wolfe listed the same three courses and teachers and observed, "In the Correspondence School, the Denomination has a medium through which to make possible, along with our Colleges, a fully equipped Ministry inasmuch as no one need go without a preparation for his life's work." The report continued to note that tuition was free and the only cost was a total of $6.75 for the books required. To that point there had been enrolled twelve students who were taking all three courses. Wolfe

---

98 Minutes of the Co-operative General Association of Freewill Baptists for 1916, 3.
99 Minutes of the Co-operative General Association of Freewill Baptists for 1916, 7.

felt he had been somewhat hindered by his relocation to Tecumseh and the responsibilities of setting up the college, as well as by the fact that all supplies of the Butler-Dunn theology book had been exhausted.[100] (More about this below.)

Wolfe's 1918 report indicated a total cost of $10 for books and that twenty-two students were enrolled. Some of these were taking all three courses, some just one. The courses and faculty were the same as before.[101] In his column in the *Morning Star* in 1919, Wolfe would observe, "Little did we think of the help the Biblical Correspondence would be to many a brother who has not had the opportunity of a College training, but in this way can receive with no cost except the books, a good next to a College education."[102]

The 1922 minutes of the Association indicate that the Reverend W. E. Dearmore was added to the Correspondence School faculty.[103] By this time, Wolfe was back in Nebraska and had little to do with the Association or the College. The 1923 minutes list Wolfe, Dearmore, and Waterman as the Correspondence School teachers.[104] In neither of these years do the minutes include a report on the Correspondence School. The few issues of the *Morning Star* that we have for 1924, 1926, and 1927 (one each) contain no advertisements for the Correspondence School—as had the issues for 1918 and 1919. Apparently Wolfe, at home in Nebraska, was conducting the school on his own terms.

Indeed, a 1923 publication refers to "the School of the Bible, as conduct-

---

100 Minutes of the Co-operative General Association of Freewill Baptists for 1917, 17-18 (unnumbered).

101 Minutes of the Co-operative General Association of Freewill Baptists for 1918, 13-14 (unnumbered).

102 *The New Morning Star*, February 1, 1919, 2.

103 Minutes of the Co-operative General Association of Freewill Baptists for 1922, 4.

104 Minutes of the Co-operative General Association of Freewill Baptists for 1923, 2.

ed by Rev. John H. Wolfe."[105] The same publication, in 1928, promoted the School of the Bible as a means by which "competent christian teachers may give instruction to those who wish to better prepare for ministerial work or any Christian Service."[106] A year later a similar promotion urged prospects for the course to contact Wolfe "and receive the literature about the course and begin the work as soon as possible, to be better prepared to handle the Word of God."[107]

By 1930, there were four courses (not named), not just three[108]—still free, except for the cost of books and $2 to cover registration and postage. The promotional pitch urges:

> Bible Study by Correspondence is a great joy in life, that one may get an understanding of the great truths of our Lord's second coming, of justification by faith, of the substitutionary character of our Lord's work upon the cross, and the person and work of the Holy Spirit. An hour's lesson a day devoted to the study of God's word, brings refreshment and rest. Those who have a hunger for a deeper and fuller spiritual life should take a course in Bible study at once. It will lead you to the Bread and Water of Life.[109]

One item of interest, related to the Correspondence School, was the republication of *Lectures on Systematic Theology* by J. J. Butler and Ransom Dunn. As noted above, this was the text Wolfe used in his course in theology. It had been originally published in 1892 by the Morning Star Publishing

---

105 *Free Will Baptist Quarterly* 6:3 (October-December, 1923), 3.

106 *Free Will Baptist Quarterly* 10:3 (July-September, 1928), 4.

107 *Free Will Baptist Quarterly* 11:2 (April-June, 1929), 4.

108 A letter from Wolfe to Morse dated February 22, 1929, includes this: "Bro. Latimer and I have outlined a new Correspondence Course which I will get in shape and send you a copy as a member of the Committee."

109 *Free Will Baptist Quarterly* 12:2 (April-June, 1930), 3.

House in Boston,[110] but supplies were limited—as noted above. Wolfe had this republished in Pawnee City, Nebraska, by "The School of the Bible," which was the name he had given to the Correspondence School.

The publication date was apparently in 1931.[111] An early 1932 publication contains this:

> For years the School of the Bible has been handicapped because the Butler-Dunn Systematic Theology was out of print, and could not be obtained in limited numbers. But now the one-thousand edition is off the press and can be had for $2.50 postpaid. This book should be in the hands of every Free Will Baptist minister, as it is the Standard for our people.[112]

I am assuming this means that he had 1,000 copies printed at this date and that he had not had any printed earlier. Perhaps he had been able, earlier, to obtain some originals from Northern sources.[113] In a letter to Morse dated July 25, 1929, Wolfe had said, "Interest is growing in the School of the Bible and perhaps we had better use, for the time, some of the money in hand for the reprint of the Theology. Of course the money gotten for the sale of the books could be returned into the treasurer's hands as it came in."

---

110 Actually, the original work included lectures only by Butler and was entitled *Natural and Revealed Theology*, published in 1861 in Dover, New Hampshire by the Freewill Baptist Publishing Establishment—which became The Morning Star Publishing House when it was relocated to Boston. The 1892 publication included additional lectures by Dunn, and it was this volume that was republished by Wolfe in Nebraska.

111 As of May 13, 1929, when he wrote a letter to Morse, Wolfe was wishing for the reprint and working toward lining up the money for this project.

112 *Free Will Baptist Quarterly* 14:1 (January-March, 1932), 4.

113 The minutes of the Nebraska Y. M. for 1915 approved purchasing and keeping on hand "for sale at cost as least twenty-five dollars worth of 'Butler-Dunn' Theologies, so they were still available at that date. In 1922, as recorded in their minutes, the Nebraska Y. M. recommended that the Star office publish one or two chapters of the book at a time for use in the College and Correspondence School, saving from 500 to 2000 copies to be bound later when all had been printed. I assume this was not done.

Most of the copies of the Butler-Dunn theology that have been in the possession of non-merging Free Will Baptists since the early nineteen hundreds were from this republication by Wolfe. To be candid, this was not a very good work on systematic theology, but it has had considerable influence among Free Will Baptists, mostly because it was the only theology text published for the denomination until fairly recent times. We can thank Wolfe and his Correspondence School for its availability.

Foreign Missions

A missions program was not part of Wolfe's grand plan for the work. Nonetheless, there was an interest in missions and an official program. I will briefly describe that.

Beginning in 1891, the Reverend Miss Sarah Antionette Esterbrook had gone to the island of Barbados in the West Indies as a missionary.[114] When the Randall movement merged into the Northern Baptists in 1910-11, presumably the American Baptist Home Mission Society had been asked to consider the sponsorship of her work. But that body, in a report presented to the General Conference Board on July 15, 1913, declined this undertaking, "since the field is so well occupied by other denominations."[115]

The Nebraska Y. M., however, adopted Miss Esterbrook's work and promoted financial support for it.[116] Then the Co-operative General Association, when it was formed at the end of 1916, had acted: "Resolved, that we

---

114 See the *New Morning Star*, December 15, 1917, p. 1. I assume she represented Free Will Baptists from the start, but I have no information about her origins. *Free Will Baptist Quarterly* 10:1 (January-March, 1928), 3, says she had completed thirty-six years there.

115 Minutes of the General Conference of Free Baptists for 1913, 17.

116 This had happened *at least* as early as 1915, as shown in the minutes for that year. As early as 1910 a letter from Miss Esterbrook was read and received by the Nebraska Y. M., perhaps indicating that she was a member of that body?

adopt the Barbados Islands as our foreign mission field, and Rev. Miss S. A. Esterbrook as our foreign missionary."[117]

Furthermore, H. M. and Lizzie McAdams had gone for the purpose of assisting Miss Esterbrook in that effort. The *New Morning Star* for May 1, 1918, reported that they, with their four-year old daughter Naomi, were making preparations to go "to Sister Esterbrook's relief," as soon as funds could be raised.[118] Five months later, in the issue for October 15, we read,

> OUR Missionaries, Revs. Hiram and Lizzie McAdams sailed from New York for the Barbadoes on yesterday. ... Sister Esterbrook has been faithful and has built up a wonderful work there, and will be so glad to have these consecrated helpers on the field with her, and if possible give her a much needed rest.

The McAdamses stayed in Barbados only for a short time. The *New Morning Star* for March 22, 1919 announced that they had returned to America. A brief biographical sketch simply says that "After some disappointments they returned."[119] Mrs. McAdams herself said, "We went with the intention of staying, but the work was not what it was represented to be, so we came back."[120] They went from there to North Carolina and spent two years in evangelistic work in that state, locating first at Winterville. Wolfe said, in connection with their return, "We may have to cease from our Barbados work for a season."[121] And the Executive Committee of the Co-op-

---

117 Minutes of the Co-operative General Association of Free Will Baptists for 1916, 3.

118 *The New Morning Star*, 13:8 (May 1, 1918), 1.

119 Asa Berry, *Biographical Sketch of Lizzie McAdams* (Nashville: Woman's National Auxiliary Convention, n.d.), 3.

120 Lizzie McAdams, *My Experience and Six Gospel Sermons* (Tecumseh: The New Morning Star Print, repr. and rev. 1927), 7. In a letter to the *New Morning Star*, printed in the issue for February 15, 1919, the McAdamses, soon after their arrival in Barbados, said that "the work is even better than we had expected."

121 The *New Morning Star*, April 5, 1919, 2.

erative General Association, in its mid-year meeting in June, 1919, acted "to withhold all funds for the Barbados" until the next session—scheduled for December in Nashville—and asked "all parties specially interested to appear before that body to adjust all differences."[122] At any rate, the McAdamses were back home in the West at least by 1922 when the minutes of the Co-operative General Association identified them as "national evangelists." The 1922 minutes of the Nebraska Y. M. report that they did not have a "regular foreign mission work."

It would be interesting, I think, to research and tell the story of Miss Esterbrook and the work in Barbados. She was officially sponsored by the Co-operative General Association fully nineteen years before the (Southeastern) General Conference identified with Miss Laura Belle Barnard in 1935.

The Feet Washing Issue

Although Benjamin Randall and his early followers held that feet washing was an ordinance of the church, the Northern Free Will Baptists soon decided to allow freedom of conscience on that subject. As a result, the practice did not continue indefinitely within that movement. It is not surprising, then, that Wolfe and others among the Kansas-Nebraska Free Will Baptists, soon after the 1910-11 merger of the Randallites with the Northern Baptists, were not committed to this ordinance.

When the Co-operative General Association was formed at the end of 1916, the Articles of Faith printed in the minutes of that session included the following:

> 13. **Gospel Ordinances.** Baptism, or the immersion of believers in water, and Lord's Supper are ordinances to be perpetuated

---

122 The *New Morning Star*, June 28, 1919, 2.

under the gospel; of universal obligation and to be administered to all true believers.

Nothing was said about feet washing. The influence of the Northern treatises is clear.

However, in the next minutes, for 1917, the article read as follows.

> 13. **Gospel Ordinances. Baptism**, or the immersion of believers in water, and the **Lord's Supper**, are ordinances to be perpetuated under the gospel; **Feet Washing**, an ordinance teaching humility, of universal obligation, and to be administered to all true believers.

Feet washing had been added. It would apparently stay in article thirteen as long as the Co-operative General Association continued to exist.[123]

Indeed, as has been noted above, the *New Morning Star* published an edition of the *Freewill Baptist Treatise* for the Co-operative General Association, apparently in 1918. In the chapter on the ordinances, feet washing is included as the third ordinance.

> 3. *Washing the Saint's Feet.* This teaches humility, purity of body as well as soul willingness to serve every Christian in any way we possibly can to promote his spiritual welfare and advance the cause of Christ. It is the duty, and happy prerogative of every believer to observe this sacred ordinance.

A footnote was attached to this, which read, "Concerning the washing of feet as a Gospel ordinance, each member shall have the right to wash feet or not, as he can best answer his own conscience to God."

---

123 I say "apparently" because we have so few (as listed earlier) of the minutes of this organization. It is included in all the minutes we possess after 1916: namely, 1917, 1918, 1923, 1934, 1937, and 1938—except for 1922 which did not include the articles of faith.

In the 1918 minutes of the Co-operative General Association, the report of Tecumseh College President Wolfe included a reference to this addition and the footnote:

> The book was printed as per vote with the exception the body was made to correspond with our General Association policy and the addition (by vote of the Board) of the Foot-washing clause along with the Foot-note which has done more to harmonize our people than any other one things. The "give and take" method that must be used in all this unifying work is one that we feel is prompted of the Lord to assist in getting these thousands of Free-will Baptists in a good harmonious working condition where as one man we can move forward in this great Field and Work. We feel grateful for the harmony thus produced and for the prospects of the ultimate coming together of all of our people.

Obviously, the decision to include feet washing was seen—by Wolfe, at least—as a means of promoting harmony more than from conviction that this was a true ordinance.

In a letter to Morse dated December 14, 1922 (referenced earlier in this chapter), Wolfe was critical of the situation during Samra Smith's tenure as president at Tecumseh College. In one observation he said, "If we who do not practice foot-washing are crowded out, ..." He was apparently alluding to the Oklahoma Free Will Baptists, who in the *New Morning Star* had characterized themselves as "GENUINE Free Will Baptists"—evidently (at least in part) because they practiced feet washing.

Wolfe's personal view of feet washing is referred to in a letter he wrote to M. L. Morse on November 4, 1927. He had recently had a letter from R. E. Tripp of Ayden, North Carolina. Tripp had been a student at Tecumseh while Wolfe was there and was now on the faculty at Eureka College in Ayden. Wolfe wrote: "In the letter he expressed the wish that I might become a teacher in the College there, but said, 'You would meet with a good deal of opposition on account of your attitude on Feet Washing as an Ordinance'." Assumedly, then, Wolfe respected those who wished to practice feet washing, but refused to regard it as an established ordinance.

It may be that Wolfe's attitude was not as critical as that of his colleague M. L. Morse. In a letter to Wolfe dated in 1928, Morse reported on his recent visit to the Southern Illinois Yearly Meeting. He had made an unsuccessful attempt, while there, to persuade that group to take part in the Inter-State Conference of Free Will Baptists that he and Wolfe were promoting. Article X of the Constitution of that organization read, "FEETWASHING: The question of Feet-washing whether an Ordinance or not or the practice thereof shall never enter into consideration, neither locally nor nationally." Presumably, this meant—however poorly worded—that the subject would be left to each person and church to determine and could not be made a subject of divisive discussion. But Morse reported that the Illinois brother who had led the discussion against participation, a Reverend Allen, "continually represented that it barred them from talking about FEET-WASHING in their local churches or practicing the same if they wished." Morse's assessment was that "they were too narrow to understand ARTICLE 10 and too stubborn to try to see it." He went on to say, "Now we are out with the Illinois Brethren, is there any show to get in with any of the Ohio or Indiana Brethren? Feet-washing is all the talk in the south and is working up north."

At the same Illinois meeting, apparently, someone had handed Morse a compromise resolution on the feet washing question, suggesting a change in Article X. It read,

> Be it Resolved, That the question or practice of footwashing in the General Conference, or any yearly or quarterly Conference a part of the General Conference, shall never be allowed to enter into, or in any way be a part of business for such conference, the practice of feetwashing to the individual member or to a church a

part of such Conference to be left in their hands: Therefore, the practice of it can never be, or a cause to be, a means of division.

Morse had responded that the Constitution could not be changed then and there but that he would take this home.[124] His own opinion, however, was indicated by his next words: "This amendment No. 1 suggested, what will be the next?"

The folder in the Morse papers that includes these letters also includes a one-page outline on the subject of feet washing, martialing evidence that it was never intended or understood to be an ordinance. It is not clear whether this was Morse's or Wolfe's outline, but it was probably Wolfe's.

At any rate, it was apparently this matter of feet washing that kept the Co-operative General Association from becoming the national organization for all Free Will Baptists. As has been noted above, both North Carolina and Tennessee Free Will Baptists first joined in with the Co-operative General Association. But by 1919 it was clear—to the Free Will Baptists of the Southeast, especially—that they could not expect the organization to take a strong stand for feet washing. Here are the words of John L. Welch, of Tennessee, in a 1971 interview, about that.

> When we met at Nashville [in 1919], we found that the Co-operative General Association would not take a definite stand on the matter of feetwashing. John H. Wolfe, you know about him from Nebraska. He was a part of the old Northern Free Will Baptists. ... He was at the head of this Co-operative Association and he didn't teach or practice feetwashing; the Free Wills of the north didn't. Well, he had a man named Samra Smith, he was his right hand or left hand man in that movement and Smith wouldn't agree. And they had another man named Waterman, Ira Waterman. He didn't

---

124   The constitution had already been adopted by the Northern Kansas and Nebraska Yearly Meetings, and so the organization had been finalized.

go along with it so they wouldn't agree to take a stand on it, they wanted to leave it an open question. The North Carolina and Tennessee people wanted it as an ordinance, you see. Well, the result of the argument was that the North Carolina group and our group pulled out from the Co-operative. We had been accepted in this 1919 meeting at Cofer's, but we pulled out over this question of feet washing.[125]

The *New Morning Star* for January 10, 1920, in a report of the 1919 session of the Co-operative General Association in Nashville, had this to say: "The North Carolina delegation and the Cumberland Association delegation withdrew from the Association on the ground that they make feet-washing a test of Church fellowship. We were indeed sorry to lose these two Associations."[126] This led the Free Will Baptists of the Southeast to form another General Conference in 1921, and it was that organization that ultimately merged with the Co-operative General Association to form the National Association of Free Will Baptists in 1935. By that time, both organizations were ready to agree on how to word the *Treatise* statement on feet washing.

Conclusion

It is difficult, after a hundred years, to assess the character and ministry of a man. For the most part, the activities reported in this chapter will speak for themselves. Even so, some things about John H. Wolfe are obvious. For one thing, he was firmly committed to the Free Will Baptist cause. It seems clear

---

125 The transcription of this interview of Welch, conducted by the writer of this chapter, is in the FWB Historical Collection.

126 The report went on to say the Alabama State Association had joined and that the Co-operative General Association had thereby gained more members than were lost in the withdrawal of North Carolina and the Cumberland of Tennessee; but that was probably an erroneous conclusion.

that he was never tempted to submit to the merger of the Randall movement into the Northern Baptists and to the resulting loss of a distinctive Free Will Baptist identity.

He must also have been a man of great determination. To be sure, many of the circumstances he faced would easily have discouraged most people. If nothing else, the gradual decline of the work in Kansas and Nebraska, where he invested most of his ministry, must have been heart wrenching. But he labored on, never relenting, until his death.

Certainly, he was a person of vision, and that led him to father one of the two broad associations of Free Will Baptist churches that ultimately resulted in the formation of the National Association. He also envisioned a College for the Free Will Baptist people and led it to early success, as well as a denominational paper that flourished for a while. And even past his disappointments in those ventures he continued to offer almost free ministerial education, by correspondence, to people who had little opportunity for it.

He was not able, finally, to save the work in Kansas and Nebraska for the Free Will Baptists, although without his efforts the churches there would not have carried the name for anything like the decades they did. But he was the clear leader in developing a broader outlook and new optimism. He brought together a disparate people and helped establish a sense of unity that lived on past the time when the Co-operative General Association had fulfilled its purpose.

He was especially concerned about the need for education among those entering the ministry, and he labored faithfully in that cause. Even long after his disappointment in the Tecumseh project, he continued to offer courses by mail and touted the importance of Bible study.

Damon Dodd called him a man of great faith. He was that.

Postscript

One of the churches involved in all this was the Hickory Grove Free Will Baptist Church of Haddam, Kansas—also known as the "Blocker" church—which has been mentioned occasionally in the account above. The record book of this church indicates that it continued to have a pastor until August 1952. After that, there were no regular services. A small number of members, including the clerk, Mrs. Iva Eichman, continued to maintain records, report to the association (the Northwest Missouri and Northeast Kansas Association of Free Will Baptists), have official meetings for routine business, and sponsor meetings each Memorial Day, for example. The activity included sending some gifts to Free Will Baptist causes.

Finally, in 1968, the group determined to sell the buildings, which were unused and deteriorating. A public auction netted $310 for the church, $90 for the parsonage, $19 for the garage, $60 for the church bell, and $26.25 for miscellaneous items: total, $505.25. Subtracting $16.50 for the unreimbursed or undonated expenses of the sale left $488.75. A check for this amount was sent to the Free Will Baptist Bible College for the building fund. Ultimately, the church's record books were also sent to the College and are part of the FWB Historical Collection.[127] So, too, was the silver communion set that had been given to the church by the Reverend John H. Wolfe. It is now on display at Welch College.

---

127 The Rev. Robert Sharry, in an email to me dated 6/30/14, related that he and the Rev. E. E. Morris visited the church clerk while he was a home missionary in Kansas in the early 1960s and urged her to send the records to the college, and gave her the college address. She obviously heeded their appeal.

7

Singing for Jesus and the College: The Story of the FWBBC Traveling Quartets, 1949-1954

I suspect that most Free Will Baptists have only vague memories, if any memories at all, of the early days of Free Will Baptist Bible College (now Welch College) and the promotional efforts that went into making it a successful educational institution. As one who lived through that period and sang in the quartets, I can speak first hand of the "adventures" we experienced. I decided to record some of the story for posterity, confident that some will find it interesting. Indeed, many may be surprised about the fundraising methods we used.

As will soon be clear, the first of the quartets toured for the college in the summer of 1949. At that time, the college was seven years old. As a fledgling institution, it had struggled—successfully enough, given the circumstances—to raise sufficient funds and recruit students. There had been some leadership changes. The Reverend L. C. Johnson, 1942 to1945, first filled the president's office. He was temporarily replaced by the Reverend L. R.

Ennis, 1945 to 1947, and then returned to lead the institution again. The original Business Manager-Treasurer, who focused on fund-raising and financial management, was the Reverend J. R. Davidson. He was also replaced in 1947, by the Reverend Henry Melvin. I do not think it too speculative to say that there was need of fresh, new methods of fund-raising and promotion. Melvin set himself to that task, making his home in Nashville and traveling extensively in the cause. The picture below is of Melvin near the time of his coming to Nashville.

Among the ideas given shape by him was using a quartet of men, FWBBC students, to travel and promote the college during the summers. From the first, these quartets sang *a capella*: that is, without instrumental accompaniment—although Melvin himself played the piano and sometimes did so for the first quartet or two. His son, Billy, who was a member of the first group, is confident that Melvin invented the name, the *Gospeliers*, which was worn by the first several quartets. That name, by the way, sometimes got fouled up: I remember one newspaper article that had it *Gospel Spellers*, and I think another source made it *Gospel Liars* (!), but perhaps that was a typographical error.

Melvin also traveled with the quartets at first, speaking in the services on behalf of the college. Perhaps it was during these tours that he came to be known, affectionately, as "Pop." He personally scheduled the tours, and much of the time there were as many as eight or even nine services a week: weeknights Monday through Saturday and three on Sunday. He and the groups usually stayed in the homes of people in the churches. That, too, was part of the "public relations" benefits of the tours.

No doubt, Melvin also originated the method of fund-raising that was used by the first quartets. Of course, free-will offerings were taken. In addition, as he (later, others) presented the needs of the college, he would urge individuals to give monthly, emphasizing the need for regular support even if the amount each month was small. In order to provide for this, he devised a method by which cash or check could be used. As he ended his presentation, he would ask those who would give $5 per month to raise their hands and the members of the quartet would pass out cards to those who did. Likewise, he asked for those who would give $2.50 per month, and then $1 per month; and they, too, would be given cards.

The printed cards, which Melvin had prepared in advance of the tour, said something like this: "With God's help, I will give $_____ each month to Free Will Baptist Bible College"; the individual filled out the amount and then his name and address. After the offering and the final song, Melvin would ask those who had received cards to bring them to one of the members of the quartet following the benediction. Those who had pledged to give in cash were given a packet of twelve business-reply (postage paid) envelopes to use in mailing their gifts. Those who preferred to give by check were given "checkbooks" with twelve blank checks, which they could fill out on the spot, pre-date for each month of the coming year, and turn in then and there so that they could be cashed each month in Nashville.

All those who responded to this challenge to give monthly were assured, publicly, that no one would ever dun them for the gift, and that the commitment was strictly between them and the Lord. At any given service, a number of people might respond. I remember, when we started out in the summer of 1950, that Melvin suggested a goal for the summer tour—so many to give monthly at each level—and that we prayed for this. People today will no doubt be surprised that we asked folks to raise their hands publicly to give and that we took the cards to their seats at that very moment. For many years, the mail brought many such business-reply envelopes, with cash (or check) to the college each day; and the monthly check plan is still used effectively.

247

There were other purposes for these tours, of course, and other means of promotion from time to time. I will reserve further details for the year-by-year accounts to follow.

The First Gospeliers, Summer, 1949

The first of the FWBBC male quartets traveled in the summer of 1949. This edition of the Gospeliers included (left to right in the photograph above) Myrtis Carnes, Wesley Calvery, Derald West, and Billy Melvin. The quartet did not represent the college's music "department," as such—there was no such department at the time—but was sponsored, directed, itinerated, and accompanied on the road by Melvin. I assume that he selected the students for the quartet, one of them being his son Billy. Melvin could play the piano and sometimes accompanied the group, but mostly they sang *a capella*, getting the starting note either from a pitch-pipe or from Melvin at the piano.

1. *Myrtis Carnes* (first tenor) was from Darlington, South Carolina, in his second year at the college in 1948-49. After that year, he returned to his

home area (the college only offered a two-year program at the time) and remained an active layman in his FWB church until his death in 1993.

2. *Wesley Calvery* (second tenor/lead) was in his second year, from Waco, Texas, and returned the next year. He would subsequently be one of the college's first B.A. graduates in 1950. He and his wife Aileen, also an FWBBC graduate, from Arkansas, spent their ministry as FWB missionaries in Japan. Wesley died in 2002.

3. *Derald West* (baritone), from Detroit (Van Dyke), Michigan, was in his second year at FWBBC in 1948-49 and would spend two more years at the college. Afterward, he returned to his home area and remained a faithful layman until his death (year unknown). I understand that he was serving as a deacon in a Baptist church at the time.

4. *Billy Melvin* (bass) called Durham, North Carolina, home at the time, since his father had been pastor at Edgemont FWB Church there before moving to Nashville to promote the college. He was also in his second year at the college in 1948-49 and went on to graduate from Taylor University two years later. After some years as a FWB pastor, he became Executive Secretary of the National Association of Free Will Baptists. In 1967, he became Executive Director of the National Association of Evangelicals. He retired from that position in 1995 and lives in Florida with his wife Darlene.

Of this first quartet, Billy Melvin (I refer to him as Billy to keep him distinct from his dad) is the only one still living. I asked him to make some notes about his experience. This is the way he summarized the purpose of the group.

> Our mission as a quartet was simple and straightforward. First and foremost our desire was to bring honor to Jesus Christ as we shared the gospel in song.
>
> Second, we sought to explain the mission of Free Will Baptist Bible College. In those days education was viewed somewhat with suspicion, so we talked a lot about a "God-called" ministry. The

college's role was to equip or prepare those who had been called by God.

Third, we sought to recruit young people who might consider attending the college. Happily there were those who did visit the college and eventually became students as a result of their contact with the Gospeliers.

Fourth, and this should come as no surprise, we sought to raise money in support of the college. In addition to the nightly offerings received, we promoted systematic giving, providing a packet of 12 envelopes for the donor to mail a check [more often, cash] each month or a packet of 12 checks that were signed by the donor and deposited each month by the college.

This summary would be appropriate for all the quartets to follow.

Billy also noted that "Looking presentable each night was a real challenge since our nightly dress included a starched white shirt and a black bow tie." Before the tour began, Melvin took the four men to a local uniform provider and each was outfitted with several white shirts, several pairs of white duck pants, a denim coat, and the black bow tie. At any point along the way, the shirts and pants could go to a laundry and be washed, starched, and ironed in one-day service.

The 1949 summer tour included churches in Illinois, Missouri, Oklahoma, Texas, and Arkansas. Billy remembers that the very first service was in Ina, Illinois, a town that "claimed a population of 900" at the time. (The photograph shown here was made in Illinois, at the home of Reba and

250

Maurine Edwards, left to right in the front with Ronald Creech, also visiting at the time.) He also remembers a service in Blue Eye, Missouri! Most FWB churches, at the time, were in the country or in small towns. The minutes of the National Association of Free Will Baptists, meeting July 12-14, 1949, in Columbus, Georgia, show that this quartet sang at several services during that meeting, using songs from their repertoire: "I Love Him," "Were You There," and "All upon the Altar." The tour apparently ended following that convention; if so, it lasted about six weeks. Billy does not remember what the quartet members were paid, only that at the end of the tour they were given a cash gift and bus tickets home!

The summer tours were not without some problems. Here is another note from Billy:

> What was our greatest challenge as we traveled each day, sleeping in a different bed each night? That's easy: the heat! This was 1949 and air conditioning was a rarity. Our Chevrolet van had no air conditioning, and neither did the churches where we were singing or the homes where we spent the night. Occasionally there would be a fan or two, but not often. Lack of inside plumbing complicated our battle with the heat. Showers were hard to come by, but we always seemed to manage, accepting with thanksgiving whatever hospitality was extended to us.

Here is Billy's conclusion to his memories of that tour: "Looking back, I realize that my association with the Gospeliers in the summer of 1949 was a great training ground for my future life and ministry. I thank God for the experience and many lessons God taught me along the way."

I have no doubt that all the members of the various quartets would give a similar testimony.

This writer remembers well that first quartet. Having just completed my senior year in high school, I traveled with my Mom from South Carolina to

251

the National League Conference in Tulsa, Oklahoma, June 14-16, 1949. At that convention, I heard them sing and was impressed by their demeanor, testimonies, and harmony. I thought how neat it would be to sing in such a quartet, and that helped settle my decision to attend FWBBC in the fall of that year. I know others who were influenced at that convention, by the quartet, to attend the college. Of their ministry there, Billy says, "It was an honor to share with hundreds of youth from across the nation."

The Second Gospeliers, Summer, 1950

When time came for a quartet to tour for the college during the summer of 1950, the group was entirely new. The four were (left to right in the photograph above) Irvin Hyman, Billy Sherrill, Bobby Picirilli (this writer), and Reedy Saverance. The name was still the Gospeliers. The methods and circumstances described above, for the first group and their tour, remained essentially the same.

1. *Irvin Hyman* (first tenor) was from near Florence, South Carolina. He first enrolled in the spring of 1949. After two years at the college, Irvin went on to serve as pastor of a number of Free Will Baptist churches, and his ministry included writing Christian literature. Now retired, he lives in Albany, Georgia.

2. *Billy Sherrill* (second tenor/lead), from Flat River, Missouri, was a second year student in 1949-50. He would later be drafted into the military during another summer tour (see 1951, below) but would subsequently return and graduate in 1958. I have no information about his life after that; he died in 2006.

3. *Bobby Picirilli* (baritone) was a freshman from the Mt. Elon FWB Church community near Pamplico, South Carolina. He graduated in 1953 and after graduate school spent his ministry as part of the faculty and administration at the college. He is now retired and lives in Hermitage, Tennessee.

4. *Reedy Saverance* (bass) was also from Florence County, South Carolina. Already married, he enrolled in the fall of 1949 and was the first married man in one of the college's traveling quartets. Reedy, now retired and living near Pamplico, South Carolina, served a number of Free Will Baptist churches as pastor.

As in 1949, Henry ("Pop") Melvin began the summer's tour traveling with the quartet to speak for the college and make the appeal for support. But during the tour he passed this leadership role to his son Billy Melvin (see 1949, above). On one occasion, Billy was heard to say to a congregation, urging their participation, that "Saying Amen to these boys is like saying *Amen* to a hound dog!" Perhaps by this Billy equaled his dad, who said, during another sermon that summer, that the Lord said, "Moses, take off your *feet*, for the ground whereon you stand is holy ground!"

The snapshot shown below is of this group on tour, with Billy Melvin and the 1949 maroon Chevrolet station wagon in which they traveled. The tour lasted for six weeks or more, beginning when school was out on June 2 and going until mid to late July. Irvin remembers that we were each paid $120 at the end of the tour and that he gave the $12 tithe to the college and had $108 left to get married on, on August 4!

A printed program, prepared in advance, was used in the services: a sheet made into a four-fold. The front says "Free Will Baptist Bible College presents ... the Gospelier Quartet in sacred concert." On the back is a list of "Quartet Personnel," adding Henry Melvin as Director and Billy Melvin as Assistant Director. Inside is a "Program" listing the 16 songs the quartet might sing, which included the standards "Just a Little Talk with Jesus" and "On the Jericho Road." One number, "I Want My Life to Tell for Jesus," was something of a theme, not just for this group, but also for some of the other quartets. Also inside were "Facts about F. W. B. B. C.," with information about the programs offered and the college's distinctives, rating, objectives, faculty, graduates, and—at the end, for emphasis—its needs. This part concluded with an appeal for prayers and gifts. In subsequent years, the need to send students would make a third appeal.

The college also sent to the churches, in advance, printed posters to use for publicity. They included a picture of the quartet and spaces to fill in the time and place of the service. A scan of one is shown below (reduced from its original 11 x 9 inches). The information filled in on this one, now faded, shows that the service announced was at Bethlehem FWB Church (near Ashland City, Tennessee) on Sunday, May 28, at 7:30 p.m. This was before the school term was over on June 2. (Similar posters were used for most of the early quartets, but few others have been preserved.)

FREE WILL BAPTIST BIBLE COLLEGE *presents . . .*

The
GOSPELIERS

in Sacred Concert

FREE WILL BAPTIST CHURCH

DATE	TIME

One feature of the services during this summer was different from the previous year and from any years that followed. This was the showing of a film called, in the program, "A Day at F. W. B. B. C." It was a "home movie" (no sound) that had been made during the 1949-50 school term by John Barrow, a student, son of college faculty member Jesse P. Barrow. We were careful to ask the pastor, in advance, if we could show the film. Some would not permit it and some would let it be shown only in an auxiliary building, not during the main service. The film gave a "slice of life" on campus and was narrated by one of the group when it was shown. We carried a projector with us, and it was my responsibility to operate it.

Irvin says we toured in Tennessee, North Carolina, Ohio, Virginia, West Virginia, Missouri, Oklahoma, and perhaps more states. He remembers in particular a service in Sulphur, Oklahoma, where W. S. Mooneyham was

255

pastor. Irvin was sick and Mooneyham practiced with us in his place that afternoon and sang that evening! Irvin's testimony is: "The summer of 1950 was one of the most inspiring and helpful periods of my 63 years as a representative of the Lord Jesus Christ. It helped prepare me for the work the Lord called me to, as pastor, teacher, and evangelist." Reedy recalls a service when, to our complete surprise, the pastor's wife shouted in the middle of our song, "The Old Ship of Zion." He also remembers (in addition to having an accident with the station wagon) that we sang at the National League Convention in Norfolk, Virginia, in June (see the section regarding the Girls' Quartet, below)—probably because his wife and her mother also came from South Carolina to be with him there!

In the section about the 1949 group, above, I included Billy Melvin's observation that many Free Will Baptists of that time were suspicious of education and that the quartet emphasized a God-called ministry. I recall a part of both Melvins' presentation of the college that they used frequently. It originated with Henry Melvin, who would say,

> Recently, one of our pastors asked me, "Well, Brother Melvin, just how many preachers did you turn out this year at that college?" I said, "Not a one, brother, not a one! We don't turn out preachers. Only God can make a preacher. We just try to help those whom God has called to prepare to preach more effectively."

Along the same lines, Melvin would often say that a man could cut more wood if he sharpens his axe. Or that you wouldn't want an untrained doctor operating on you. I remember once when he led in a prayer, he began, "Lord, you know how when the old cow gets sick ..." and we wondered what was coming next. It was, "We send for the best-trained veterinarian we can find." Indeed, we often encountered resistance to the message of the college, and many felt that educating preachers would be harmful, not helpful.

The Girls' Quartet, Summer, 1950

For the first and only time, the college also sent a girls' quartet on tour during the summer of 1950. Their relatively short tour began when school was out in the spring, on June 2, and lasted for about two weeks. The college president, the Reverend L. C. Johnson, traveled with the girls and spoke for the college.

The personnel of the group were as follows (left to right in the picture).

1. *Beth Davidson* (pianist) was a freshman from Davis, North Carolina, the daughter of the founding Business Manager-Treasurer of the college, J. R. Davidson. Beth returned to her home the next year and later married a Baptist layman, Bill Harrison. They lived in Clarkston, Georgia, where she died in 2011.

2. *Jane Reeder* (tenor), from Fort Worth, Texas, was a freshman at the college. After two years as a student, she returned to her home, married James Trout, a FWB layman, and with her family participated in the ministry of several churches—including a FWB church plant in Irving, Texas. Widowed since 1994, she lives in Stockton, California.

3. *Wanda Edwards* (soprano), from Desloge, Missouri, was a second-year student during 1949-50, daughter of Eunice Edwards, a leader among FWB women. Following another year at the college Wanda returned to her home area in Missouri where she married Joe Stumbo and became a nurse. She

died relatively young, from primary pulmonary hypertension; I do not know the year.

4. *Virginia Hales* (alto), another freshman, was from Norfolk, Virginia, daughter of a well-known FWB pastor, W. A. Hales. She did not return to the college in the fall of 1950, but returned to complete another year there after marrying Henry VanKluyve. The two of them now live in Hermitage, Tennessee, after Henry's retirement from the FWB Foreign Missions office and many years as pastor of FWB churches.

5. *Lucy Wisehart* (bass) was from Myrtle, Missouri, and enrolled for the first time in the fall of 1949. After graduation in 1953, Lucy served as a missionary in Cuba, married Felix Lima and served with him in Texas, and after his death married Irvin Hyman (see the Gospeliers for 1950), with whom she lives now in Albany, Georgia.

Like many of the traveling quartets, this group formed itself. During the school year, as they remember it, they were with some girls in the college parlor, singing, while Beth was playing the piano. Most girls sing either soprano or alto, but Jane recalls starting to sing the tenor line and Lucy chimed in with the bass to round out the harmony. Things developed from there. The ladies remember that both Mrs. Sawyer, who taught music, and Beth were of help to them. The group often sang on campus and in local churches, sometimes driven in the college van by fellow student Joe Ange. By the time the school year was nearing its end, the college's administration had the idea to take the girls on tour. Virginia, Lucy, and Jane assume that this originated with President Johnson.

Before the tour began, the girls were taken to a "low overhead" outlet store where they were fitted, under the supervision of Wanda Edwards, the sophomore in the group, with two outfits each. One was blue and white, the other green. One was washable, the other required dry-cleaning. Virginia remembers that Henry Melvin took them there.

Given Johnson's involvement, the quartet went to churches where he knew the situation well, including Mississippi, where he had been pastor, and churches in and around his home area in Georgia. In Mississippi, they remember singing in three churches: Tupelo, Amory, and New Gauley. In Georgia, they sang in several more churches, including Johnson's home church near Alma and in Glenville. Virginia remembers that they met Sammy Wilkinson there, who enrolled in the college in the fall and said that the girls' quartet influenced him to go.

Lucy recalls that they, like the boys (above), showed the film, "A Day at F. W. B. B. C." on their tour. She ran the projector and Dr. Johnson did the narration.

The quartet finished their tour singing at the National League Conference in Norfolk, Virginia, June 13-15. The printed program shows that they were featured, scheduled to sing several times. A song especially selected for the program was "Mighty Army of the Young," and the girls recall that they changed the words of the chorus from "Jesus lives" to "Christ controls" to fit in with the conference theme. They were also scheduled to sing, "Praise Ye the Lord," "What Will You Do with Jesus?" "Ready," and "All Upon the Altar." Also in their repertoire were "Wonderful, Wonderful Jesus," and "Wonderful Peace." The 1950 Gospeliers were also scheduled to sing in one slot at the conference, using "There's a City Foursquare"—a song I don't even remember!

Lucy thinks that some of the appeal of the Girls' Quartet was that most people had never heard a female quartet! Jane remembers their singing, and Johnson speaking, on a local radio station in Norfolk at the time. She also recalls the long bus ride home to Fort Worth after the conference.

One of the interesting things involving the girls' quartet is that they had teamed up with the Gospeliers (who also traveled that summer; see above) to sing as a "double quartet" in a program during the spring semester. The picture below shows the group, all dressed up to sing for a vespers program.

259

(The order of the girls, left to right, is Edwards, Reeder, Hales, and Wisehart.) I believe we sang "Tis Midnight and on Olive's Brow," but I wouldn't guarantee that!

The Gospeliers, 1950-51 Term

When the 1950 summer tour was over and the fall term began in September, 1950, the quartet situation became different in two ways. First, the Gospeliers who had traveled during the summer experienced personnel changes. Irvin Hyman was replaced by C. H. Overman, and Reedy Saverance by George C. Lee, Jr. The new members enrolled in the fall of 1950, as did Frank Sexton, who sometimes played the piano for them at functions in Nashville during the 1950-51 term. No "official" photograph of this group exists; the snapshot shown here is from the college's 1951 yearbook, *The Lumen.* They are, left to right:

THE GOSPELIERS

1. *C. H. Overman* (first tenor) was from Kenly, North Carolina. Following his years at the college, he became a Free Will Baptist pastor, taught school, and served many years as editor at the Free Will Baptist Press in Ayden, North Carolina. C. H. died in 2012.

2. *Billy Sherrill* (second tenor/lead). See the summer, 1950.

3. *Bobby Picirilli* (baritone). See the summer, 1950.

4. *George C. Lee, Jr.* (bass) was from Calhoun City, Mississippi, the son of a leading Mississippi FWB minister, the Reverend G. C. Lee, Sr. George was already experienced in a professional group, the All American Quartet. George went on to serve as a home missionary in Nebraska and as pastor of a number of Free Will Baptist churches. He is now retired and living in Goldsboro, North Carolina, where he is pastor of a Friends Church and writes Southern gospel music for several publishers.

5. *Frank Sexton* (pianist) was from Winfield, Alabama. He earned his doctorate in education and has retired from a career in teaching. He lives now in Pensacola, Florida, where he still sings in the choir and teaches Sunday School in a Baptist church.

This quartet did not travel, as such, during a summer tour. They sang for various functions during the 1950-51 school term, but were soon replaced by the freshman group described in the following paragraphs.

261

The Freshman Quartet, 1950-51 Term

The other change during 1950-51 was more significant. Four freshmen, standing in registration lines together in the fall, began to sing gospel songs, perhaps partly for the enjoyment of singing and partly to relieve the tedium. This group, with some subsequent modification, would go on to become the best known Gospeliers among Free Will Baptists for years to come. At first, however, they were simply known as the Freshman Quartet, as another snapshot from the 1951 college yearbook, *The Lumen*, shows. This, too, was not an "official" photograph. The fellows are as follows, left to right.

FRESHMAN QUARTET

1. *Ray Turnage* (first tenor) came from Florence, South Carolina. After graduation, Ray went on to serve in various ministries for Free Will Baptists; these included leading the National League work and the Tennessee Free Will Baptist Children's Home in Greeneville, Tennessee. Now retired, he lives in Edmond, Oklahoma, with his wife Lissie (Chaudoin) from Oklahoma.

2. *Bobby Jackson* (second tenor/lead) was from Kenly, North Carolina. Even as a student, Bobby's preaching laid the foundation for his lifetime ministry as an evangelist. He is semi-retired and lives in Greenville, North Carolina, with his wife Jane (Ketteman) from Illinois. His memoirs, *Yesterday*, include a chapter on the Gospeliers.

3. *Eugene Waddell* (baritone) was also from Kenly, North Carolina, a cousin, and friend of Bobby's from elementary school days. Eugene served several Free Will Baptist churches as pastor and ultimately became director

of the denomination's Foreign Missions program. He died in 2007 and is survived by his second wife, North Carolinian Genevieve (Johnson), who lives in Nashville, Tennessee. Eugene's first wife, Leah (Nichols), also from North Carolina, died of cancer in 1962.

4. *James Earl Raper* (bass), from Goldsboro, North Carolina, spent much of his childhood in the Free Will Baptist Children's Home in Middlesex, North Carolina. His ministry included several pastorates and a period of time as Superintendent of the Tennessee Free Will Baptist Children's Home. He is retired, with his wife Doris (Borden) of Oklahoma, and they live near Turbeville, South Carolina.

All four of these were graduated from the college in 1954. From the moment they began to sing together, during the fall of 1950, it was obvious they were very *good* and that people enjoyed their singing and their personalities. It is no surprise, then, that by the end of the first semester Henry Melvin had plans for them. The college was raising funds to build an auditorium, one they hoped to complete—and did!—in time for commencement in 1951, and a tour with these fellows seemed sure to help with that campaign. So this "Freshman Quartet" became the first of the college quartets to tour *during* the school year. Melvin took them out for two (three?) weeks at the start of the second semester in January. They traveled primarily in Eastern North Carolina and were especially effective in representing the college and appealing to prospective students.

One sidelight of this special tour was the question of the fellows' room and board charges during the time they were traveling. At first, the college billed them the same as all the other students. The quartet members protested that they had not lived on campus or eaten in the dining room during the time they were out. In the end, the college cancelled their board charges for the period. Otherwise, there was no "salary" for them as there had been for quartets traveling during the summer.

The Gospeliers, Summer 1951

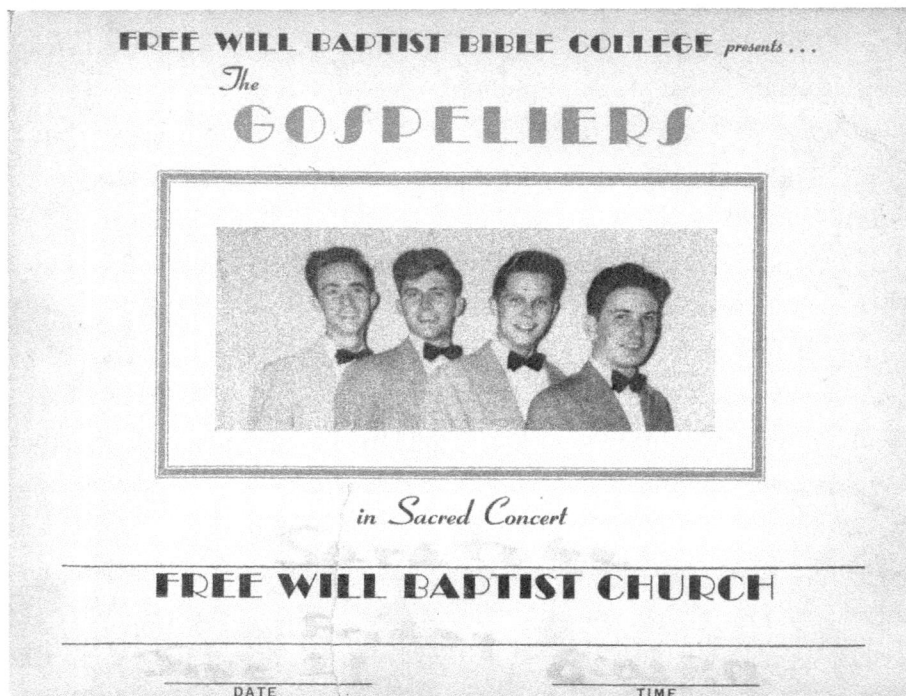

FREE WILL BAPTIST BIBLE COLLEGE *presents* ...

The

GOSPELIERS

in Sacred Concert

FREE WILL BAPTIST CHURCH

DATE   TIME

The freshman quartet of 1950-51 was such a hit that they became the Gospeliers and went out on tour at the beginning of the summer of 1951. The poster reproduced above was used during that tour. The information written in (but too dim to reproduce) is for a service at the Saratoga (North Carolina) Church on June 29 at 8:00 p.m.

But the summer wasn't that simple: there were three stages, representing personnel changes. (All of the individuals have been identified in the preceding sections.)

Stage 1. The four fellows in what had been known as the freshman quartet, described in the preceding section—Turnage, Jackson, Waddell, and Raper— traveled between the end of the spring term and the National Association in Nashville. The poster above was used during this part of the tour (and perhaps for the rest of the tour, as well!).

Stage 2. At the National Association, Billy Sherrill and this writer
replaced Bobby Jackson and Eugene Waddell. I remember well
the strong feeling I had during
the National Association, hearing the four who had toured up
to that point. I realized just how
good they were, and I said that I
wished they could just go ahead and finish out the summer. It was a shame to change the group. But this had been prearranged; both of the ones replaced were wanted at home to help with harvest on the farm, and Jackson had some revival meetings scheduled. So the plan was that the modified group—Turnage, Sherrill, Picirilli, and Raper, would finish the summer tour. The pic-
ture here shows them in that order, with Pop Melvin behind them.

Stage 3. But Billy Sherrill was
unexpectedly drafted for military
service before the tour was over
and Eugene Waddell came back
in his place to finish the tour. The
final four, then, were Turnage,
Picirilli, Waddell, and Raper, as
shown in the picture above, left to right, with leader Billy Melvin. (The sign in the station wagon window reads, "No trespassing—No hunting.")

Once again, as during the previous summer, Henry Melvin was along to represent the college only part of the time. His son Billy filled this role during most of the summer. James Raper kept a record of all the places the three groups traveled that summer: from June 4-30 in North Carolina; then back

265

to Nashville; from July 14 to August 5 in Oklahoma; and from August 6-21 in Missouri. We finished the tour in Kirksville, Missouri.

People in the churches were hospitable and often did extra things for us. Ray Turnage remembers, for example, an "ice cream social" after the service at Holdenville, Oklahoma. And all of us remember a party the young people in Tulsa gave us at the home of Barbara Hancock one Saturday night after service.

The Gospeliers, 1951-52 Term

It soon became clear, when school began again in the fall of 1951, that the group that had been the freshman quartet during the previous year (who had toured for the college for the first part of the summer) were determined and encouraged to stay together. One change in personnel took place, even though all four had returned for the new school term.

The change resulted from a combination of circumstances. During this school term, for the first time, the Gospeliers began traveling for the college, frequently, on weekends. Ray Turnage needed to work regularly in order to be financially able to remain in school, and that presented a problem for weekend tours. As a result, this writer took Turnage's place in the group, now wearing the name Gospeliers regularly. Waddell became the first tenor for all the songs, singing the part that Turnage had previously sung—although the two of them had sometimes alternated before.

During this school year, college officials decided that in light of our experience with the quartets, we did not need anyone else to travel with us and represent the college. Gradually, this responsibility fell on this writer. I had heard Henry Melvin and Billy Melvin make their presentation enough that I knew it by heart! Perhaps that is how I gradually became the spokesman for the Gospeliers.

The Gospeliers, Summer 1952

When scheduling for the summer of 1952 began to take shape, two of the group just described could not travel for this purpose. James Raper was planning to attend summer school full time, and Bobby Jackson had revival meetings lined up. As a result, two other students were drafted to sing in their place. The foursome who toured this summer, then, were as follows.

1. *Eugene Waddell* (first tenor). See the Freshman Quartet, 1950-51.

2. *Carlton Lambert* (second tenor/lead), a sophomore, was from Brilliant, Alabama, son of well-known pastor A. J. Lambert. After graduation, Carlton served the denomination in the role of superintendent of the Free Will Baptist Children's Home in Eldridge, Alabama. He died in 2011.

Gospeliers Cover 9,000 Miles During Summer Itinerary

The Gospeliers, who have just returned from a summer tour for the College, covered 9,000 miles of Free Will Baptist territory in five states during the ten weeks they were out.

"It was a thrilling experience," said Bobby Picirilli, leader of the group, in recounting some experiences of the summer. "We saw many definite signs of increasing support for the Bible College. The picture is very encouraging," he added.

From 74 services in North Carolina, Virginia, Texas, Oklahoma and Arkansas the offerings totaled $16,440.67 in cash and pledges. The average per service was $221.75.

Besides Picirilli, members of the quartet who made the tour were Carlton Lambert, Eugene Waddell and Bill McClintock.

The amount given by each state and the number of services is shown below:

	No. Services	Amount
North Carolina	34	$6,649.12
Virginia	2	1,314.80
Texas	14	3,433.97
Oklahoma	19	3,616.40
Arkansas	5	1,416.38

3. *Bobby Picirilli* (baritone). See the Gospeliers, Summer 1950.

4. *Bill McClintock* (bass) was a freshman from Highland Park, Michigan. Much of Bill's ministry was at camps for abandoned boys. He also planted and pastored a FWB church in Doniphan, Missouri. He died in 2012.

267

As a rising senior, I was placed in charge of the quartet during this summer tour—during which the candid shot shown here was taken. That meant I had to speak for the college in the services, keep up with the offerings and pledge cards (as described in the introduction to this chapter), and make such decisions as were required about our activities.

This writer is the only one of these four still living. While I do not remember all the places we visited during this summer, the very first issue of the *Free Will Baptist Bible College Bulletin*, published in September 1952, includes a brief report of the tour; the article is reproduced on the previous page.

In his memoirs, Bobby Jackson observes that most of the time the quartets stayed in the homes of the people in the churches when they were on tour, hoping to save money and to make friends for the school. He adds, "The few times [we] were blessed to get a motel room with the privacy and convenience were highlights along the journey." It was during this 1952 tour that at the end of one evening's service the pastor raised the question as to who wanted to take the quartet members home for the night. When a painful silence resulted, one man finally said he would pay for us to stay in a motel! Little did he realize how we welcomed that: we enjoyed being with the people, but an occasional night in a motel was a treat!

I remember our singing for the National Association at Shawnee, Oklahoma, July 8-10, and touring in Texas. I also remember our final service at Grubbs, Arkansas, on the way back to Nashville. Both Gene Waddell and

I were favorably impressed with the warmth of the people there toward us. (We were *not* positively impressed by the mosquitos, prevalent in that rice-growing area!)

The Gospeliers, 1952-53 Term

During this school year, the previous year's foursome was restored: Waddell, Jackson, Picirilli, and Raper. We traveled on many weekends to represent the college.

The photograph reproduced here is from the December 1952, issue of the college *Bulletin*. The caption with the photograph reads,

> Meet the Gospeliers—A group of boys, who in the minds of thousands of Free Will Baptists, typify the dozens of consecrated students at the Bible college, are the Gospeliers. This male quartet, with varying members sometimes, has traveled over many thousand miles of Free Will Baptist territory presenting the cause of the Bible college. They have also appeared on the programs of many national conventions. From left to right, the members of the quartet are Eugene Waddell, junior, Kenly, N. C.,; Bobby Jackson, junior, Fremont, N. C.; Bobby Picirilli, senior, Pamplico, S. C., and James Earl Raper, Junior, Snow Hill, N. C.

This seems an appropriate place to describe a weekend mini-tour, which usually included five services: Friday evening, Saturday evening, Sunday morning, Sunday afternoon, and Sunday evening. An attempt was made to

269

schedule services for Friday evenings in churches we could reach after classes and for Sunday evenings in churches that were not so far away that we could not be back at the college by midnight or so. But it was sometimes the case that we would have to drive all night Sunday night and be in class at 8:00 a.m. on Monday mornings. The clipping shown here is from the February 1953 issue of the college *Bulletin* and describes a typical weekend tour. A college official—in this case Dean Light-

Quartet Makes Brief Georgia Itinerary

The Gospeliers, along with Rev. Ralph Lightsey, Dean, made a week end itinerary in south Georgia recently. According to Mr. Lightsey the ministry of the quartet was enthusiastically received.

Besides the many intangible things, a total of $1,281 in cash and gifts to be sent in monthly was given.

The churches visited were New Light, Morgan; Zion, Hilton; New Salem, Colquitt; Midway, Moultrie; and Pleasant Hill, Vienna. The young men also sang over Radio Station WGRA, Cairo, Georgia, Sunday morning and for the service celebrating the anniversary of Rev. K. V. Şhutes' broadcasting from Cairo.

sey—sometimes accompanied us to speak for the college, but not always.

It was during this term that the college first began to pay quartet members for weekend travel. That came about as a result of an initiative taken by the quartet. We were conscious of the fact that weekend tours made it even more difficult to find part time employment to help with college expenses. I have already made reference, in describing the 1951-52 term, to Ray Turnage's need for income, a need that led to my replacing him in the quartet. We decided to make a case to the college officials to consider some sort of pay for us during our weekend travels.

The plan we devised was to use what we were paid during the previous summer tour as a basis, dividing the total weekly "salary" by eight to represent an average "per service" honorarium. That came out, as I recall, to about $3 per service. We explained this formula in writing, and the quartet decided that I should be the one to present this as a request for consideration to the college officials. I remember handing the paper, with some explanation, to E. B. ("Mack") McDonald (a senior like myself, who was serving as

270

keeper of the books—unofficially, the treasurer—for the college). He did not give much response!

Gospeliers to Make South Carolina Itinerary

The Gospeliers, a widely-known male quartet from Free Will Baptist Bible College will make a brief tour in South Carolina in the interest of the Bible College, March 12-15. Churches to be visited on the tour will be:

Lebanon .... March 12
Salem .... March 13
Darlington .... March 14
Horse Branch ....(Sunday 11:00 a.m.) March 15
New Town .... (Sunday 3:00 p.m.) March 15
Bethany .... (Sunday 7:30 p.m.) March 15

Rev. Charles Thigpen, Registrar, will accompany the quartet. Mr. Thigpen is a native of South Carolina.

Soon, however, the four of us were called into the office to meet with Mack and President Johnson. Perhaps Dean Lightsey was also in the meeting. I don't remember much about it except that Dr. Johnson wondered aloud if we were being "mercenaries." At any rate, they decided that the request was reasonable and from then on, we were remunerated at the rate we had suggested. Perhaps that is one reason we preferred to have five services on a weekend rather than a lesser number!

I note that this story is also recounted in Bobby Jackson's memoirs, *Yesterday*, pages 326-327. If there are differences between the two narratives, they are not substantive and the reader can consider the defective memories of the octogenarians involved! Anyway, all the subsequent quartets that were paid for traveling during the school year have us to thank!

The clipping shown here is from the March 1953, issue of the college *Bulletin* and shows a weekend that started on Thursday rather than Friday. The next issue of the *Bulletin* reported that a total of $2,300 in cash and pledges was raised.

Bobby Jackson has reminded me again, of what he said in his memoirs: the quartet evangelistic services, during which he usually preached, "opened many doors for revival meetings and the beginning of an evangelistic ministry that continued for over 50 years."

There is no question that traveling for the college and ministering in these services helped us all—and this would apply to all the quartets—become better known in the denomination and contributed toward our opportunities for

271

ministry. The tours likewise helped us become much better acquainted with our denomination and its people.

The Evangeliers, 1952-53 Term

The Gospeliers were not the only quartet to travel for the college on weekends during the 1952-53 school year. Four students formed yet another group and took the name *Evangeliers*. They are shown here in a clipping from the college *Bulletin* issued in February 1953.

1. *Doyle Hawkins*, (first tenor) a sophomore from Brilliant, Alabama, a newcomer

The Evangeliers—Last month you were introduced to the Gospeliers, the original male quartet of the Free Will Baptist Bible college. This month we would like for you to meet the Evangeliers, a singing group organized last year. Along with the Gospeliers, these boys have visited many churches presenting the work of the Bible college. Members of the quartet are (left to right): Doyle Hawkins, sophomore, Brilliant, Ala.; G. C. Lee, Jr., junior, Calhoun City, Miss.; Carlton Lambert, junior, Florence, Ala.; and Bill McClintock, sophomore, Detroit, Michigan.

in a traveling quartet. Doyle spent his career with the Social Security Administration in Birmingham, where he lives in retirement and is a widower. At 88, he sings and is active in the Forestdale Church in Birmingham.

2. *G. C. Lee, Jr.* (second tenor/lead). See the Gospeliers, 1950-51 term, above.

3. *Carlton Lambert* (baritone). See the Gospeliers, summer 1952, above.

4. *Bill McClintock* (bass). See the Gospeliers, summer 1952, above.

5. *Frank Sexton* (pianist, not shown) also played for this group. See the Gospeliers, 1950-51 term, above.

The clipping shown here appeared in the May 1953 issue of the college *Bulletin*, as the school term drew to a close. It refers to the weekend tours of the Gospeliers and the Evangeliers during the 1952-53 school term.

The article also shows awareness, on the part of college officials, of the importance of the ministry of these quartets. The same things could be said of all the quartets that toured for the college at any time, whether during the school term or during the summer.

Doyle Hawkins thinks that their very first service was in Cordova, Alabama, and remembers services in Mis-

College Quartet Visits Five States

Outstanding results have been realized in the last few weeks from services conducted by two quartets from the Bible College. Week end services have been conducted in five states: Georgia, Alabama, Kentucky, West Virginia, and Tennessee. Rev. M. H. Millette, Hilton, Georgia, arranged one of these week end itineraries for southwest Georgia and southeast Alabama. Rev. Homer Willis, Paintsville, Kentucky, arranged another such itinerary in eastern Kentucky and West Virginia. Churches visited in Tennessee were near Nashville. Approximately $10,000 has been raised this school year by the week end itineraries of these quartets.

The College administration appreciates the work of the young men who have gone out on these itineraries, and the people who have so graciously received them.

sissippi where G. C.'s dad was pastor, and in Columbia, Tennessee, with Pastor W. B. Hughes. He adds, "I think our most memorable service was at the church in Highland Park, Michigan, where Brother Raymond Riggs was pastor. We sang over his radio program on Sunday, and he took us to the Greater Detroit Gospel Singing Convention that same day, where we sang two songs, I think." Doyle expresses the desires that he (like all the quartets) had for the services, that there would be decisions for Christ and to attend the college and to support the college.

Of note is the fact that, when the college celebrated its 50th anniversary in 1992, this quartet was one of the groups who came back and sang for the occasion.

273

The Gospeliers, Summer 1953

Quartet Summer Itinerary Being Planned

An itinerary is now being worked out for a quartet to go out this summer. For the past five years the Bible College has had a quartet on the field during the summer months. During these years quartets have visited practically every state where there is organized Free Will Baptist work.

Dean Lightsey stated that the purpose of sending the Quartet is threefold: "1. To present a gospel service that will exhalt Christ. 2. To give firsthand information about the Bible College. 3. To present the needs of the Bible College and receive gifts which people wish to make."

The clipping reproduced here appeared in the March 1953, issue of the college *Bulletin*. Lightsey's summary of the purpose of such tours sounds very much like Billy Melvin's, given above in connection with the first tour in the summer of 1949.

For various reasons, most of the members of the previous groups could not travel in the summer of 1953. This was particularly true of the Gospeliers, with three of them (Jackson, Raper, Picirilli) planning weddings. We did manage to schedule some revival meetings as a group (not sponsored by the college): in the Winterville, North Carolina, FWB Church (Henry Melvin, pastor), in the Winterville High School gymnasium, at Memorial FWB Church near Surrency, Georgia, and in Flat River, Missouri, in a tent meeting.

But two of the Evangeliers were available and two new members were recruited to form the quartet that would travel during the summer of 1953.

The four members of the group were as follows, left to right in the poster photograph that appears here (used in Kilsyth, West Virginia, July 5).

1. *Carroll Alexander* (first tenor), son of FWB minister D. W. Alexander of North Carolina. Carroll was a sophomore in 1952-53 and went on to graduate and spend his ministry as a FWB pastor. He retired in Columbia, South Carolina, and died in 2014 while I was preparing this chapter.

2. *Carlton Lambert* (second tenor). See the Gospeliers, summer 1952, above.

FREE WILL BAPTIST BIBLE COLLEGE *presents...*

The

GOSPELIERS

In a Program of Gospel Songs and Sermons

KILSYTH

FREE WILL BAPTIST CHURCH

SUNDAY

JULY 5   8 P.M.

Date   Time

3. *George C. Lee, Jr.* (baritone). See the Gospeliers, 1950-51 term, above.

4. *Marvis Lee* (bass), also a sophomore, was from Springfield, Tennessee. After graduation and a period of time as a FWB minister, Marvis spent ten years in pharmaceutical sales and now has a Tax Professionals business in Knoxville, Tennessee, where he lives.

An article in the college *Bulletin* for June 1953, gave a good description of the tour that was scheduled. I quote it in its entirety.

> For the past four years the Bible College has sent out a young men's quartet to visit churches in almost every state where there are Free Will Baptist people. Usually these visits have been made during the summer vacation period, but occasional short trips have been made during the school term.

The quartet this summer will visit churches in North Carolina through most of June with some visits in Virginia the latter part of June; after this visits will be made in West Virginia, Illinois, and Missouri during July and August. While in Illinois, the members of the quartet will attend the National Association.

The purpose of the College in sending out the quartet is four-fold: (1) To acquaint our people with the College, its work, and its needs; (2) To appeal to Free Will Baptist youth to consider the Bible College in planning their Christian training; (3) To seek the support of our people in assuring the financial success of the College; and (4) To present a program of gospel songs, testimonies, and a message from God's Word with the prayer that His blessings will be upon the service to the end that souls may be saved and that Christians may be revived.

This ministry of the College quartet has been very successful in supplementing the income of the College as hundreds of people volunteer to support its work of training our young men and women for full-time Christian work. Another distinct benefit of the quartet's visits is the attracting of many Free Will Baptist young people to the College, for in the young men of the quartet is seen the Christian training and character they themselves want.

The churches that have been visited previously by the quartet are enthusiastic in receiving them again. Of course, it has been impossible to visit all our Free Will Baptist churches; but through this medium the College is becoming acquainted with more and more of our people.

Not only have the churches been visited, but the young men are usually entertained in the homes of the church members. Here they have been treated like kings as they share in Christian fellowship and the comforts of home life. These visits in the homes give opportunity to talk with young people who are interested in coming to the Bible College as well as affording opportunity of dealing with those who have never been Christians. Several conversions have been reported in the services, and many young people have testified to decisions of consecration.

We know that the churches visited this year will enjoy the quartet and that the Lord will bless with wonderful services.

These observations sum up well the ministry of all the quartets. It seems clear that the particular anticipations expressed were, indeed, realized. In the *Bulletin* for August 1953, a report of the tour was given, with cash and pledges received as follows:

North Carolina (30 services), ... $6,517.17	Northeast Missouri (5 services),.. 932.32
Virginia (4 services) 1,298.25	Illinois (8 services).................. 1,228.23
West Virginia (9 services), ... 1,037.11	Missouri (16 services) 1,853.68
Ohio (6 services) , ... 1,826.55	Total $14,693.31

Carlton Lambert was the student in charge during the tour. Interestingly, his widow has preserved some letters that were sent to Carlton from E. B. McDonald at the college office during the tour. A letter dated June 15, 1953, provides the schedule of services for the rest of June—seven each week—in North Carolina and Virginia and promises a schedule for West Virginia

to follow in July, concluding, "If you should run completely out of an appointment where we have not advised you, call us collect and we will mourn with you"! Sure enough, a letter dated June 24 gives the West Virginia schedule—June 30 through July 7—as it had been arranged by the Reverend R. H. Doan. Enclosed with the letter were "a new Pure Oil Credit Card" and the news that the Gulf Card had not yet come in! Yet another letter, dated July 22, acknowledges receipt of Carlton's report for recent services and observes, "You surely had a crackerjack of a service at Hazel Creek Church. Those check books really look good! Keep up the good work." (If the reader gathers that arrangements for services were often not finalized until shortly before the quartets arrived, that perception is correct! This was true every summer.)

George remembers an unusual event in Beckley, West Virginia, that summer: "A large Southern Baptist Church had evangelist Hyman J. Appleman at their church for a revival meeting, and somehow we were asked to sing for a Sunday afternoon service. I got Appleman's signature in a New Testament that I still have. He signed in English and Hebrew."

Marvis Lee was the preacher during the quartet services. He recalls the experience as a "terrific influence" on his life, one that afforded him much growth and opportunity for dealing with people. The growth included improving his usage of English as a result of the suggestions offered by fellow quartet members Carroll Alexander and Carlton Lambert. As an example, he remembers that he preached a sermon on "Where Art Thou At?" until they explained that the extra "at" was not necessary!

The Gospeliers, 1953-54 Term

When the 1953-54 term began in September, all four of the men who had sung together during the 1952-53 term were back except for this writer. (I had graduated and gone on to enroll in graduate school.) George C. Lee, Jr. took my place in the group as baritone, which had now come to think of the name *Gospeliers* as belonging exclusively to them! (Another word about that below.) The picture reproduced below shows them in official pose: Waddell, Jackson, Lee, and Raper.

As in 1952-53, then, the Gospeliers traveled for the college on weekends. One thing was different: a member of the faculty was enlisted to play the piano for them and make the trips with them. He was Wendell Babcock, affectionately nicknamed "Little Man" by the quartet, a very capable pianist, and

his accompaniment added flair to the quartet's music. Babcock was originally from Flint, Michigan, but had come to the college from Timmonsville, South Carolina, where he served as pastor of Bay Branch FWB Church. Before that, he had played for Youth for Christ and gospel quartets in the North. This was the first version of the Gospeliers to travel with a pianist. (No picture of the quartet with Babcock is available.)

In addition to Babcock's contribution, George Lee's experience in gospel quartets and gospel music enabled him to make a number of adjustments in the songs' arrangements. Between Babcock and Lee, then, the songs took on an added quality that made them sound more polished. I was able to attend one of their services near Greenville, South Carolina, one weekend, and I was impressed with the musical growth of the group. Those same arrangements would continue to be part of the Gospeliers' repertoire for the rest of their singing days.

Although a faculty member, Babcock did not lead the service or present the college. Other members of the group, usually Waddell or Raper, shared that responsibility.

George Lee reminded me of one of the experiences of this group that I have heard some of the others relate. They left the college early one Friday morning for a service that evening in Pensacola, Florida. They thought they had time to go by New Orleans, where Mardi Gras was in full swing. But by the time they got to New Orleans they realized just how far they had to go and after making one quick turn down Bourbon Street they fled for Pensacola. Changing clothes in the van as they traveled, they barely made the service.

At commencement in 1954, this group sang a song that was especially appropriate for the occasion: *I Know Not What the Future Holds (But I Know*

279

Who Holds the Future). When the school year ended, all four graduated and went their separate ways in Free Will Baptist ministry. Yet another group would have to be recruited to travel for the college in the summer of 1954. Indeed, they were, and their names were Willis Wilson (North Carolina), Carroll Alexander (North Carolina), Galen Dunbar (West Virginia), and Dale Burden (Oklahoma). After them, a whole new quartet enrolled in the fall of 1954, from Fairmount Park FWB Church in Norfolk, Virginia. They were the *King's Messengers*: Bill Gardner, Blant Ferguson, Randy Cox, and Joe Creech. The college no longer used the name *Gospeliers*. But I have finished the story I set out to tell, about how things were with the college's traveling quartets during the first five years.

Well, maybe not quite finished. Some concluding observations seem worthwhile.

1. One of these is to answer a question that some will probably raise: namely, did people actually send in those $1 and $5 monthly gifts they promised? The answer is yes, many did. As I went through the issues of the college *Bulletin* during the years I have covered, my attention was caught, more than once, by letters from givers printed in various issues. I use the August 1953, issue as just one example.

A letter from Florence, Alabama, said: "Enclosed you will find $3 on my pledge. I thank God for the wonderful work our College is doing."

Another was from Ashford, Alabama: "Enclosed is $5, my August offering. ... I think it does more for our College for these young men to come into our Free Will Baptist Churches and prove what is being done in College. I never thought too much about it until the Gospeliers came to Prospect Free Will Baptist church at Dothan, Alabama. I did believe we should help but I didn't have the desire I have now."

Yet another came from Ewing, Illinois: "We are sending our pledges for April, May, June and July, which we have failed to send until now. The College quartet was at the Ina Free Will Baptist Church Tuesday, July 21. It is so wonderful to know that young people such as these boys are willing to give up everything to follow Christ."

One was from Norfolk, Virginia: "When the Bible College quartet came to the Fairmount Park Free Will Baptist church, I said I would give $5 a month for the College. I want to tell you that all of us got a real blessing out of their singing and preaching."

From Cove City, North Carolina, came this: "Enclosed find $3 on my pledge for three months' period."

One from Huntington, West Virginia, said this: "Enclosed is a money order for $2.50 which I am paying for the month of July. It gives me a great blessing to know that I might help to promote the work of the Lord Jesus Christ. My prayers are that some day I too might be able to attend the Bible College."

It would be unrealistic to suggest that the traveling quartets raised all the money that FWBBC required. But it would also be wrong to take lightly the fact that this particular method of fund-raising, at that time in our history, contributed greatly to the college's early financial stability.

2. It is important to remember that the quartets—like all traveling student groups since then—were effective in recruiting students for the college, and that this had implications for the number of young people who have gone into various ministries in the life of our denomination. I remember making contact with a number of young people when I was on tour, some of whom I wrote letters to afterward, encouraging them to consider attending the college. The 1950 Girls' Quartet had influence on Sammy Wilkinson, as mentioned in that part of this story. Not only did he become a FWBBC student, he became one of our missionaries. And that is an example that could be multiplied many times over. It remains true that students are the best recruiters of more students.

One of the things that I have noticed, in writing this piece, is that most of those in the quartets themselves have gone on in faithful and effective service for the Lord in our ranks.

3. I would also mention the evangelistic impact of the quartet services. Perhaps that was not necessarily a part of the original purpose for the tours. At least it did not get mentioned widely at first, and for the first couple of summers or so the services did not usually include sermons. But by the time our quartet began to travel on weekends in 1951-52 or 1952-53, when we were on our own, we determined to make evangelistic preaching a part of our regular services. One or the other of us would bring a message aimed at bringing people to Jesus. The other three of us knew very well that Bobby Jackson was the best at that, and so he was the speaker more often than not. Regardless, many people came to know the Lord in those services, and that tradition has continued.

For my final conclusion, I trust I may be excused for focusing on the implications of all this for one particular group of men who came to be known, permanently, as the Gospeliers. Bobby Jackson has written some of our story in a chapter in his memoirs (pp. 321-361), ostensibly written by our pitch pipe, nicknamed "Sackbut." I will not attempt to retell that story here. Still, one of the lasting effects of the quartet ministry of the college was in forging a relationship that ultimately came to have a large impact on the lives of four—more broadly, six—men.

We loved to sing together. After we had finished FWBBC, in 1954-55 the four of us were in graduate schools in South Carolina, not far apart, and continued to travel on weekends *for the Bible College*, just as we had done before, during the fall semester. We reached out to churches within a reasonable distance, still having four or five services a weekend and still being paid per service; the college raised the amount during the semester, by the way, and we did not ask for it! Our wives would stay together while we were gone, and they too began to forge a strong bond.

Indeed, the college *Bulletin* reported on this in the issue for October-November 1954, saying:

> The Gospeliers Quartet is still going strong! Having sung as the College quartet the past four years, the singing of Eugene Waddell, James Earl Raper, Bobby Picirilli, and Bobby Jackson has become known denominational wide. They have continued their quartet work this year although they graduated from the Bible College last June. All four are in graduate school in South Carolina—Waddell at Columbia Bible College, and Raper, Picirilli, and Jackson at Bob Jones University—and on weekends they have represented the College in some of the near-by Free Will Baptist churches.
>
> During the months of September and October the quartet made 6 week-end itineraries in South Carolina, Georgia, and North Carolina, totaling 26 services with a good measure of response of offerings and pledges. Also there were several decisions for Christ resulting from the services.

After that semester, when such travel was no longer possible because of our individual involvements, we continued to get together to sing whenever opportunity was afforded us. If we were all at some meeting, for example, we soon gathered in somebody's hotel room—or even in a convention center restroom!—just to sing for our own pleasure. As Waddell and Raper became pastors, they arranged weekend revival services for Bobby to preach and the four of us to sing. At various times other pastors arranged for Bobby to preach and the other three to come so we could sing for the meetings. I have already mentioned four revivals we conducted during the summer of 1953, for example. Sometimes we would be invited for conferences and all four of us would preach as well as sing together. This went on for years. Indeed, there were not many years that passed but that we were together to sing in at least one meeting. Somewhere in there, my daughter Jean became a good pianist and started accompanying us, which helped us stay on pitch and covered up some of our failings. She played for us for about 35 years.

It would be a mistake to think that our close friendship issued solely from our singing together while we were students. That was just how it began. It was years and years of being together that forged a bond of love that is stronger than the bond between blood brothers. It is a Christian thing, of course, and all Christians can understand this to some degree. But it is more than most Christian relationships, too.

In the year 2000, at Cofer's Chapel in Nashville, Waddell decided we would have a 50-year weekend celebration of our quartet, harking back to the fall of 1950 when the four of *them* were in registration line and started up singing. We invited Ray Turnage and George Lee, too, and we had a great time. A few people came from some distance to be with us in the celebration, although we did not publicize it widely. By that time, some of the notes had started going sour a little—although I have to say that as I took my turn on the bench and listened to one or the other of the foursomes I thought we had not lost it entirely.

Anyway, Jackson started losing his hearing and Waddell started having more trouble hitting the high notes. (None of us were ever really gifted singers, anyway, except perhaps for George!) We did not necessarily *decide*, but we came to realize that our singing days were numbered. So we decided that we would have an annual week's "retreat," the four of us and our wives, just to get together. We started that about ten years ago, and the photograph shown below was made at a restaurant on one of those annual get-togethers. The purpose did *not* include singing; I think that in all of these years, at our retreats, we only sang *one* song *one* time. We just like to be together, talk (sometimes about old times, of course), pray together, play together (which includes our own version of Trivial Pursuit, the men against the women), and eat together.

I guess the last time we sang was when Cofer's Chapel had a Gene Waddell day, not long before his death, to praise God for his long ministry to the church and the denomination. Well, we did try to sing at his graveside, with his son Michael taking his part, singing *Peace in the Valley*. We really fouled it up, and it was all I could do to keep from laughing, thinking how Waddell must be splitting his sides at the horrible sound (it was not Michael's fault)!

It is not quite the same, now, with Waddell gone, and my Clara, but it is still good. One day before long we will all be together again in the Father's house with the Jesus we sang for, thanks in part to the college we sang for. There is no telling just what that will be like. Whatever our joy, we will share it with all those who are likewise partakers of God's grace.

The life's stories of the other quartets who sang from 1949 through the spring of 1954 are not all exactly like ours, of course. But for all of them, as for us, the experience made a difference, a difference that affected the college, lots of other people, and—most of all—the singers themselves for the rest of their lives.

A special thanks to almost everyone mentioned in this piece—except for those who have passed on, of course—for lots of help putting all this together and obtaining pictures. Thanks guys and gals. I hope you enjoy your story.

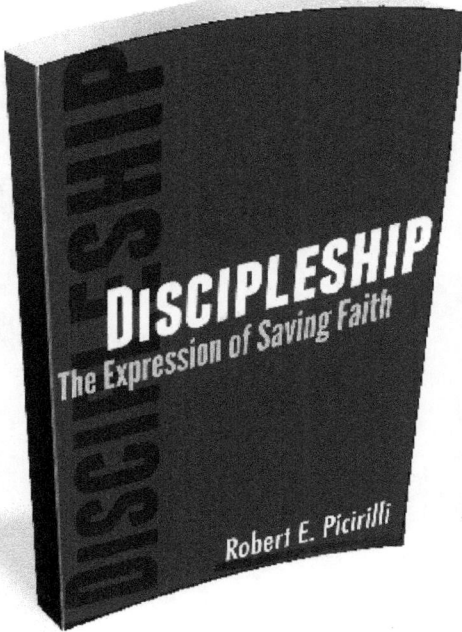

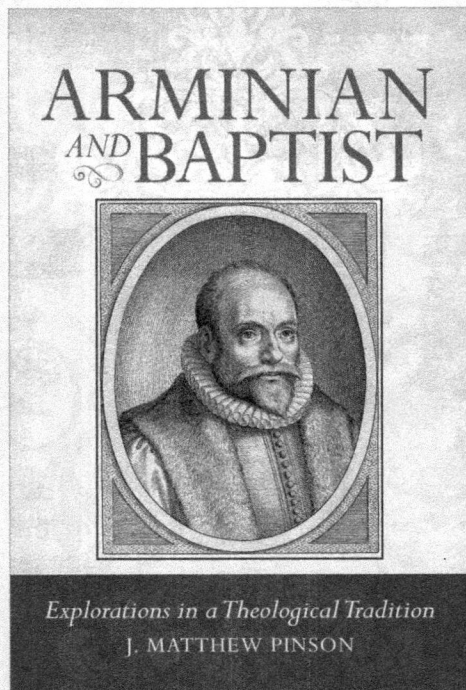

What is **D6?**

BASED ON DEUTERONOMY 6:4-7

A **conference** for your entire **team**

A **curriculum** for every age at **church**

An **experience** for every person in your **home**

D6 CONFERENCE
ONCE A YEAR

Connecting
CHURCH & HOME
These must work together!

DEFINE & REFINE Your Discipleship Plan

ONE HOUR
A WEEK

POWER OF
PARENTAL INFLUENCE

www.d6family.com